Edward the [...] unto [...] ower [...]

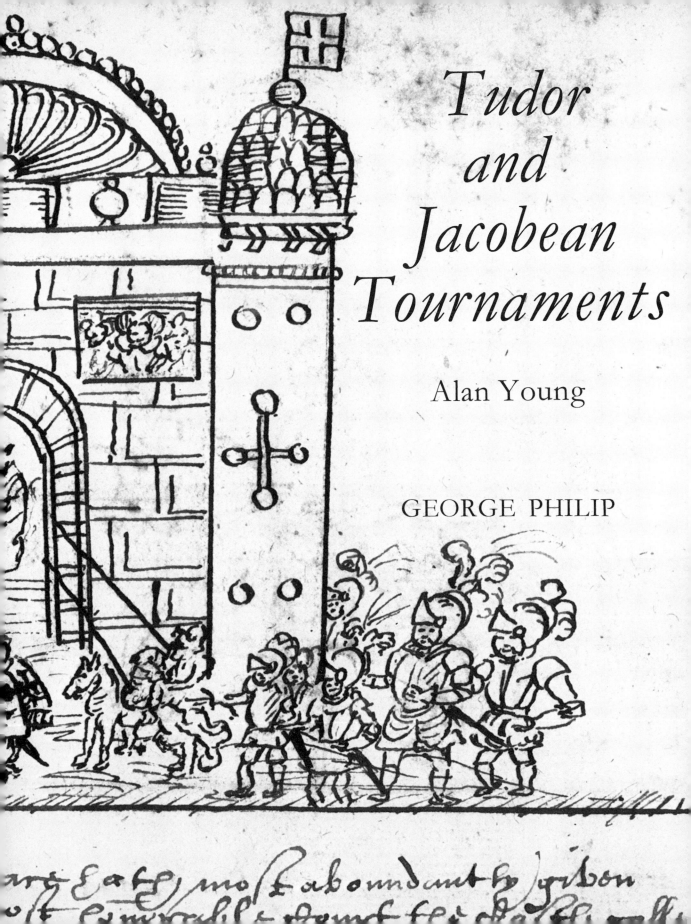

Tudor and Jacobean Tournaments

Alan Young

GEORGE PHILIP

To Eleanor, Eric, and Julian

British Library Cataloguing in Publication Data

Young, Alan
    Tudor and Jacobean tournaments.
    1. Tournaments—England—History
    2. England—Social life and customs
    —16th century   3. England—Social
    life and customs—17th century
    I. Title
    796'.0942   DA320
ISBN 0-540-01120-7

© Alan Young 1987

First published by George Philip,
27A Floral Street, London WC2E 9DP

Filmset and printed by BAS Printers Limited,
Over Wallop, Hampshire

ILLUSTRATION ACKNOWLEDGEMENTS

Aerofilms Limited pp. 111, 114; *Ashmolean Museum, Oxford* pp. 104, 108, 109, 112, 119; *Bibliothèque Nationale, Paris* pp. 51, 84; *Bodleian Library* p. 93; *British Library* pp. 10, 18, 19, 26, 32, 39, 45, 47, 57, 80, 82, 132, 133, 147, 156, 161; *British Museum* pp. 130, 182; *College of Arms* pp. 49, 53, 87, 97, 99, 126, 127; *Devonshire Collection, Chatsworth* pp. 90, 129, 178, 179, 180; *Earl of Plymouth Estates* p. 71; *Duke of Roxburghe* p. 117; *Guildhall Library, City of London* p. 91; *Hampton Court (HM the Queen)* pp. 28, 114; *Lambeth Palace Library* p. 166; *By permission of the Master and Fellows Magdalene College, Cambridge* p. 120; *Metropolitan Museum of Art, New York* pp. 15, 17, 20, 63, 167; *Museum of London* pp. 81, 105, 121; *National Gallery of Ireland* p. 137; *National Library of Scotland* pp. 188–9; *National Maritime Museum, London* pp. 37, 139; *National Portrait Gallery* pp. 24, 29, 31, 33, 151, 155; *Nelson-Atkins Museum of Art, Kansas City, Missouri (courtesy of the Starr Foundation)* p. 138; *Pierpont Morgan Library* pp. 75, 77, 94; *Private Collections* pp. 34, 78, 79, 89, 118, 142, 171; *The Armouries, Tower of London (Crown Copyright Reserved)* pp. 12, 13, 16, 35, 60, 61, 64, 65, 66, 141; *Royal Collections (HM the Queen)* p. 181; *Royal Commission on Historical Monuments (England)* p. 21; *Sir John Soane's Museum* p. 113; *University of Utrecht* pp. 112–3; *Victoria & Albert Museum* pp. 59, 62.

Contents

Preface

THIS BOOK ORIGINATED from an attempt to provide a history of the role of the tournament in the political and social life of the courts of Elizabeth I and James I. However, the history of the tournament between 1558 and 1625 can only be properly seen in the context of the special aspirations of the Tudor court as it developed during the reigns of the first Tudor monarchs, Henry VII and Henry VIII. Consequently I begin my story in 1485 when Henry VII provided the funds for a tournament to celebrate his coronation. In dealing with this earlier period, I am inevitably much indebted to the work of Sydney Anglo, Gordon Kipling and Glynne Wickham, who have written not only about individual tournaments and their staging, but have discussed the place of spectacle and pageantry as an aspect of Tudor national policy, showing also its debts to European influences.

However, this first full-length study of the Tudor and Jacobean tournament contains much that is new and comes to a number of conclusions that differ somewhat from those of previous scholars. Its chief value, I believe, is that it makes clear that the Tudor and Jacobean tournament, though somewhat ignored by cultural historians, was of major significance in the court calendar. Money lavished upon it far surpassed that spent on disguisings, pageants, masques and plays, and its public nature made it far more suitable than these much-studied types of entertainment as a vehicle for the expression of royal magnificence, the ideals of courtly virtue, and the unity of the body politic. In tracing the history of the English tournament from 1485 to its demise in 1625, I have attempted to give it back its due place within the rich and varied fabric of Tudor and Jacobean court pageantry. Once this is done, we can better comprehend its relevance to the revival of chivalric values, so important to an understanding of men such as Sir Philip Sidney and the Earl of Essex and of literary creations such as the *Arcadia* and *The Faerie Queene*. Above all, we can perceive the tournament as an event of high political seriousness.

In the course of writing this book, I have received a great deal of help from many institutions and individuals. Among the former, I owe a special debt of gratitude to the following: the Acadia University Library, the Ashmolean Museum, the Bodleian Library, the British Library, The College of Arms, The Folger Shakespeare Library, The Greater London Record Office and History Library, the Landesbibliothek und Murhardsche Bibliothek (Kassel), The Metropolitan Museum (New York), the Museum of London, The Carl H. Pforzheimer Library, The Pierpont Morgan Library, The Public Record Office (London) and the University of London Library. Among the many individuals who have been particularly kind and supportive are the following: Joyce S. Acton, Peter Daly (McGill University), I. A. Grimm (Landesbibliothek und Murhardsche Bibliothek, Kassel), John Orrell (University of Alberta), Sir Roy Strong (Director of the Victoria and Albert Museum), Sir Anthony Wagner (Clarenceux King of Arms) and R. C. Yorke (Archivist at the College of Arms). Finally, I would like to thank Wendy Katz for her enduring tolerance and constant support during the past few years.

Alan Young

A Note On Sources

The most important primary sources for this study are to be found among the documents in the great manuscript collections of the Bodleian Library, the British Library, the College of Arms, the Guildhall Library, the Lambeth Palace Library, and the Public Record Office. Wherever possible I have gone directly to these sources; however, a number of them have been printed and on occasion I have been obliged to quote from the published versions, as has been acknowledged in my notes. Among the most useful of these published versions are those contained in the works listed in the table of abbreviations under the following names: Anglo, Brown, Chamberlain, Collins, Cripps-Day, Feuillerat, Gairdner, Jordan, Leland, Lodge, Machyn, Nichols, Walker and Winwood.

I

To Them That Honour Desyreth

 YOUTH MUST HAVE seen his blood flow and felt his teeth crack under the blow of his adversary and have been thrown to the ground twenty times.' Only then will he 'be able to face real war with the hope of victory'.[1] So wrote the twelfth-century chronicler Roger of Hoveden in justification of that brutal medieval cross between sport and warfare known as the tournament. The origins of the tournament are obscure, but the form which Richard I legalized in England in 1194 came from France. In its earliest manifestations, the tournament was regarded primarily as training for war. It had first appeared in England, according to various chroniclers, some time during King Stephen's reign (1135–54), but many English knights had already gained familiarity with it on the Continent. In its most straightforward, but to us perhaps least attractive, form the tournament consisted of a single event involving two large opposing groups of knights who fought each other at some agreed upon time and place (usually midway between two towns or villages) in answer to a formal challenge. There was frequently no predetermined boundary to the combat area and fighting might range across considerable tracts of country and even through the streets of nearby towns and villages, presumably to the distress of any farmers and householders in the vicinity, though there is some evidence to suggest that the local inhabitants sometimes welcomed such an event as a source of potential revenue. The fighting in a tournament could be fierce, bloody, without judges to see fair play, and virtually without rules, though some kind of truce was supposed to be observed before and after the fighting and some form of neutral area was usually assigned to each side for prisoners and the wounded. The combat would continue until nightfall, until both sides were exhausted, or until one side had clearly won.

When we think of the early tournaments that were held throughout Europe, we must dismiss from our thoughts all romantic and chivalric associations. Nothing protected one knight from being attacked by a group of opponents, and nothing protected him if he lost his weapons or was wounded. If a knight was unhorsed, he or his horse (or both) were liable to be seized by an opponent's retainers and dragged off to await ransom. Ruses such as using men on foot to cut an opponent's stirrups or to ambush him in some out-of-the-

1 The tournament as sin. Moralists in the Middle Ages frequently condemned tournaments. In this fourteenth-century treatise devils prepare to seize the souls of knights killed in a tournament.

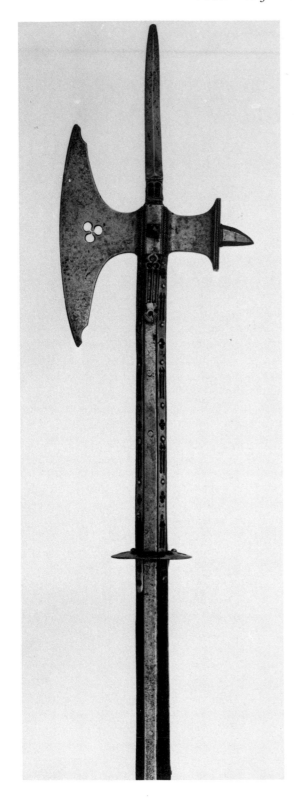

way place were common, as was the practice of wresting a knight's reins from his hands and galloping off with him in tow. Loss of life or limb was common, and not surprisingly the Church objected. Beginning with Pope Innocent II's ban in 1130, successive injunctions appeared until 1316 prohibiting participation in tournaments. Those killed were even denied Christian burial, although the mortally wounded could still obtain the last sacrament and extreme unction. On occasion, too, all the combatants in a tournament might be subject to excommunication (Fig. 1). However, the number of injunctions issued by successive Popes when compared with the number of tournaments known to have taken place shows that the Church was ineffective in discouraging those knights who travelled far afield to risk life and limb wherever a tournament might be held. Rulers too were prone to impose bans, primarily because they feared large assemblies of armed men, especially those led by powerful and at times recalcitrant feudal barons, but also because the loss of a valuable fighting man in mock warfare meant one less assistant in the business of real war. Yet even those rulers who themselves imposed bans in their own domains were often keen participants elsewhere whenever they got the opportunity. Furthermore, it would appear that their bans, like those of the Church, were often ignored.

The vicious nature of tournament practices was often matched by the unengaging motives of participants. All too easily the tournament could become a disguise for feudal war, in which case the death of an opponent would be no great cause for regret. However, the tournament seems principally

2 *English pole-axe (late fifteenth century). Foot combats were a popular feature of many tournaments and before the Tudor period the pole-axe was a favourite weapon in such combats. Henry VIII delighted onlookers in 1510 when he fought at barriers with a pole-axe.*

to have been valued for the financial profit to be derived from ransoms and booty. A defeated opponent, in fact, was best taken alive, since he could then be ransomed. Henry III's friend, William Marshal (William le Maréchal), was very successful at outwitting, defeating and capturing his opponents at tournament after tournament during his travels in Europe. On one occasion, for example, he and his men captured 103 knights between Pentecost and Lent along with horses and equipment.[2] Such prisoners were then held hostage for fat ransoms. Clearly, we are a long way from the kind of tournaments familiar to generations from Walter Scott and the celluloid images of Hollywood.

Such bloody business was, however, increasingly subjected to formal controls, both in England and elsewhere, and was softened by the inclusion of safer forms of mock combat. These two developments broadly speaking led to the Tudor and Jacobean tournament with which we shall be concerned in this book. The earliest signs of control in England were the various restrictions imposed by Richard I when he licensed tournaments in 1194. From this date, permission from certain of King Richard's officers had first to be obtained before any tournament could be held. Each event had then to be attended by two knights and two clerks, and these men then administered an oath in which combatants promised to keep the peace and not pursue private feuds. Those who participated also had to pay a sizeable tax for licence to enter their names. During the next century and a half a general change in the character of the tournament can be traced throughout Europe in keeping with the formalities of such rules. The number of partici-

3   A staff weapon from the Tower of London Armouries. Edged and pointed weapons were rarely used in Tudor and Jacobean tournaments.

pants, at one time regularly amounting to hundreds, decreased, and a knight's retinue might be restricted in size and forbidden on pain of imprisonment to carry arms in an attempt to prevent them from joining in the fray.[3] Equally significant was the introduction of the increasingly popular and highly-skilled form of single combat known as jousting, and with this the presence of heralds and judges empowered to see that rules were obeyed and scores carefully kept.

Jousting, which was to become the principal event at later tournaments, is mentioned as early as 1141 by William of Malmesbury. Its great advantage was that it offered the individual knight a much better opportunity than the usual mêlée to display his skills to an assembly of beholders. Furthermore, it provided a form of competition that was relatively easily judged. The victor in a joust could be clearly identified, whereas it was difficult to determine which side had won in a bloody, chaotic free-for-all between scores of knights pursuing each other all over the countryside. Initially, however, the joust provided only a minor supplement to the tournament, often preceding it as a kind of preliminary exercise performed by apprentice knights who fought with rebated (blunted) lances. Yet jousting gradually gained popularity and prominence, eventually becoming the main event for the chief participants.[4] Potentially it was a very dangerous form of combat. Rebated lances, first heard of at some unknown date before 1200, might be used by squires but they were not necessarily used by everyone else. The use of sharpened lances, and the possibility of riding down an opponent by outmanoeuvring him and charging him, horse to horse, when he was in a disadvantageous position were key elements among the dangers involved.

We can assume that those events employing the sharpened weapons of war were the most dangerous, though they were the most highly regarded since they offered a supreme test of courage (Figs 2 and 3). However, from a quite early date we hear of weapons of 'courtesy' being used—and it seems clear that tournaments began to be categorized according to the types of weapon used. Commonly, from the middle of the thirteenth century, distinctions are made between jousts *à plaisance* (later called jousts of peace) and jousts *à outrance* (jousts of war). As safety began to be of more concern (Fig. 4), rebated weapons became increasingly more common. Virtually all Tudor and Jacobean tournaments were to employ such weapons of 'courtesy', their main event usually being the 'Jousts of Peace' (i.e. jousts with rebated lances). Yet, even then, the temptation to try the old ways was too much on at least one occasion. At the Westminster tournament held by Henry VII in November 1501, to welcome Katherine of Aragon to England at the time of her marriage to Prince Arthur, the participants at one point charged against each other in the open area of the tiltyard with sharp lances.[5] Undoubtedly, however, rebated weapons had by this time become the norm, and everyone knew why. As the articles of combat for the tournament at the Field of Cloth of Gold explained, 'In consequence of the numerous accidents to noblemen, sharp steel not to be used as in times past, but only arms for strength, agility and pastime'.[6]

Equally important, and also part of a growing emphasis upon safety, was the introduction of the tilt barrier and the use of heavy plate armour, carefully designed to offer the maximum protection to the tournament participant. Among the earliest references to the tilt are those by the chronicler Monstrelet in his descriptions of jousting at Arras in 1429 and at Dijon in 1443.[7] At first the device seems to have consisted of a long cloth or piece of canvas hung upon a stout rope across the centre of the tournament area dividing it into two parts. Two opposing riders, one on either side of the tilt, would charge each other with lance in right hand and barrier to the left, the lance pointed across the body past the left ear of the horse and across the top of the barrier. Points were awarded according to the number of lances broken and the types of contact made with the opponent, but as a discouragement to those who might otherwise break the rules points were deducted for fouls (striking an opponent's horse, for example). The use of the tilt barrier prevented collisions between horses and also ensured that the consequences of an impact between a knight and his opponent's twelve-foot lance were less serious. The lances were carried at an angle of approximately 20 to 30 degrees to the path of the oncoming rider so that on contact they would probably snap, and indeed were expected to. The higher the barrier, the greater the safety. Early sources mention heights of five to six feet and later (see Chapter 3) a height of about six feet—enough to protect most of the horse and the lower part of a rider—seems to have become standard. A barrier of cloth or canvas, of course, provided only token protection, and wooden partitions soon tended to be preferred.

The adoption of plate armour and the special features designed for use in the tiltyard are of paramount importance in the historical development of tournaments. In the earliest tournaments knights wore mail on body and legs and metal caps for the head, but in the thirteenth century at the time of William Marshal such head coverings began to be replaced by helms or *heaumes* (heavy head-pieces covering the entire head) (Fig. 5). Not later than the beginning of the thirteenth century, we also begin to hear of the use of breastplates, and it is known that Richard, Count of Poitou (later Richard I of England), wore one when he tilted with Guillaume des Barres.[8] By the mid thirteenth century the use of plate armour was increasingly common, and by the third decade of the fourteenth century it had been universally adopted by those who could afford it. From the early fifteenth century, the great European schools of armourers, in quest of maximum safety, were able to build made-to-measure suits of plate armour totally encasing a knight from head to toe (Fig. 6). Such armour was carefully shaped, polished and curved to make sword and lance blows

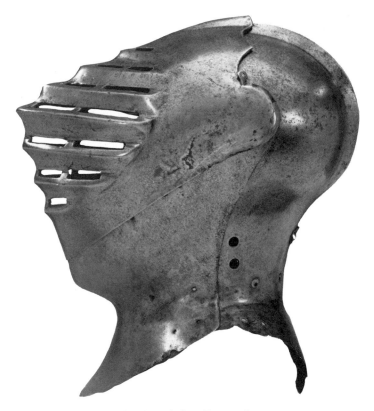

4 *Foot combat helm (English or Burgundian, c. 1500). For sparring with swords or pole-axes, helmets with multiple slits for vision and ventilation were used. Thrusting was illegal, so in theory these vents did not make the knights more vulnerable.*

glance harmlessly off. For jousting the left side of the body had extra protection, something which rendered the shield obsolete, and for foot combat other specialized types of plate armour were introduced. Further developments occurred in the design of head pieces. Understandably special care was taken to protect the head and eyes of those engaged in jousting. Seeing an opponent sufficiently clearly to aim a lance when riding along a tilt barrier must often have been very difficult because the aperture provided for the eyes was so small, but at least there was less risk of the tragic fate of King Henri II of France. In 1559 he had been killed at a tournament

5 The 'Brocas' helm (probably south German, c. 1490). This frog-mouthed style of jousting helm enabled the rider to see his opponent and, if he raised his head slightly, his eyes were protected from the opponent's lance.

FAR RIGHT
6 Locking gauntlet. The locking gauntlet, a device often banned from earlier tournaments, permitted a knight in a tourney to lock his sword into his hand so that it could not be lost. By the time of Henry VIII, the device was an accepted part of tournament equipment. Here is an example from a suit of armour dated 1527 that was made for a French ambassador, the Vicomte de Turenne, by Henry VIII's workshops at Greenwich.

when his opponent's splintered lance poked through his visor and hit him above the eye. A knight's saddle gave him additional protection, in that it was designed to hold him in place while tilting. Even if he received a blow from his opponent's lance, the high back of the saddle would prevent him from being forced backwards. Building up the saddle in front protected the vulnerable groin area and attaching side pieces in front of each leg and boot-like stirrups was a further extension of such safety measures.

Developments of this kind no doubt had much to do with the changed nature of warfare itself. The fast-moving mounted warrior, a Norman innovation made possible by the invention of the stirrup, had become outmoded with the development of heavier armour and of a type of cavalry ill-suited to fierce pursuits across country. Of key significance was Edward III's decisive victory over the Scots at Halidon Hill in 1333, which was achieved partly by the use of defensive positions and archers, and partly by using knights and men-at-arms in foot combat. After they had dismounted, their horses were sent to the rear. The spectacular success of that day completed the evolution of a form of battle strategy combining archers and heavily-armed foot soldiers, soon to be put to the test in Europe at Sluys and above all at Crécy. Indirectly, however, it marks the demise of heavy cavalry. Consequently the older form of tournament with its emphasis on speed and pursuit became largely obsolete as a training for war, and the feudal horseman something of an anachronism.

All the above, however, is as nothing in comparison to the impact of chivalric ideals. The change brought by this transformation in sensibility is exemplified in the somewhat fantastical early thirteenth-century figure of Ulrich von Liechtenstein. For Ulrich the display of individual gallantry and the honour achieved in the service of one's lady became ends in themselves and the tournament then developed as part of the apparatus of courtly love.[9] In the wake of such a transformation,

skill and grace in the martial arts were given high value and began to take precedence over brute force, cunning and endurance. Under the influence of chivalry, the tournament also came to be more of a social diversion, and an occasion for pomp, pageantry and conspicuous expenditure. The influence of the literary romances was particularly important, and they in turn were influenced by the tournaments. In the thirteenth century, the awarding of exotic prizes, the presence of women as the supposed *raison d'être* for the knights' chivalrous exploits, elaborate feastings, dancing, minstrelsy, and sumptuous costumes all became familiar features of tournaments throughout Europe (Fig. 7).

All these developments are features of the eroticism which so characterizes the events of the late Middle Ages (Fig. 8).[10] The tournament offered the perfect vehicle for the expression of male desire, male conquest, and the deliverance of virginity, this last often the literal or figurative prize awarded to the successful knight. The latent symbolism inherent in a knight wearing the veil or dress of his lady, in the use of such motifs as knights besieging fortresses inhabited by women, and in the award of a kiss or a ring as prize, is unmistakeable. As early as 1226, for example, a knight by the name of Waltman announced that he would joust against all-comers at Mercersberg. In what was probably an imitation of the romance of Guy of Warwick, he offered as prizes to anyone who defeated him, his horse, his hawk, his hound, his harness, and his young lady. She, however, in

Necelle faifon et entretant que les trieues fe tenoient en france et en angleterre par mer et par terre et que les angloie et leure fubiectz les wuloient bien tenir referue auaine pillare qui eftoient en auuerfhne Ceulx article de mar che heriotent le pate et fes pourf yene deca la riuiere de doudone et deta maie les fouuernee cappitanee qui eftoient rendue par traicte et par compofition nauoient pue leure fourfait maie fen diffimuloient grande ment et quelque diffimulaton quil yeuft pour le fommage

que le pue Sauuernhe en receu noit les plantee en renoient a pute eut confeil le roy de fran ce denoyer denere le roy dangle terre et lui efcripre et fummier tout leftat de cee mauuaie pil lare qui guerre faifoient en ce purtee et pue enclobe en la pury foubz lombre de leure mete lagle chofe ne fe pouoit ne denoit bon nement ne leaument faire. En trextant que cee chofee fe deme noient et re cuy bien que le roy angleterre fen enuifa car temte eftoit de ce faire et de y pouueyr. Lee troie cheualliere def fue nommiee dont noftre hiftoi re fait mention qui auoient en

7   Parading the lists before the tournament at St Inglevert in 1390 (ABOVE LEFT), and jousting at the same event (ABOVE). This famous tournament was attended by English knights who had the choice of fighting with sharp or with rebated (blunted) weapons. *The illustration of the parade shows the typical highly decorative horse bards and arming pavilions. The importance of female spectators is also evident.*

a departure from romance necessary no doubt for contemporary decorum, could free herself by the gift of a ring.[11] For the Church and for moralists, this aspect of the tournament was as much to be condemned as the lack of concern with the sanctity of human life exhibited in the vicious mêlées during its earlier history.

A further particularly striking innovation in the tournament is the use of disguise. Ulrich von Liechtenstein, for example, appeared as King Arthur in 1240, but other more extreme fictional roles, such as knights appearing as women or monks, are recorded. In England during Edward III's reign, disguises, the use of Arthurian motifs, and processions were common.[12] The King and his court on one occasion, for example, disguised themselves as Tartars, and at another tournament English knights jousted disguised as the Pope and twelve cardinals. Such disguises also tended to make use of allegory through which a knight would explain his

8 Knights storm the Castle of Love (French ivory casket, early fourteenth century). The latent erotic element in tournaments is exemplified in this love allegory in which knights catapult sweetmeats and are in turn bombarded by ladies with roses.

arrival before his lady. The elaborate speeches and pageant cars that played a major role in Tudor and Jacobean tournaments are the direct result of these developments. The so-called Round Tables, about which much has been written yet little is known, appear to have provided a particular incentive to disguises (Fig. 9). These were festive occasions involving tournament-like events but employing only 'weapons of peace' (rebated weapons). They seem to have involved a conscious attempt to replace the older, more dangerous form of tournament with something safer and more carefully regulated. They flourished in England and on the Continent in the thirteenth century and on into the fourteenth, their connections with Arthurian

9 *Round Table in the Great Hall, Winchester Castle. Though popularly associated with King Arthur, the table (eighteen feet in diameter) was probably made for Edward III in the fourteenth century. It was probably first painted in the Tudor colours of green and white and decorated with a central Tudor rose in 1522 at the command of Henry VIII.*

romance (though in origin they may have preceded the Arthur story) providing added inspiration for the common use of Arthurian disguises.[13]

But we should not be misled. Chivalric civility went only so far. All the developments just described were intermingled with what was still potentially a violent and dangerous activity. The fighting at tournaments, though more carefully controlled as time passed, remained real enough, as is evidenced by the steady number of casualties. Even when the tilt barrier was introduced in the fifteenth century, fatalities still occurred on occasion. It is perhaps wiser to think of the late thirteenth- and fourteenth-century tournament as very mixed in nature, still exhibiting some of the violence of its origins, yet softening somewhat with the accretion of many of the trappings of chivalric romance which may themselves owe something of their subject-matter and character to the tournament. We should be cautious about accepting any account that proposes a swift and clear-cut evolution from brutality to civility. Unfortunately past historians frequently seem to have over-simplified the development of the tournament in just this way, ignoring its mixed character during much of its early history.[14]

If such explanations of the development and character of the tournament are sometimes open to question, other factors are perhaps less problematic. In England, the tournament seems to have been officially recognized as a fully-fledged social institution with a dominant place in court affairs by the time Edward I came home from the crusades. However, it was Edward III, the victor of Halidon Hill and Crécy, his grandson Richard II, and Edward IV, who most fully developed the potential of the tournament as a vehicle for courtly pageantry, lavish display, and chivalric festivity. Moreover, Edward IV was the first to draw upon the models of the magnificent Burgundian tournaments that were to so touch the fancies of the first two Tudor monarchs, Henry VII and Henry VIII.

The great dukedom of Burgundy, far more powerful than France itself, was politically and culturally the most dominant power in northern Europe during the fifteenth century. Through skilfully-contrived dynastic marriages and territorial expansion, what we know today as the French province of Burgundy in eastern France had become a vast ducal domain that reached northwards to the sea and included Franche Comté, Luxembourg, Hainaut, Picardy, and Artois, not to mention almost the entire area now known as Belgium and the Netherlands. At this time an endless round of festivities—banquets, revels, tournaments—provided a model of matchless splendour which was the envy of the rest of Europe, and the court of Philip the Good and of his successor Charles the Bold was the focus for an unparalleled revival of chivalry and fascination with romance. Close ties between the English and Burgundian courts were made when Edward IV's sister, Margaret of York, married Charles the Bold in 1468. The marriage was celebrated at Bruges with a tournament, the *Pas de l'Arbre d'Or*, a gigantic spectacle befitting the wealthiest ruler in Europe. The many Englishmen who attended must have been amazed by the continuous pageantry, the rich costumes, the portable pavilions, and the general opulence displayed in every detail. Indeed, one Englishman remarked in a letter home to his mother that the richness of it all was such as 'I herd nevyr' and that 'as for the Dwkys coort, as of lords, ladys and gentylwomen, knyts, sqwyers, and gentylmen, I hert never of non lyek to it, save King Artourys cort'.[15] Following the alliance created by this marriage and by Edward's pact of friendship and defence with Charles, Charles' court was the obvious place for King Edward to take refuge a few years later during his brief exile from England (1470–71), though Charles at the time had little use for Edward the powerless refugee, and gave him less than a warm welcome at first.

Other obvious connections between the English and Burgundian courts arose from the fact that Edward's wife, Elizabeth Woodville, was the daughter of Jacquetta of Luxembourg. Her brother Anthony not only assisted in the marriage negotiations for Edward's sister but fought in a famous London tournament against the Grand Bastard of Burgundy in 1467 and a year later went to Bruges to fight in the *Pas de l'Arbre d'Or*. Not surprisingly, English interest in and imitation of the court of Burgundy during Edward's reign touched many aspects of cultural life: education, literature, the collecting of manuscripts and books, and the revival of chivalric ideals.[16] Following the brief interruption of Richard III's reign, Burgundian influences were renewed when Henry VII consciously set out in a far more consistent manner than Edward to model many aspects of the newly-established Tudor court upon that of Burgundy. Among the numerous signs of this was the sudden transition to a new tournament style in November 1501 when the participants entered the tiltyard in Burgundian pageant cars, hung their shields from a Tree of Chivalry like that of the Grand Bastard in Bruges in 1468, and apparelled themselves in various symbolic guises.[17]

This brings us to the most essential point about the kind of tournaments staged at Henry VII's court. Throughout Europe, but particularly at the Burgundian court, the tournament had become recognized as the public spectacle *par excellence*, which a national leader could use in the profoundly serious political exercise of displaying his or her magnificence. Courtesy books and books of advice for rulers make much of this virtue, emphasizing that lavish display and expenditure of wealth were both proper and necessary as signs of status and pre-eminence. At the same time, whenever foreign visitors were entertained, whenever a ruler or that ruler's representative travelled abroad, or whenever some occasion put national prestige at stake, that prestige could be defined in large measure by the richness of outward trappings, from clothes, jewellery, horses and weapons to the number of retainers, buildings, ships, gifts, banquets, and masques.

The tournament as it had become by the fifteenth century, with its accompanying banquets, dances and rich prizes, offered an unparalleled opportunity for combining many of these ingredients. Knights and horses could be equipped with impressive and extremely expensive plate armour, which for purposes of national prestige was ideally made by native armourers. Over that armour the knights might wear elaborately decorated and bejewelled costumes, while their horses might be arrayed in embroidered caparisons often decorated with a motto and emblematic picture (the knight's impresa). A single knight might have many retainers, all richly dressed in their master's colours. They would accompany him in procession to the tiltyard, carrying his lances and weapons, and leading his spare horses. To accompany a knight's entry into the tiltyard, there might be expensive and elaborate scenic devices, perhaps involving actors and musicians and the performance of some form of dramatic presentation that at times could imbue the subsequent fighting with allegorical significance.

All these elements, so typical of the great tournament festivals in Burgundy and at the various courts of the Hapsburgs, the Valois, the Bourbons, and the Medici, were also adopted at the Tudor and Jacobean courts. Underlying these displays of magnificence were the political motivations from which they derived. The tournament was more than mere sport and its place in the court calendar based on more than entertainment. Only political motivation makes sense of the fact that Henry VIII spent £4000 on the Westminster tournament of 1511, almost double the cost (£2300) of his 900-ton warship, the *Great Elizabeth*. Unfortunately historians and commentators from Puritan times on have tended to see the later English tournament as little more than a self-indulgent and

ephemeral pastime, and a rather expensive one at that. This has led to a view of it as somehow decadent, a falling-off from some supposed ideal, but the reality is otherwise, and viewed in its social and political context, however alien that may be to us, the tournament had an important role to fulfil.[18]

Although that role was not solely or even principally that of preparation for war, the Tudors none the less liked to pretend that the tiltyard could be a nursery for real combat. The challenge for the 1501 tournament to celebrate the marriage of Prince Arthur and Katherine of Aragon, for example, spoke of the 'exercise and faictes of the Necessary discipline of armes', and when Sir Rowland de Vieilleville received a fanciful challenge in 1507, it spoke of how the ensuing tournament would serve to provide 'exercise to them that honour desyreth and to make folkes more apte to serue ther prince when cawses shall require'.[19]

Late in Henry VIII's reign, the same theme was still being reiterated. When a tournament was held in May 1540, the challenge spoke of how in the past such 'feats of arms have raised men to honour, both in God's service against his infidel enemies and in serving their princes'.[20] Such sentiments would have appealed to both Henry VII and his son Henry VIII. The older Henry came to the throne after years of civil strife (Fig. 10), and he knew very well that the crown he had gained on the field of Bosworth could only be retained by uniting opposing factions within his kingdom, if necessary through force of arms. Tournaments might not provide a very relevant form of martial training, given the changed military realities of the sixteenth century, but none the less they must have been reassuring in their expression of *esprit de corps* and their assertion of willing service to the monarch through combat at arms.

Yet this perceived value of tournaments comes nowhere near explaining their place in Henry's policies. To understand this we need to see his tournaments as part of a broad strategy aimed at achieving national unity and an unshakeable royal dynasty. His marriage to Elizabeth of York, for example, was a crucial step, for it joined the key rival houses of York and Lancaster. The Tudor dynasty was then secured by the birth of Prince Arthur, since Edward IV had had no surviving male issue.

To further strengthen his position and help unify potential domestic rivals, Henry needed his countrymen to share a strong sense of the reality of his kingship. A united nation was a strong one, and Henry employed various approaches to achieve his purpose. He made effective use of the royal progress, that 'traditional instrument of royal propaganda' by means of which the king, 'with an impressive retinue, could show himself at various key points of the realm, and thereby impress the populace with the reality of an authority which must, frequently, have seemed very remote'.[21] At the same time, he encouraged the use of appropriate symbolism, particularly the white and red rose, signifying the union between the houses of York and Lancaster, and the red dragon, signifying his Welsh ancestry. The dragon also indicated his supposed fulfilment of the prophecy recorded in Geoffrey of Monmouth's *Historia Regum Britanniae*, that the red dragon (the British) would triumph over the white dragon (the Saxons). Henry also encouraged the veneration of his Lancastrian uncle Henry VI as a martyr and source of miracles, thereby strengthening his own status; and he contributed to the development of a powerful Tudor mythology that included such concepts as the return of King Arthur. In addition, Henry strengthened his position through the careful use of patronage and the placing of allies in positions of power throughout the country, while systematically removing his enemies. Parliament's aid was enlisted to confirm his title and to establish a strong tax base, and successive small rebellions were methodically put down, each success strengthening his hand against any further threat. Though he disbanded his

10 *Portrait of Henry VII by Michiel Sittow (1505). After defeating Richard III at the Battle of Bosworth, Henry VII united the Houses of York and Lancaster by marrying Elizabeth of York. He fully understood the potential of tournaments as instruments of prestige propaganda.*

mercenary troops, Henry did form his own permanent military force, the Yeomen of the Guard. Small in numbers, they were apparently none the less sufficiently impressive to add further strength to his grip on the throne.

As a plank in his overall strategy, Henry used public display to impress the authority of his presence upon his subjects. He began this process with his carefully-timed triumphant entry into London twelve days after his victory at Bosworth, the event climaxing with the presentation of his three banners at St Paul's, one of which was the fiery red dragon so important in the new national mythology. His coronation, which followed the customary, but in this instance very grand, procession from the Tower to Westminster Hall, was more magnificent than that of any previous king, for Henry spent over £1500 on it in a calculated and very successful bid to gain the admiration of his people. Then came the traditional coronation banquet, a sumptuous affair at which Henry entertained representatives of the Law, the City of London, the Church, the Lords temporal and other knights, and prominent citizens.

The conspicuous and expensive showmanship Henry displayed on this occasion and on similar occasions throughout his reign has always seemed something of a paradox, in view of the fact that Henry is often alleged to have been parsimonious and lacking in flamboyance, even perhaps introverted. Yet Henry clearly knew when it was politically expedient to spend, and spend he did. There was his marriage to Elizabeth, the celebration of Prince Arthur's birth, the coronation of Elizabeth, the ceremonies and festivities marking the creation of Prince Arthur as Prince of Wales and Prince Henry as Duke of York, the marriage of Arthur to Katherine of Aragon, the celebration of the league between Henry and the King of the Romans, the meeting between Henry and Philip of Burgundy, and the betrothal of Princess Mary to Charles of Burgundy. Henry also spent amply and judiciously on feasts, plays, pageants and other such events appropriate to the regular court holiday celebrations of Christmas, New Year, Shrovetide and May Day. As those of his account books to survive also show, Henry spent heavily on building works, clothes for himself and his retainers, jewels, gifts, and the general entertainment of foreign visitors and ambassadors.

At the court of any powerful Renaissance prince, expenditure on foreign guests was of especial importance, and it is clear that Henry fully appreciated that his prestige abroad, as at home, was in part dependent upon his policies of conspicuous display and magnificence. That he was singularly successful in establishing for himself and his country the kind of image he no doubt hoped for is apparent from the descriptions of chroniclers and from ambassadorial despatches, both of which often seem almost obsessively concerned with noting details of clothing, jewellery and pageantry.[22]

Henry VII's policies of calculated display were not unusual for a Renaissance ruler, though in his case there was a particular need to establish the authority of his kingship. As we shall see, his English successors followed him by celebrating the major festivals of the calendar as of old with due munificence, and by ensuring that important events such as coronations, royal marriages and births, military victories, treaties with other nations, and visits by foreign dignitaries were appropriately marked by magnificent show. In terms of propaganda to bolster the status of the monarch, Tudor and Jacobean tournaments were the most frequent and lavishly financed form of spectacle to be used for this purpose. They were never mere entertainment (though entertaining they certainly were), extravagant fantasy, or archaic exercises of obsolete military skills.

The political motives behind Henry VII's tournaments were evident in those of his successors; but with some qualifications. Henry VIII, for example, was a vigorous and skilful participant, and there is no doubt of the delight he took in the tournament *per se* and of the means it provided for him to display his athletic prowess (Fig. 11). Though he remained in the royal viewing stand at his coronation tournament in 1509, he made his first public appearance several months later in January 1510 in the tiltyard at Richmond. Unlike his father, Henry VIII seems to have felt no urgent need to bolster his hold upon the throne, but as if to compensate, his attitude to foreign affairs was singularly aggressive, and, whether planned or not, his prowess at tournaments quickly earned the admiration of foreign ambassadors. Their reports not only conveyed the usual details of sumptuous finery and impressive show, but tended to add comments on Henry's martial skills and valour as a fighter. The fol-

lowing description by Sebastian Giustinian, the Venetian ambassador, is typical. Speaking of the May Day tournament at Greenwich in 1515, he said:

After dinner, a stately joust took place, at which his Majesty jousted with many others, strenuously and valorously; and assuredly, most serene Prince, from what we have seen of him, and in conformity, moreover, with the report made to us by others, this most serene King is not only very expert in arms, and of great valour, and most excellent in his personal endowments, but is likewise so gifted and accomplished with mental accomplishments of every sort that we believe him to have few equals in the world.[23]

No doubt Henry's father would have approved. Not only was the money laid out for the tournament getting a proper return, but here was a son whose personal reputation as a brave and able combatant, made evident by his feats in tournaments, was being enhanced in all the proper foreign quarters, accompanied by praise for his mental accomplishments. Here was an English prince to be reckoned with.

Henry VIII's active participation in tournaments, in which he was often chief challenger and/or a prize-winner, lasted until 1527, after which time he seems to have resigned himself to being a spectator. However, he had much to look back on. His most memorable tournament must surely have been that in 1520, the legendary Field of Cloth of Gold, at which he and King Francis I spent staggering sums of money to achieve the maximum show of magnificence in what seems to have been a sincere, though doomed, attempt to solve some of the major European political problems by a show of good will and chivalric brotherhood

(Fig. 12). In the course of this vast public display, the two Kings fought side by side in a lengthy and complex tournament that symbolically transformed past hostility, as if by a process of sublimation, into the genteel 'sport' of chivalric encounters in the lists.

During the latter part of Henry's reign the number of tournaments decreased considerably. Perhaps, like many a retired athlete, he preferred not to have to watch the prowess of others younger and more active than himself, and perhaps the inspiration flagged with the fall of Wolsey, the chief architect of many of Henry's most stunning spectacles.[24] England's increasingly insular situation, following Henry's break with Rome in the early 1530s, may also be significant. The aggressive foreign policy of former times, with its theme of universal peace, and its vision of England as the arbiter of Europe, was clearly no longer relevant. Furthermore, when his old desires for military glory revived and Henry invaded both Scotland and France in the 1540s, the chief consequence was the ruin of the English economy. Prodigious expenditure on prestige propaganda would in future no longer be so easy. Whatever the full explanation for the dearth of tournaments in the latter years of the reign, there was, as will be clear in a moment, little to match the grandeur of his earlier tiltyard displays in the years that followed his death in 1547 until the accession of his daughter Elizabeth in 1558.

The reign of Henry's son, Edward VI (Fig. 13), began in February 1547 with the customary royal entry into London, elaborate coronation ritual, and celebratory banquet in Westminster Hall, with the Royal Champion appearing on horseback to issue the traditional challenge against all who disputed the King's rightful succession. As was customary also, there was a tournament. At the time Edward was nine years old and he was to live only another six years. His untimely death appears to have led many historians to overemphasize his supposedly weak constitution. Sydney Anglo, for example, noting Edward's youth, his 'only

11 Henry VIII as warrior knight. His broken lance suggests that he has just jousted successfully. His horse wears a shaffron, a crinet and a bard decorated with Tudor roses.

moderate health', and the difficult political situation in England, has suggested that there were 'but a handful of tilts and tourneys' during the reign and that the tournament did not enjoy a revival.[25] But the evidence would appear to suggest that it was really only Edward's youth that imposed limitations. In fact, it can be argued that Edward was initially a fairly robust, even athletic child, whose brief kingship saw far more tournaments than the closing fourteen years of his father's reign, during which only three tournaments took place. Edward was instructed in the art of tilting and managing horses, and he delighted 'in every sort of exercise'.[26] However, his appearances at tournaments were restricted, as we might expect, to the moderately safe running at ring. This was a form of exercise recommended in treatises of the time as a

12   Henry VIII's meeting with Francis I at Guisnes (June 1520). The Field of Cloth of Gold, one of the most extravagant diplomatic exercises ever, included a tournament. The specially built tournament ground with its great Tree of Chivalry can be seen in the top right corner.

means of practising tilting, the opponent being replaced by a ring suspended from a post beside the tilt barrier. Participants would take turns to ride along the tilt, the winner being whoever speared the ring with his lance the most times after a set number of turns (or courses). Edward performed in such competitions in April and May 1551 and again in May 1552. Had he been older, he would no doubt have emulated his father by tilting against mounted opponents, though there is

no telling whether his skills would ever have matched those of Henry.

During Edward's reign and in addition to the events just mentioned, there was a running at ring at a reception for ambassadors, a combat at barriers to celebrate the New Year and a water tournament at Deptford, all in 1550, and there were tournaments in 1548, 1550 and 1552 (two separate events on 3 and 17 January) to mark the festivals of Shrovetide and New Year, and the marriage of the Earl of Warwick's son to the Duke of Somerset's daughter. For a reign generally lacking in royal betrothals, weddings, births, coronations of consorts, and major foreign treaties, this record is fairly substantial. Furthermore, the elaborate debate and ensuing combat at barriers between the Champions of Youth and the

13   Portrait of Edward VI (studio of William Scrots, c. 1546). Though many historians have stressed Edward's ill-health, he was a keen student of the martial arts. Tournaments and running at ring were common during his brief reign.

Champions of Riches in January 1552 and the May running at ring and tourney with swords the year before also indicate that a degree of appropriate magnificence was by no means lacking.

Edward himself has described the 1551 event in which he and his followers competed against a party of men led by the Protector's son (the Earl of Hertford):

The challenge at running at ring performed, at the
  which first came the King, sixteen footmen, and

ten horsemen, in black silk coats pulled out with white silk taffeta; then all lords having three men likewise appareled, and all gentlemen, their footmen in white fustian pulled out with black taffeta. The other side came all in yellow taffeta. At length the yellow band took it twice in 120 course, and my band tainted often—which was counted as nothing—and took never—which seemed very strange—and so the prize was of my side lost. After that, tourney followed between six of my band and six of theirs.[27]

To this we can add the diarist Henry Machyn's description of this 'grett tryhumpe at Grenwyche', with its 'trumpeters, hats, clokes, and baners blacke and whytt, and speres'.[28] Edward's father would probably not have thought much of his son's performance at this event, but the point is that, within the limitations imposed upon him by age, Edward appears to have ensured by his presence at tournaments that they continued as a vehicle for kingly magnificence, even if circumstances did not permit events on the mammoth scale employed by his father and grandfather. Just how consciously such displays were manipulated as instruments of policy during the Regency is, however, difficult to say. Apart from the general inferences to be drawn by spectators from the sight of the young Edward practising his martial skills so as to prove his potential as a military leader of his people, there is little evidence of any specific connection between tournaments and policy.[29]

When Edward's sister Mary became Queen in July 1553, there was the usual pomp and pageantry attending her coronation. Given her close escape from the Earl of Northumberland's conspiracy to place Lady Jane Grey on the throne in her stead, and given some initial opposition to her catholicism, she might have been tempted, after her grandfather's pattern, to do everything in her power to make her coronation festivities enforce the image of the reality of her accession as fully as possible. But though both her entry into London and her coronation certainly followed ancient custom, there is no record of them being marked by the traditional tournament. Such an event would have permitted all her subjects public access to her presence in the Whitehall tiltyard, where they would have been able to gaze at will (if only from afar) upon their newly-crowned Queen as she presided over the martial feats of her knights. Not that Mary's welcome to the throne was anything less than warm, but her rapid shift away from religious moderation and tolerance soon began to undermine her popularity, a process accelerated in 1554 by her marriage to Philip of Spain (Fig. 14), a Roman Catholic and heir to the Spanish throne. Though Mary and Philip's marriage and their triumphal entry into London were accompanied by costly and lavish festivities, including the ceremonial drawing of twenty cartloads of Spanish gold through the streets, the opportunity for a tournament appears once more to have been neglected. Meagre as the evidence is, it would seem that Mary was not particularly interested in feats of arms and the political benefits that she could derive from them.

Yet her reign was not completely without such events. The motive behind them appears to have been the somewhat naïve hope of creating a healthy spirit of bonhomie among English and Spanish through their joint participation in the chivalric sports of the tiltyard. The idea had something in common with the tactics of Henry VIII and Francis I at the Field of Cloth of Gold and of Catherine de Medici, who attempted to use court fêtes and tournaments as an instrument of political appeasement by drawing together rival factions in pleasant and harmless recreations.[30] Mary and Philip's motives were commendable, for the English, notorious in the sixteenth century for their xenophobic tendencies, had quickly become hostile and actively antagonistic towards all things Spanish with the presence of so many Spaniards in England. Thus it was, perhaps

14 *Portrait of Philip II of Spain by an unknown artist (c. 1580). Whereas Mary Tudor appears to have had little taste for tournaments, her consort, whenever in England, attempted to use them as a means of overcoming the hostility between the English and the Spanish at court.*

as something of a calculated risk, that in November 1554 Don Frederick de Toledo, Lord Strange, Don Ferdinando de Toledo, Don Francisco de Mendoca, and Garsulace de la Vega issued a challenge to fight on foot at the barriers against all-comers at Whitehall (Figs 15 and 40). The wording of the challenge endeavoured to remind everyone of the traditionally international nature of tournaments, it having 'bene a custome, that to the Courts of Kings and great Princes, Knights, and Gentlemen, of divers nations have made their repaire for the triall of knighthood, and exercise of armes'.[31]

The event itself took place on 4 December and was judged by two English and two Spanish tournament judges. Philip himself answered the challenge and came second in the award of the prize (a brooch) for 'the fairest and most gallant entry' and first in the combat with foils.[32] Two weeks later another 'grett tryhumph' was held in which Philip and both English and Spanish knights participated 'on fott with spayers and swerds at the tornay'.[33] On January 24 there was another such event, and a few weeks later there was a great dinner (a midday meal) to celebrate the marriage of Lord Strange and Lady Cumberland, followed by jousting and a tourney on horseback with swords. This was in turn followed by supper and a game involving canes, the *Juego de cannes*, a Spanish novelty which characteristically seems not to have found much favour with English spectators.

Such efforts to bring English and Spanish together in feats of arms continued the following month. On 25 March, which was Lady Day, there was, so Machyn informs us, 'as gret justes as youe have sene' in the Whitehall tiltyard.[34] The challenge was shared between a Spaniard and Sir George Howard, whose men and horses entered trimmed in white. They were followed by Philip and many others in blue trimmed with yellow, their helmets sporting blue and yellow plumes. Mingled in among them were various other retainers in exotic Turkish

costume. After Philip left for the Netherlands in September, such events ceased until his return to England in 1557, but in December of that year possibly the most spectacular tournament of Mary's reign occurred. The young Princess Elizabeth, soon to be queen, sat with Philip and Mary to watch a grand spectacle at which some two hundred spears were broken.

Thus, tournaments continued after Edward's death, but they seem to have occurred only at the instigation of Mary's consort, and their purpose seems to have been largely confined to the hopeless task of improving Anglo-Spanish relations. Mary's general lack of enthusiasm may have had something to do with this policy, but probably it had more to do with the depleted state of the crown coffers, her subjects' increasing lack of enthusiasm for her reign, her own sickness and private unhappiness, and the disastrous decline of England's prestige abroad, culminating in the loss of Calais to France. All these factors collectively worked against the holding of such joyful public extravaganzas as her father had initiated in the tiltyards of Greenwich, Westminster Palace and Whitehall. During the long reign of Mary's sister Elizabeth (Fig. 16), however, all this was to change.

Like her father, though in very different and quite novel ways, Elizabeth discovered how to exploit the tournament as an instrument of propaganda to her maximum advantage.

When Mary died on 17 November 1558, there was little in the way of national grief. Elizabeth's ceremonial entry into London and her coronation early in the New Year, on the other hand, were accompanied by an extra measure of heartfelt rejoicing. Although the tournament scheduled to follow the day after on 16 January had to be postponed for twenty-four hours because Elizabeth was in a state of exhaustion, it was none the less a full-scale affair lasting two days, and it employed what had become virtually the standard format for both English and European tournaments. The combats were preceded and concluded by elaborate processions of the Challengers, Defenders, and their various retainers. Within this framework, which allowed for a full display of pageantry and the participants' finery, there were three categories of combat. The first and most important event was the Jousts Royal, or tilting. Then followed the tourney. The procedure generally adopted for this event in the latter half of the sixteenth century can be seen in the Elizabethan illustration of the three types of combat (see Fig. 17). This shows one

LEFT

15   Foot combat at barriers with swords. Large numbers of such weapons might be required for a tournament and baskets of spare swords can be seen in the background.

BELOW RIGHT

16   Portrait of Elizabeth I by Marcus Gheeraerts the Younger (c. 1592). The so-called 'Ditchley' portrait alludes to the relationship between Elizabeth and her Champion, Sir Henry Lee. It also exemplifies the elaborate fantasy created by the cult of Elizabeth and given full rein in the tiltyard.

knight running at another without a tilt barrier to separate them, a form of combat which presumably originated in the early medieval open mêlée. Finally there were foot combats, usually fought across a barrier, first with spears and then with swords. Occasionally variations were introduced into this tripartite arrangement—(Henry VIII fought with axes on foot at one tournament)—but in general this was the conventional Renaissance pattern. During Edward's and Mary's reigns, for the various reasons cited above, this pattern had often been discarded, but with Elizabeth's coronation tournament it was once more restored and remained the convention for English tournaments as it had been during the first two Tudor reigns.

The eight tournaments during the first seven years of Elizabeth's reign appear to have served primarily as an opportunity for some of her aspiring courtiers to vie for her favour by impressing her with feats of arms and lavish display. It would seem that it was not so much a case of the monarch attempting to impress her subjects as a matter of them seeking to gain her attention. Particularly prominent were the two Dudley brothers (Fig. 18), Ambrose (the Earl of Warwick) and Robert (soon to be Earl of Leicester and perhaps already an aspirant for Elizabeth's

hand in marriage). At the beginning of her reign, the Dudley family was in a somewhat precarious position. After their treasonous involvement in the Lady Jane Grey conspiracy, it had only been because of their conspicuous military service at the siege of St Quentin that Mary in 1557 lifted from them the act of attainder that had marred the fortunes of the entire family. Both Ambrose and Robert had been friendly with Elizabeth in earlier days, and they were doubtless more than relieved when she came to the throne and their political fortunes began to flourish. For them the tiltyard offered opportunities for public displays of loyalty and martial talent.

Such motives were to set a pattern for future young hopefuls at Elizabeth's court,

the most memorable of these being Sir Philip Sidney (Leicester's nephew) in the 1570s and early 1580s and the Earl of Essex (Leicester's stepson) in the 1580s and 1590s. Such young men of the second half of Elizabeth's reign appear to have been further attracted by the chivalric ideals so colourfully passed on to them in the literature of the romances. These ideals were revitalized in such fashionable contemporary works as the *Amadis de Gaule*, Ariosto's *Orlando Furioso*, Tasso's *Gerusa-lemme Liberata*, Sidney's *Arcadia*, and Spenser's *Faerie Queene*. Handbooks of courtly behaviour, exemplified by Castiglione's widely-read *The Courtier*, also played a part in this process. For Sidney, who once confessed that he 'never heard the old song of *Percy* and *Duglas*', without finding his heart 'mooved more then with a Trumpet',[35] or for Essex, who at the siege of Lisbon thrust his pike into the city gate and offered to break a lance in honour of his mistress (Elizabeth) against

17 *This Elizabethan illustration is a unique record of a tourney. The knights fight one on one with blunted and rebated swords.*

anyone daring to come out and face him, the tiltyard and its associations with chivalric romance must have been irresistible.

The naïve and egotistic behaviour of Essex, flying in the face of contemporary realities, makes sense in the context of an era which modelled private morality and public duty on an ideal image of the past. Nowhere is this better exemplified than in Spenser's *Faerie Queene* and the figure of Prince Arthur, who is described in Spenser's prefatory letter to Sir Walter Raleigh as 'perfected in the twelve private morall vertues, as Aristotle hath devised'. In his quest for the Faerie Queene (Elizabeth), Arthur is intended to represent the virtue of magnificence by his

18 *Jousting close helmet of the Earl of Leicester (c. 1576). The helmet, like the remainder of the armour, is etched with the ragged staff motif of the Dudley family. The visor has breathing holes on the right-hand side only, so that the side of the face nearest to an opponent is completely protected.*

deeds. Mythic history (the Arthur story), the chivalric ideal, and contemporary reality are thus combined.[36] At the same time, the attraction of the tiltyard may also have had something to do with the fact that the Tudor regime had no place for the aristocracy's hereditary sense of power and pride, and some outlet for the old aggressions was needed. The tiltyard could still be a place where, disguised in the surface appearance of chivalric gentility, pride could be vindicated and aggressive energies released.[37] For her part Elizabeth seems to have responded warmly to her subjects' tiltyard antics, especially when these were part and parcel of a display of ritualized service, though as always she was cautious in bestowing her favours in return, as both Sidney and Essex discovered.

In the course of her reign, the earlier tournaments so dominated by the Dudleys were followed by tournaments designed to mark two types of public occasion. As in her father's reign, tournaments were vehicles for prestige propaganda. However, though they were still held to celebrate such events as important weddings (two in 1565 and one in 1572), a military victory (1588), and the festivals of Shrovetide (1595) and Christmas (1564–65), there were few such tournaments compared to the corresponding occasions in her father's reign. Instead, the Elizabethan tournaments from about 1570 onwards were usually of two kinds. Either they were special events to honour visiting foreign dignitaries, or they formed part of the regular annual celebration of Elizabeth's accession each 17 November.

With the first type of tournament, Elizabeth ensured that her magnificence, her subjects' loyalty, and her warriors' prowess in feats of arms were duly reported by foreign visitors in their despatches to other European courts. Such had been the policy of both Henry VII and Henry VIII, and, like them, Elizabeth seems to have been singularly successful in achieving her aim, judging from the glowing descriptions of some of her foreign guests. Typical of Elizabeth's policy in action were the special preparations she demanded when a visitor from Russia happened to be in London at the time of her Accession Day tournament in 1600. Rowland White, in a letter to Sir Robert Sidney, remarked: 'I heare that this yeare her Majesty wold have very great care taken that her Coronacion [i.e. Accession] day be with gallant solemnyties at tilt and turney observed, to the end the embassador of Russia may hold yt in admiracion.'[38]

Tournaments also provided Elizabeth with a means of consolidating and maintaining domestic unity and regal authority at home, a perhaps more important function than their potential in building her reputation abroad.

The Accession Day tournaments were a novel institution admirably suited to just such aims. Precisely when they began is not completely clear. According to William Segar, the herald and painter, 'these annuall exercises in Armes, solemnized the 17. day of Nouember, were first begun and occasioned by the right vertuous and honourable Sir *Henry Lea* [. . .] who of his great zeale, and earnest desire to eternize the glory of her Maiesties Court, in the beginning of her happy reigne, voluntarily vowed (vnlesse infirmity, age, or other accident did impeach him) during his life, to present himselfe at the Tilt armed, the day aforesayd yeerly, there to performe in honor of her sacred Maiestie the promise he formerly made. Whereupon the Lords and Gentlemen of the sayd Court, incited by so worthy an example, determined to continue that custome.'[39] That Sir Henry Lee was the instigator is confirmed by his epitaph, which refers to his 'Honouringe his highlye gracious M[ist]ris with Reysinge those later Olimpiads of her Coronation Justs and Tournaments', and by one of his own tiltyard speeches in which he refers to himself as the 'first Celebrater, in this kind, of this sacred memory of that blessed reign'.[40]

In spite of Segar's claim that the Accession Day tournaments date from the beginning of Elizabeth's reign, they probably began somewhat later. William Camden says that the November anniversary was first celebrated with a tournament following the twelfth year of Elizabeth's reign (17 November 1569 to 16 November 1570),[41] and its origins may hence have had something to do with the general rejoicing following the suppression of the Northern Rebellion in 1569–70. The earliest actual evidence of an Accession Day tournament dates from 1577 when the Earl of Arundel, Lord Windsor, Philip Sidney and Fulke Greville, as challengers, fought against twelve defenders, among whom was Sir Henry Lee, and there is also some inconclusive evidence of similar tournaments in 1578 and 1579. Certainly, by 17 November 1581, Accession Day tournaments were well established as 'the ordinary exercise of Armes' yearly used.[42] As surviving records then show, an Accession Day tournament was held every year of Elizabeth's reign from 1581, apart from one year (1582) in which an outbreak of the plague prevented the court from

coming to London. Furthermore the Accession Day tournament was always held in the same place, the Whitehall tiltyard, apart from 1593 when the court stayed at Windsor because of the plague and held the tournament there.

The November 17 tournaments were only one mode of celebration marking what was a major and highly popular national holiday. Throughout the land Elizabeth's day was marked by sermons, bell-ringing, firework displays, the firing of guns, the lighting of bonfires, the distribution of alms to prisoners and bread to the poor, the keeping of open table in great households, and the publication of literary tributes to England's virgin Queen. The holiday seems to have had a particularly anti-papal flavour, which was all part of a growing cult of Elizabeth as the saviour of the reformed Church. That cult involved an elaborate pattern of ritual and ceremonial affecting not just tournaments but the Queen's formal progresses through the countryside, the annual feast of the Garter, and a whole variety of other court festivals.[43]

For saints' days and the religious pageantry and festivity often associated with them in the past, the Elizabethans substituted Accession Day, a new holy day of Elizabeth to surpass 'all the Pope's holidays'. For the court and for Londoners, its centrepiece, the tournament, combined the imagery of chivalry and religion in expressing her loyal knights' dedication to her service. The following extract from the tiltyard speech of a knight who arrives at a tournament accompanied by a group of countrymen typifies the sentiments commonly expressed each 17 November:

Now most gracious Q[ueen] as they were of late makinge merye with this homely melodye, [. . .] one that came from the Church told them, how the Curate had shewed his p[ari]shioners of a holdaye wich passed all the popes holidays, & that shold be kept the Seaventeenth daye of Nouember, The Knight remembringe then the vowe he had made, w[hi]ch was whilest he cold sett on a horse, & carye a staff in his hand, to

19 Portrait of James I (attributed to John de Critz). James, though a lover of horses and hunting, rarely participated in tournaments. None the less, tournaments were frequent during his reign, and he fully appreciated their value in enhancing the prestige of himself and his country.

sacrefice yearly the strength of his arme in honor of her that was m[istress] of his hart, Told these his neighbours, he must goe from [them] a while, ney by St marye q[uoth] they then wee will goe with you, & take such p[art] as you doe, so shall we see for the spence of a few pence the godliest ladye (god blesse her) that eu[er] man sett eie on.[44]

In a curious but completely characteristic fashion, the attitudes expressed in such speeches were further extended following the victory over the Spanish Armada in 1588. In that year the normal events of 17 November

flowed over into a second tournament which was held on what was coincidentally the most appropriate of Saints' days. As one contemporary explained: 'Every year on the 17th November the Queen celebrates the feast of her coronation; and this year on the 19th, which is St Elizabeth's Day, she determined to hold another festival, in celebration of the recent events [i.e. the Armada victory]. There was a great public procession, jousts, and great bonfires all over the city.'[45] Records of further tournaments on St Elizabeth's Day exist for 1590, 1594, 1596 and 1598. On each of these occasions the Earl of Essex acted as a principal challenger (in 1594 he was the only challenger), and one suspects that he somehow adopted this extension of the Accession Day celebrations as an opportunity to show himself to maximum advantage, making the day as much Essex' Day as Elizabeth's.

If Essex tried to steal the limelight on such occasions (as he later almost stole the crown), he none the less had no discernible effect upon the general adoration of Elizabeth which so dominated the tournaments of her reign, as will emerge later. What will also become apparent is how Elizabeth, having received a near-empty treasury from Mary, skilfully managed to shift onto others much of the financial burden of staging tournaments. As one of her subjects so tellingly put it after the 1590 tournament: 'These sports were great and done in costly sort, to her Majesty's liking, and their great cost.'[46]

With the reign of James I (Fig. 19), the nature of English tournaments changed once more. Elizabeth had made full use of her sex and virgin status to play the role of lady of honour when presiding in the tiltyard, and it might have been expected that the King, as a male, would make some attempt to enter the tiltyard as soldier-knight, as in the days of Henry VIII and Edward VI. But this was clearly not at all to James' taste. Though he loved the outdoors and would spend hours on the back of a horse when out hunting, and though in his treatise for his son, *Basilikon*

Doron, he recommended the art of jousting, James kept his participation in tournaments to a minimum. During the visit of his brother-in-law, King Christian of Denmark, in 1606, for example, the two Kings ran at the ring, but in the tournament held the next day to celebrate James' escape from the Gowrie conspiracy, it was only King Christian who entered the lists to tilt against armed opponents.

Other forays against the ring were made by James in 1609 and 1613. This latter event was part of the celebration of the wedding of his daughter, Princess Elizabeth, and it involved the King, his son Prince Charles, and his son-in-law, together with members of the English nobility and their foreign counterparts. By all accounts it was a splendid show, but the truth remains that James had neither the temperament nor, probably, the skill to follow the example of his great, great uncle, Henry VIII. None the less, his reign saw a steady succession of tournaments. Although no coronation tournament was held in July 1603 because of the plague, annual Accession Day tournaments took place thereafter each 24 March, with very few exceptions. In addition to the Accession Day tournaments, special events were held to celebrate weddings in 1606, 1613, and 1614, and there were tournaments to entertain important foreign visitors in 1606 (the King of Denmark), 1607 (the Prince de Joinville), 1610 (the Prince of Brunswick), 1621 (French ambassadors), and 1622 (Philip, Landgrave of Hesse).

Superficially, then, the pattern of tournaments would seem to be very similar to that of Elizabeth's reign. However, it is clear that the fervour of admiration for Elizabeth, transformed into a complex chivalric cult in the tiltyard, was never transferred to James. His dislike and fear of crowds, his inability or unwillingness to participate in tournaments, and his many failings that so lessened his general popularity, all worked against him. None the less, in the eyes of his people, he offered one special

asset not shared by Elizabeth—he had two sons. Furthermore, as the two boys became older, they showed considerable enthusiasm for tournaments, thereby for a time giving such events new life and reviving the whole chivalric apparatus that had dominated Elizabeth's tournaments.

This was particularly evident in the case of James' elder son, Prince Henry (Fig. 20). For this aptly-named youth, who was only nine years old when his father succeeded to the throne of England in 1603, there was from the first enormous popular enthusiasm in all ranks of English society. Rapid disappointment in James hastened the elevation of Henry into a cult figure. He would be the perfect king, a warrior like his namesake Henry V, a wondrous embodiment of the chivalric virtues, a knight-defender of Protestantism, and a hero in whom the peoples of the new Great Britain could invest their hopes and dreams of national greatness. As early as 1606, during the visit of his uncle, the King of Denmark, Prince Henry made a public appearance that seems to have been designed to offer the spectators in the tiltyard an image of a warrior-king-to-be.[47] During the same visit, the Prince also ran at ring, and three years later he again participated in this sport in a match against his father. But his real debut as a participant in martial spectacles was on Twelfth Night, 1610, when he and six assistants fought a combat on foot at barriers against fifty-six opponents in the Banqueting Hall at Whitehall.[48]

At this event, there seems to have been a conscious attempt to create, or perhaps consolidate, the chivalric cult that had developed around the fifteen-year-old boy. In his challenge, delivered at court on 31 December, he named himself Meliadus, Lord of the Isles, and addressing 'the valorous knights, of ye Courte of greate Bryttayne', he invited them to the 'accomplishm[en]t of highe enterprises'.[49] As William Drummond of Hawthorden later explained, Henry's chosen name was an aptly-chosen anagram, *Miles a Deo* (soldier of God).[50] Henry's entry

Par Achillis, Puer vne vinçes .

20 *Prince Henry as martial hero. The popularity of Prince Henry at the beginning of James I's reign amounted to an extravagant cult. Among other things, Englishmen perceived him as a future warrior-knight who would defend England and the cause of Protestantism. Comparisons with his predecessors, Henry V and Henry VIII, were common.*

into the Banqueting Hall in the presence of the King and Queen and the ambassadors of Spain and Venice was planned as a spectacular piece of ceremonial. As if this were not sufficient to show the world the young prince's promise for the future, there was also a dramatic *mise-en-scène* composed by Ben Jonson to accompany the event, with scenic devices by Inigo Jones.

In no uncertain terms, Jonson revived the Tudor mythology of Arthur. First the Lady of the Lake appeared, lamenting the decay of chivalry since Arthur's time, but then Arthur himself was revealed to prophesy that a knight was at hand 'that by the might/And magic of his arm' would restore the 'ruined seats of virtue'. Merlin then arose from his tomb and Meliadus was presented as the epitome of knighthood ('Glory of knights and hopes of all the earth'). Henry's presence caused Chivalry to wake from her slumber, at which point the combat began.[51] The young prince was introduced by Merlin as the true successor of England's earlier warlike kings, since the chivalric glories of Arthur would be revived in him.

In future developments of this kind,[52] King James, though given due veneration as a virtually god-like figure, was almost completely side-stepped. Prince Henry and his knightly promise for the future were what caught the emotions and hopes of English subjects. Had it not been for Henry's untimely death in November 1612, there is no doubt that, once he had become old enough to participate in jousting, the tiltyard would have provided the perfect setting for a popular cult of adoration, equivalent to that which had once developed around Elizabeth. Whether the young prince would ever have had the political abilities and qualities of character to sustain the role is another question.

After the young Prince's death, the outpouring of national grief was extra-ordinary, akin perhaps to the sense of shattered dreams that accompanied the aftermath of President Kennedy's assassi-nation in 1963. For a replacement for Meliadus, Britain would have to look to his younger brother Prince Charles, but the revived chivalric cult that had flowered so strongly around Henry never seems to have taken firm root around Charles. Yet, in some respects, Charles was equally well qualified to satisfy his compatriots' desire for a knightly hero. In 1613 he had participated in running at ring before a great crowd in the Whitehall tiltyard in honour of his sister's wedding. A contemporary account of his appearance records that 'the braue yong flower, and hope of England, Prince *Charles*, mounted as it were vpon a Spanish Jennet, that takes his swiftnes from ye nature of the winde, most couragiously, and with much agillitie of hand, tooke the Ring clearely foure times in fiue courses, which was in the eye of the Kings Maiestie and the Nobilitie, there present, a sight of much admiration, and an exceeding comfort to all the land'.[53]

Somewhat surprisingly Charles did not participate in the barriers held in November 1616 to celebrate his creation as Prince of Wales. Indeed, one source indicates that the decision to make the Inns of Court responsible for the event was a deliberate ruse to exclude Charles.[54] However, there were apparently no such concerns in 1620 when, on his father's Accession Day, Prince Charles made an impressive first entry into the Whitehall tiltyard. Accompanied by the Earl Marshall and the heralds, there was first a long and colourful procession to the tiltyard from Denmark House. It included the 'Princes Band of his Artillerie yarde, [. . .] many of the Knight Marshalls men well suited with Tronchions in their handes,' twelve trumpeters, numerous of the Prince's retainers dressed in his colours (green, yellow and silver), some of whom carried the Prince's staves, the Master of the Prince's Horse, and three spare horses 'with plumes, and rich embrothered Caparisons of his Cullors led by Queries or officers of the Stable'.[55] Once in the tiltyard, the prince entered 'a most rich and stately Pauillion' in his colours and decorated with his arms and badges.

A similar entry followed in 1621 and all was prepared for the same thing to be repeated in 1622, but the King was ill, and this tournament had to be cancelled. Thereafter Charles does not seem to have participated in a formal tournament again,[56] but his two appearances in 1620 and 1621 clearly impressed observers, and the Venetian ambassador, Girolamo Lando, wrote to the Doge and Senate of the 'marvellous grace, bravery, splendour and pomp' displayed by the prince and his fellow combatants, and he mentioned that jousting and horsemanship were the prince's 'chief delights'. On another occasion he said: 'In all corporal exercises he is admirable, not resting content with mediocrity. He excels at tilting and indulges in every other kind of horsemanship, and even if he were not prince one would have to confess that he surpassed others.'[57]

Yet this was not enough, and in retrospect we can see that, with the death of Prince

Henry, the desire to create a national mythology based on the imagery of chivalry and using the tiltyard as a venue and focus for prince and knights was at an end. Tournaments continued, ambassadors and subjects continued to be more or less impressed, but some essential ingredient was missing and without it the English tournament was doomed. As far as I can determine, the last of the Stuart tournaments occurred at the outset of Charles' reign, to celebrate his proxy marriage to Henrietta Maria of France in May 1625. Some time after the Queen consort's arrival in England, there were held *des très-belles joustes, & quantite de jeux & de combats a Barriere*.[58] Why, we may wonder, were no further tournaments held after this date? Various factors have to be considered in answering this question.

The matter of cost was probably of key importance. In the main James had adopted Elizabeth's method of financing tournaments by passing many of the expenses on to the participants. Such expenses could be very high, and as Burton remarked in his *Anatomy of Melancholy*, the 'riding of great horses, running at rings, tilts and tournaments' caused many gentlemen to 'gallop quite out of their fortunes',[59] while Chapman in his *Middle Temple and Lincoln's Inn Masque* has Capriccio say that he has 'heard of some courtiers that have run themselves out of their states with jousting'.[60] Yet heavy expenditure, as in Elizabeth's time, was the expected norm. Individual noblemen spent over £1000 each to appear at the tournament to celebrate Prince Henry's creation as Prince of Wales in June 1610, and the Venetian ambassador remarked of the 1610 Accession Day tournament: 'The city will be *en fête* with jousts, for which they have gone to excessive expense, as is the habit of this nation, which, not even in its sports, thinks fit to use things that merely make a show but employs things of solid value.'[61] Various other contemporary comments indicate that the tournaments of James' reign could be as magnificent to the eye and as expensive to the pocket as anything contrived during the time of Elizabeth, though there are few parallels to the scenic devices that appeared in a number of the major Elizabethan tournaments.

Even so, an undercurrent of disappointment appears quite early on. Expectations of glittering and costly splendour, it would appear, were not always met. Of the Accession Day tournament in 1606, for example, one commentator remarked: 'The Tilting was performed very barely, and their whole Equipage poor and penurious, saving the Earls of Pembrook and Montgomery, that was both rich and dainty: There was more expected of Devise and Cost (at least) at the Hands of the Duke of Lenox, and the young Earle of Arundell for the Maidenhead of their running.'[62] Seven years later, two observers recorded their disappointment. One wrote that the tilting 'was as poorely worthe the seeing as any that euer I sawe in my lyfe, and very fewe runners [. . .] None made any shew at all'. The other made the following complaint: 'Some Caparisons seen before, adventured to appear again on the Stage with a little disguisement, even on the back of one of the most curious: So frugal are the times, or so indigent. The two *Riches* [Sir Henry and Sir Robert] only made a speech to the King: the rest were contented with bare Imprese.'[63] Finally, in 1621, although it was generally agreed that the Prince and his entourage made a fine show, the remaining spectacle seems to have been considered no more than 'ordinarie'.[64]

Lack of spectacle, the re-use of old materials, the unwillingness or inability to spend extravagantly, and a decline in the number of participants, all seem to point to a growing disenchantment with the tournament. Several other factors probably also contributed. There was James' perennial love of hunting and the court's growing fascination with horse-racing and wild goose chases; there was probably a decline in the numbers of those able to practise the martial skills (already long obsolete) required for the traditional events of the tournament; and there was a wakening, if not abatement, of those revived chivalric ideals that could not survive for long without the focus provided by a Queen Elizabeth or a Prince Henry. In addition, the public nature of the tournament, which involved the attendance of all ranks of society in a ritualistic celebration of monarchic and national ideals, had lost its political appeal for the Stuarts. Significantly, the complex and costly tournament spectacle of Prince Henry's barriers took place indoors and excluded the general populace. The phenomenal development of the court masque, which obviously owes much to the tradition of tournament spectacle, is a related factor here, since it appears that it threatened to overtake the tournament as the chief vehicle for display propaganda in the course of James' reign. Significantly, the annual Stuart spectacles of state each Twelfth Night and Shrovetide were masques rather than tournaments. With the use of perspective scenery, stage machines, controlled lighting, complex musical effects, and an emphasis upon speech and dance, an indoor setting was to be preferred.

In the masques, courtiers were still seen as heroes, but the monarch increasingly became a supernatural being, even a god. The actions were still largely allegorical, and the central themes were still concerned with the power and prestige of the monarchy, but the masque lacked the key element of the open-air English tournament—the watching ranks of commoners and those not immediately attached to the court. This significant omission is a prophetic sign of the social and political rift between court and people that was to lead to the events of the 1640s. The conduct of the tournament had offered an image of social and political unity, especially in the Whitehall tiltyard with its provision for many thousands of spectators. All ranks of society had engaged in a collective rite of veneration for the monarch. In contrast, the Stuart masque was exclusionary and inward-looking, and it is not without significance that its heyday occurred during a period (1629–1640) when the King adopted 'personal Rule' and barred shut the doors of Parliament. In fact, Charles had begun his reign by dispensing with a triumphal entry into London and ordering the pageants prepared by the citizens to be taken down.[65] It was one thing to spend vast sums upon a spectacle at which even the meanest citizen could bask in the display of national magnificence. It was quite another to do it behind closed doors in a period of increasing government debt in celebration of absolutist rule.

II

What Price Glory?

LEAR EVIDENCE that successive Tudor and Jacobean governments had a high regard for the tournament as an instrument of prestige propaganda is to be found as soon as one begins to explore the manner in which tournaments were organized and financed. Public events of this kind, conducted on what was often a massive scale, of necessity required the combined resources of various branches of government and involved quite considerable expenditure by both the crown and private individuals. In the next chapter we shall see how the necessary physical facilities, namely the tiltyards, were constructed, maintained, and furnished by the Office of the Works (the government department responsible for building and the physical maintenance of crown property) and by the Chamber (the department responsible for interior furnishings). This chapter is primarily concerned with the contribution of the heralds, the Office of the Revels, the armour workshops, the Office of the Armoury, and the Master of the Horse. It is also clear that there was a growing burden of costs placed upon individual participants during the reign of Queen Elizabeth. It was, as has already been suggested, a burden that in James I's reign probably contributed more than any other factor to the demise of the English tournament.

During the Middle Ages the increasing use of heralds at tournaments greatly contributed to the change in their character. That the bloody free-for-all of the twelfth century was largely transformed in succeeding centuries into a ceremonial and courtly spectacle where knights displayed their martial skills and chivalric graces and competed for prizes before an audience was very much due to the presence of the heralds. By the time Henry VII came to the throne in 1485, the tasks of the heralds (or properly speaking the Kings of Arms, Heralds, and Pursuivants) included the proclamation of challenges (Fig. 21), the accompanying of knights to the tournaments, the crying of a knight's name at his entry into the lists, keeping score (Fig. 22), and the announcing of the victor. Above all heralds were responsible for enforcing the elaborate rules that were designed to protect participants from danger and to ensure that the spectacle was ordered and in keeping with the chivalric virtues that it supposedly celebrated.

Before their all-important work in the tiltyard itself, however, the heralds were first responsible for announcing forthcoming tournaments and proclaiming challenges. This was an ancient and familiar role for heralds, who in the heyday of the medieval tournament had often travelled far and wide in Europe. Following Henry VII's accession, however, English heralds seem to have travelled abroad less frequently to announce tournaments and proclaim challenges, and English tournaments in the main do not appear to have been open to foreign knights. None the less, in 1494 the challengers for the tournament to celebrate the creation of Prince Henry as Duke of York still held to the traditional formula that they were willing 'to answer all commers of what nacion so ever they bee'.[1] Similarly, in 1500 when Henry and his courtiers met the Archduke Philip of Burgundy and his courtiers at Calais, the English heralds proclaimed a challenge for a tournament at Westminster to celebrate the forthcoming marriage of Katherine of Aragon to Prince Arthur.[2] As might also be expected, the very special circumstances of the tournament of the Field of Cloth of Gold in 1520 necessitated plans to send heralds throughout Europe. In fact, lack of time resulted in the challenge being proclaimed by King Henry VIII's heralds only at the French court and in two of the Low Countries (Zeeland and Holland), while the heralds of Henry's fellow challenger, King Francis I, appeared only at Greenwich, and at the courts of Flanders and Artois.

Once the names of the combatants were known, the heralds may have had the task of drawing up the lists of jousters. Certainly this was so in Queen Elizabeth's reign, as we know from a letter written to the Garter King of Arms by the Earl of Worcester in 1602 requesting a change in the running order.[3] However, the heralds received their list of names from a much higher authority. During James I's reign, if not before, the Keeper of the Privy Seal appears to have been involved in deciding the names of participants, since it was to him that Thomas Windsor wrote in 1618 explaining that he was not fit enough to ride in the coming tournament. That same year a list was drawn up of all those that had and all those that had not previously participated, and Robert Naughton, the Secretary of State, sent it to the 'Lords Comissioners for Cause Marshall', instructing them to contact those whose names were marked so that

those named could 'provide and put themselves in order to runne at Tilt against the 24th of March next without faile'.[4]

Just who the originating authority was is not clear, but by 1625 it seems to have been the Earl Marshal (the official responsible both for organizing ceremonial occasions and for overseeing the work of the heralds). The tone of the letter sent by the Earl of Arundel as Earl Marshal to warn those that were to participate in 1625 is like that of the few other surviving documents just cited—excuses, it seems clear, were not likely to be accepted:[5]

Sir,

I have especiall apointme[n]t from his Majesty to signify unto you that it is his majesty's pleasure that you prepare & put yourself in readyness to run at the Tilt on the [blank] day of this present March at the Court of Whitehall where you are to give your attendance on the princes Highness who then is prepared to run himself so shall you give his Majesty great Content and gain your self much honour . . .

Upon receipt of such a summons, a knight had no choice but to take part, as the Earl of Cumberland discovered in 1602 when he was forced to participate despite his plea that his injured arm would not even hold a lance and that he would therefore have to ride along the tilt barrier without any weapon.[6]

Once a tournament had been announced, the participants contacted, and the tilting order arranged, there was always the possibility of postponement or cancellation. The heralds had the unenviable task of announcing changes of this kind. Thus in 1571, one of the Kings of Arms had to proclaim that 'The Justes appoyntd to haue been p[er]formed att the Queens Ma[jes]tyes pallace att Westminster on mundaye the first of Maye' had by Queen Elizabeth's command been postponed until the following Sunday, that the tourney planned for the day after had also been postponed for a week, while 'the Course

---

*The three Kings of Arms were known as Garter, Clarenceux and Norrey.

in feild' was to be 'omitted and left vnattempted for this tyme'.[7] As might be expected, the unreliable English weather was often responsible. On 17 November 1599, for example, William Camden, Clarenceux King of Arms*, rode first into the Whitehall tiltyard and then to the Court Gate just outside to proclaim to the waiting crowds that,

21 *Heralds issuing a challenge. The role of heralds in proclaiming challenges and in the conduct of tournaments was extremely important. The surviving records of heralds are one of the chief sources of information about tournaments.*

'Whereas this daye hathe vsually byn held, wth solemne & Royall Justes for the honor of her Ma[esty's] Reigne: It is nowe her Ma[jesty's] will & pleasure (by reason of the vnseasonablenes of the weather) to defferr the saide Justes vntill to morrowe in the afternoone. And therefore all, that are here now p[re]sent, may depart vntill then.' But still the weather remained unkind, and Clarenceux was forced to carry out the same task the next day and postpone the tournament yet again.[8]

During the Middle Ages an important task of the heralds at tournaments had been the receipt, the certification, and the display (nailing up) of a participant's coat of arms. There are sporadic references to the continuance of this custom during the early Tudor period and as late as the early years of Queen Elizabeth's reign. One of the conditions for participation in the November 1494 tournament, for example, was 'that euery gentleman comer to the said Juste shall bring with him a scuction [i.e. shield] of his Armes and deliver it to the Officers of Armes then being there present before that he shall run'. We know, too, that the trees of chivalry at the tournaments in November 1501, June 1520, and May 1540 were all used by the heralds to display the arms of the combatants, and in November 1565 the challengers' shields 'were fastened upp on iiii Posts under the Queen's Window' at one end of the Whitehall tiltyard.[9] However, once it became customary at Elizabethan tournaments for a knight's page to present his impresa shield to the Queen (as distinct from his shield of arms) (see Chapter 5), the ancient custom of identifying oneself by submitting a shield of one's arms to the heralds appears to have died out, although heralds still appear to have been entitled to the traditional fee for clouage ('nailing up').

Once a herald had announced the contestants upon their entry to the lists, and once any initial speeches, pageants and presentations had been completed, the combat could begin. For this judges were appointed, usually four or five men of high rank, but it was the heralds themselves who kept score of the points achieved by each knight in the different forms of contest. What precisely the rules were from one tournament to another is often difficult to determine. None the less, from the details of the articles of the challenges and from the frequency with which heralds throughout the Tudor and Jacobean period copied out versions of the rules for jousting formulated in 1466 by John Tiptoft, Earl of Worcester,[10] it is possible to deduce the general pattern for sixteenth- and seventeenth-century English tournaments. In Sir John Harington's *Nugae Antiquae* (1779) the statement is made that Tiptoft's rules were officially adopted in 1562,[11] but unfortunately no documentary evidence for this assertion has been found. However, it may well have been so, for there is a striking continuity between the rules as set out by Tiptoft and those that seem to have been employed throughout the Tudor and Jacobean period.

According to Tiptoft, points in jousting were to be awarded for striking an opponent's helmet with one's lance, for striking the crown-like safety device (the coronel) at the end of his lance with one's own, for unseating him, and for breaking a lance by striking him in the permissible area from the waist upwards. The equivalent of demerit points were received if a knight struck his opponent's horse or saddle, if he struck the tilt itself, or if he struck an opponent whose back was turned, or who was disarmed. Tiptoft's rules only dealt with jousting, but later versions such as that in William Segar's *Honor, Militarie and Ciuil* (1602) often included rules for the tourney and for combats at barriers, their principal features being rules forbidding the use of locking gauntlets (Fig. 6) (a piece of armour that prevented one's sword being knocked from one's hand),

22 *Jousting with rebated lances. The illustration demonstrates the key role of heralds and the specially built viewing stands common at tournaments.*

and the striking of an opponent below the belt or under the barrier in foot combats.

Tiptoft's rules are difficult to intepret and do not provide for all possible contingencies,[12] but they are clear enough in indicating that a participant's score was obtained by counting the number of lances broken on his opponent and the number of contacts (attaints) made upon his opponent with his lance, even though these did not necessarily result in a broken lance. Clearly, too, lances broken and attaints involving contact with the opponent's head rather than the larger and easier target of his body earned extra points. The original scoring cheques on which heralds recorded the scores of participants are also helpful. Those from the sixteenth century on are still preserved at the College of Arms, the earliest being those for the tournament in February 1511, although there are also copies of four cheques relating to the tournament of November 1501.

The problems associated with interpreting the scoring cheques are quite complex, since the system of notation appears to have changed in the course of time and there are, furthermore, contradictions between the fairly elaborate systems set out in some of the surviving heraldic manuscripts and the scoring cheques themselves. The cheques for the jousting in the February 1511 tournament, for example, distinguish between attaints on the head, attaints on the body, lances broken on the head, lances broken on the body, and lances ill-broken, by using all three lines of the customary scoring cheque format. They also indicate the number of courses run by each knight.[13] In Elizabeth's reign, however, as can be seen from the scoring cheque for the jousting on 17 November 1584 (Fig. 23), the heralds recorded only the number of lances broken (the lines bisecting the centre line in the rectangle) and the number of courses run (the lines and/or prick holes bisecting the centre line outside the rectangle). This radical change from Henrician days (and indeed from the earlier years of Elizabeth's reign) illustrates in vivid terms the manner in

which jousting skills had deteriorated. To break a lance was all that a knight now had to do to score.

Scoring cheques for the tourney and barriers are very rare and present further problems of interpretation.[14] However, the limited evidence that they offer shows that the heralds scoring the tourney recorded the number of sword strokes, the disarming of a participant, and the breaking of swords. Scoring the barriers involved recording the number of swords and pikes broken, the number of blows delivered, and any foul blows for which a participant should be penalized.

The conclusion of a tournament was traditionally marked by the heralds' cry of '*A l'hostel*' (to lodgings). This was certainly the case for the tournaments in November 1494, in February 1511, and for Henry VIII's tournament in Tournai in October 1513. Concerning this last, Hall says, 'When ye iustes wer done, the kyng and all the other unhelmed them & rode about the Tilt and did great reuerence to the ladies, and then the herauldes cryed to lodgyng'.[15] Medieval custom was also adhered to with regard to banqueting, dancing and the award of prizes by the lady or ladies to those knights who had fared best in the lists (Fig. 24). Presumably the heralds supplied the scoring cheques to the judges, who in turn advised the ladies of honour about which participants had fared best. This certainly appears to have been so according to a herald's manuscript concerned with one of the tournaments of Elizabeth's reign:[16]

23 *An original scored jousting cheque for 17 November 1584 showing the number of lances broken by each contestant (the marks inside the rectangles) and the number of courses run (the slashes or pin pricks on the line to the right of the rectangle). The names of Challengers and Answerers are opposite each other, beginning with Sir Henry Lee and Sir Philip Sidney.*

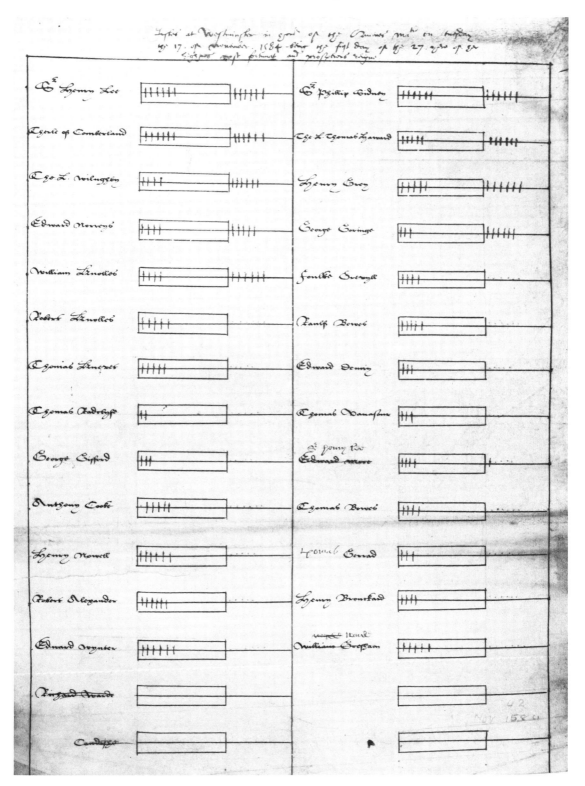

ffierst after the justes Royall. tourney. and baryers is accomplished then A dauncynge to be prepared in the presence of the quenes Ma[jes]tie during wiche dauncying the Judges Being determyned They to make report vnto the quenes highnes of their determynation And then the quenes ma[jes]tie To vse the names of a consultation with other Ladies upon the determynation of the said Judges and when the quenes Ma[jes]tie and the Ladies hathe concluded her highnes To call Clarencieuilx King of armes of that province to Bring and present the pryses.

Typical prizes during the Tudor and Jacobean period were gold rings, rings with precious stones, gold chains, and on occasion such items as a jewelled sword, a large sum of money, or an expensive jewel. On one famous occasion Elizabeth presented her favourite, Sir Christopher Hatton, with a bell on a chain in allusion to one of her pet names for him—'bellwether'.[17] The herald's manuscript just quoted also tells us that when Clarenceux was called he had to 'present the ryng of golde withe a dyamont vnto the quenes Ma[jes]tie saing most high most puysant and most excelent prynces Elysabeth by the grace of god quene of England ffraunce and Irland deffender of the faithe etc. Here is the peice the wiche your heighnes shall awarde vnto the best Juster.' The Queen then appointed two young ladies to bring the victor to her once Clarenceux had announced the winner's names according to the standard formula. Blanks had been left in the manuscript for the names of those who came third, second, and first:

Then the quenes heighnes To cause Clarencieux to call him that hathe best defended to haue the price and then so to make the oyes and saye hathe Justed well and hath Justed right well and hath Justed best for the wiche the quenes Ma[jes]tie and the Ladies hathe awarded him the pryce of the Justes Royall wiche is a ryng of golde withe a dyamont.

The prizes for the tourney and the barriers were awarded in a similar way.

Apparently it was customary to reward both the participant who had scored the highest number of points and whoever had conducted himself with most style and flair. This is clear from another surviving College of Arms document concerning the prize-giving proclamation made by Richard Lee, Clarenceux King of Arms, on the evening of 19 November 1594 following the tournament at which the Earl of Essex had challenged all-comers. It first refers to the fact that the heralds had earlier proclaimed Essex' challenge, which included provision for two prizes, 'the one for him that brake most staves in four courses, the other for him that ranne most fayrest'.[18] There follows a description of the packed room in which Queen Elizabeth was sitting 'most Royally vnder her Cloth of Estate, and all her nobillitye about her'. Lee entered to the sound of trumpets and gave the Queen three low curtsies. After delivering his proclamation, 'there was brought vnto her Ma[jes]tie present Mr Robert Knowles betwen two Ladyes and they presenting him vnto her Ma[jes]tie. She deliuered vnto him a pryse w[hi]ch was a Juell of gold set w[i]th Stones as to him that best deserved the same as the most fayrest Ronner.' Unfortunately there was no winner for the other prize, the herald's note informs us, since nine runners had all broken the same number of lances. As a result, there was further tilting the next day, the Earl of Essex being the eventual winner.

The heralds' involvement at tournaments was thus fairly considerable, but they would doubtless not have had things otherwise since tournaments provided them with one of their principal sources of income. Not only did heralds receive an annual grant from the

24 *The victor receiving his prize. It was customary for prizes to be awarded at the banquet following a tournament. The herald announced the names of he who had done well, he who had done better, and he who had done best. The prize was usually a costly jewel (in medieval times perhaps a kiss) presented by the Lady of the tournament.*

crown for various miscellaneous services, but for occasions such as coronations, which traditionally included celebratory tournaments, there appear to have been standard fees. Thus, following Edward VI's coronation in 1547, the heralds were awarded forty pounds to cover their traditional rights to clouage (the fee for nailing up a participants' coat of arms), to the hinder parts of the participant's trappers (the covering put over the horse), and to anything else, armour or weapons, that fell to the ground.[19] A similar sum appears to have been awarded following Queen Elizabeth's coronation.[20]

At other times, as had been the case in the Middle Ages, the heralds were also entitled to these rights. Thus, at the tournament on 13 November 1565 to celebrate the wedding of Ambrose Dudley, the Earl of Warwick, the heralds at one point seized both the horse and the armour of Henry Mackwilliam after he and his horse had been thrown in the tourney by Henry Knollys. There was some dispute about this, and the Earl Marshal, Thomas Duke of Norfolk, called upon the Kings of Arms to show precedents.[21] This was done and the heralds were awarded twenty pounds for the redemption of the horse and armour, a sum graciously paid by Robert Dudley, the Earl of Leicester and a fellow defender with Mackwilliam. Other participants lost pieces of armour, pieces of their bases (the skirts covering the armour), and plumes from their helmets. They too had to pay a redemption fee, twenty nobles of which was paid by Leicester and forty shillings by penalized participants.

As was also customary, the heralds later recorded the sums received in their Partition Books. On this occasion the books show that the three Kings of Arms (Garter, Clarenceux and Norrey) received a total of 245 shillings to be divided equally among them, the six Heralds (Somerset, Richmond, Lancaster, Chester, Windsor, York) received the same amount to be divided equally, and the four Pursuivants (Rouge Cross, Portcullis, Bluemantle, Rouge Dragon) received 81s. 8d.,

also to be divided equally.[22] The partition of funds was governed by a formula that was adjusted if any of the officers of arms had been absent. By the time of Elizabeth, it was customary to give each Pursuivant one share, each Herald two, and each King of Arms four.

The Partition Books, which survive from as early as 1527, also reveal other sums regularly received by the heralds for their work at tournaments. Fees, for example, were paid by participants according to their rank for their first appearance at a tournament, and frequently these sums of money were accompanied or replaced by the gift of scarves or plumes in the nobleman's heraldic colours. On 17 November 1583, for example, the Partition Books record that the Earl of Cumberland gave the officers of arms six pounds because he 'had not his Coullers to give', and the Lord Willoughby gave six silk scarves in his colours of watchet and murray. Some thirty-seven years later, in 1620, when Prince Charles made his first tournament appearance, the Prince paid twenty pounds, the Marquis of Buckingham thirteen pounds six shillings and eight pence, the Earl of Oxford and the Earl of Salisbury ten pounds each, and the Lord Compton six pounds, thirteen shillings and four pence,[23] all this according to a well-established formula governing the fees due to heralds for a participant's first appearance in a tournament.

It is apparent, then, that the all-important services of the heralds at tournaments were thus primarily paid for by private individuals and not by the crown. This practice had a long tradition and being able to pay for heralds, along with being able to maintain the proper kind of horse and weapons, had in times past been one of the criteria by which one established one's knightly credentials. None the less, the heralds were also paid a relatively significant amount by the crown in the course of each year.

Whereas the work of the heralds at tournaments was supported only indirectly by the crown, that of the Office of the Revels was

paid for directly out of government funds. The particular responsibility of the Office of the Revels (once it came into being on 11 March 1545) was to provide costumes, horse bards (coverings, often stuffed or armoured for the chest and flanks), and scenic devices. Initially, in Henry VII's reign, there was no such government department, and it was the Office of the Wardrobe which built pageants and supplied costumes for disguisings and, we must assume, for tournaments too.[24] During Henry's reign it was customary for the official who took charge of disguisings or pageantry at Christmas to be known as 'master of the revels'. This position gradually expanded in scope and importance, eventually necessitating the creation of the separate post of Master of the Revels. As Henry was anxious to offer the world English equivalents in the lists, in the disguising hall and on stage to the great Franco-Burgundian spectacles, this evolution is hardly surprising. Henry wanted to show that his court, too, was quite at home with pageant cars, complex scenic devices, and elaborate allegories.[25]

However, the first major step towards the creation of a completely independent Office of the Revels did not occur until early in Henry VIII's reign when the Sergeant of Office of the Tents was made Yeoman of the

25   *Henry VIII entering the Westminster tiltyard in 1511. This segment from the Great Tournament Roll of Westminster shows Henry in silver armour as Coeur Loyal entering the tiltyard beneath an elaborate portable pavilion decorated with the letter 'K' (for Katherine). The King is accompanied by twenty-two footmen.*

Revels as well. The principal task of the officer was to obtain any necessary materials from mercers, the Office of the Wardrobe, or the Jewel House and the Mint.[26] He had also to undertake the hiring of architects, carpenters, painters, tailors and embroiderers, and when all was ready he had to be present for any actual performances, whether at plays, disguisings, or tournaments. Afterwards he had to take custody of all costumes and properties and render a proper expense account to the Exchequer.

During most of Henry VIII's reign the position was held by Richard Gibson, formerly of the Office of the Wardrobe, and he has left us a series of detailed accounts beginning a number of years before he officially became Yeoman of the Revels. These reveal to the full Henry VIII's willingness to spend lavishly from his exchequer in order to make his tournaments such impressive spectacles that no one could doubt his magnificence and liberality. As already remarked, for Henry the tournament was the perfect vehicle for self-enhancement and for the enhancement of English national prestige (Fig. 25), based as it was on the martial arts in which he was so highly skilled. Gibson's accounts, in all their painstaking detail, show just how those desired effects were achieved and at what cost.[27]

Gibson's accounts also make clear that Henry was anxious not only that he himself should appear in full chivalric glory every time he entered the tiltyard, but also that those accompanying him—either his fellow challengers or his fellow answerers, depending on which side Henry was fighting on—should also be magnificently turned out as well. Thus, for the jousts to entertain the Flemish ambassadors during their visit to Greenwich in July 1517, in addition to all the other expenses,[28] a considerable sum of money was expended by Gibson to fit out both Henry and his horse in cloth of silver, white velvet, gold damask, black satin, and black velvet. Then there were his three spare horses trapped in white velvet, bordered with gold letters. Fourteen gentlemen fought on Henry's side and these and their horses he had fitted out in white satin, white velvet, silver damask, and their own heraldic colours. In addition there were fourteen knights and attendants in white velvet and satin, thirty-four trumpeters, stablemen, armourers and others in white damask, and forty-nine other attendants in sarcenet of various colours. Little wonder that Gibson needed some 549 yards of satin, 295 yards of velvet, 205 yards of blue damask, 26 yards of cloth of silver, 129 yards of sarcenet, 128 oz. of damask gold (worth £75 11s. 6d.) and 1531 oz. of damask silver (worth £103 11s. 4d.).[29] Furthermore, rather than having his finery returned to the royal store, Henry permitted the gentlemen challengers to keep their costumes. Likewise the various attendants, yeomen, trumpeters and armourers all retained theirs.

There are many other examples in Gibson's accounts of the fitting out of those who fought in tournaments on Henry's side. On occasion, as in October 1518, Gibson had to provide different costumes for each successive day of a tournament for Henry, his companions, and their horses. As already indicated, he was also responsible for all manner of other items. For the July 1517 tournament, for example, he had to provide a pavilion ('arming shed') in which the combatants could arm themselves, a tall mast for holding up lances when they were not in use, and bread and beer for the workmen setting up the tilt.

By far the most complex and expensive items, however, were the great mobile scenic devices that appeared at a number of tournaments. For the first day of the February 1511 tournament, for example, a forest was constructed, 26 feet long, 16 feet wide and 9 feet high, garnished with artificial hawthorns, oaks, maples, hazels, birches, fern, broom and furze. There were beasts and birds, foresters, a castle, and a maiden with a garland of roses. The pageant was drawn by a huge lion and an antelope upon which sat two maidens. Hidden inside were the four challengers whose coats of arms were placed at each corner of the pageant. For all this Gibson required twenty-seven feet of oak for mules and other beasts, seventy-eight alder poles for the forest, ten bundles of paper for moulding the beasts and the faces of the lion and the antelope, and a long list of further items that included costumes for the maidens and the men leading the pageant, canvas, paint, ironwork, leather, two dozen embossed birds, and 2400 'turned' acorns and hazelnuts. At the end of Gibson's account he notes ruefully that, although it had been intended to preserve the pageant, it was later attacked by members of the king's guard, broken up and carried off. Those who had had custody of it were beaten up, two of them having 'ther hedes brokyn'.[30]

The most ambitious and expensive tournament project in which Gibson was involved was that of the Field of Cloth of Gold. Gibson was responsible for the great tree of chivalry in the tiltyard, an enormous and elaborate affair requiring wagon loads of timber, 141 yards of satin, 512 yards of damask, 153 yards of sarcenet, 2400 cherries of crimson satin and 2000 flowers of white satin.[31] And he was of course responsible for the sum of over £3000 that was spent on the endless array of costumes for the King, his fellow knights, their attendants, the armourers, spearmaker, saddlers, stablemen, and heralds, not to mention embroidered bards for many of the horses.[32] Such were the costs of prestige propaganda in the European market.

Gibson died in 1534 and was succeeded as Yeoman of the Revels by John Farlyon in November of that year. In the patent of Farlyon's appointment he is described as 'Yeoman or Keeper of the King's vestures or apparel of masks, revels and disguisings, and of apparel and trappers of horses, for justes and turneys',[33] and ten years later these tasks were considered important enough for the officer in charge to be called Master of the Revels, a position first held by Thomas Cawarden, who was also joint-Master of the Office of the Tents, until 1559. During this period, as we have seen, tournaments did not occur on such a grand scale as some of those in Henry VIII's reign, and most of the surviving Revels documents tell us little about such events. However, the Office of the Revels conducted a regular airing (or spring cleaning) and the Clerk made an inventory of its stock at these times. The records of these airings and inventories during the reigns of Edward VI and Queen Mary provide fascinating glimpses of the materials used in tournaments.[34] In the inventory of 26 March 1555, for example, there is a list of 'Couerynges of Bardes and baces'.[35] This includes two bards made of cloth of gold and purple velvet. Each is embroidered with a silver knight riding towards a mountain. In the clouds above, a lady casts darts at him. The embroidery work also includes various gold letters and pictures of hearts. A second item in the list refers to bases of cloth of gold,

silver, and reddish brown velvet, the velvet embroidered with white roses, a black bull and letters of gold.

Such items were kept in store so money could be saved by using them again. Henry VIII, when not anxious to dazzle the world with completely new outfits, had from time to time taken used items from store,[36] and Edward VI did the same thing. On the 24 November 1551, for example, Edward signed a warrant ordering Cawarden to furnish the Earl of Warwick, Sir Henry Sidney, Sir Henry Neville, and Sir Henry Gates with whatever there was in store 'as shall be by them and you thought moost meetest and sufficient for the ffurniture of their bases and as shall appertaigne vnto their horses'.[37] The planned event eventually took place on 3 and 6 January 1552, and the Revels had to work literally night and day in preparation, for the material they had available was apparently insufficient for the needs of the four challengers, who had three great horses and three light horses each (a total of twenty-four!). Though some of the Revels' materials could be cut and altered and certain items embroidered with the King's motto could be re-worked, it appears that it was still necessary for the Revels to make and decorate twelve bards and eight caparisons and to paint in 'poesies' on these items and on the challengers' bases and shields, the entire project costing a total sum of £89 13s. 9d.[38]

During Queen Elizabeth's reign, and the Masterships of Sir Thomas Benger (1559–72), Thomas Blagrave (acting 1573–9), and Sir Edmund Tilney (1579–1610), the Office of the Revels appears to have played a far smaller role in the organization and presentation of tournaments, but this may simply reflect the lack of surviving documents from the Elizabethan Office of the Revels. As in previous reigns the Yeoman of the Revels, according to the Patent Rolls, remained the official directly responsible for the 'apparrell and trappers of all and singuler our horses ordeyned and appoynted and hereafter to be ordayned and appoynted for our Iustes and Turneys',[39] but the lack of surviving records makes it hard for us to tell whether the Revels still regularly supplied such items or continued to hold them in store.[40]

The Office also appears to have had the task of producing memorial books for tournaments. These were perhaps like those known to have been handed out at some of the later Stuart masques.[41] They were distributed among important spectators and presumably listed the events and participants, and perhaps commented on the scenic devices. Unfortunately, no such book has survived. All we know of them is that, in 1588, Tilney was paid ten shillings 'for the fayre writing of all the devises on the 17 daye of November . . . in two copies for the quene',[42] and that Philip Gawdy in a letter to his father said that he was enclosing a book 'that was gyven me that day that they rann at tilt. Divers of them being gyven to most of the lordes, and gentlemen about the Court, and one especially to the Quene.'[43]

As part of their duties, the Master and his men regularly attended all tournaments and were paid for doing so. Thus Tilney and his officers were present for the proclamation of the Earl of Arundel's challenge early in 1581 and were there also for the ensuing tournament, 'during all which tyme the master of the Revells attended for the presenting of diuerse devises which happened in that meane season'.[44] Later that same year, Tilney performed similar services for the challenge and tournament in May 1581: 'Edmond Tylney esquier master of the Revells for his chardges and certen provision, viz. ffor his Attendaunce at the proclaymyng of the challendge and the ij. dayes of the tryumphe him self and his men xxiiijs.'[45] For this event the Office of the Revels appears to have supplied forty-six impresa shields, but one looks in vain for any expenses related to the complex 'rolling trench' (see p. 158) that the challengers employed in the tiltyard.

In fact, only two events of the Elizabethan period, both combats at barriers, offer any evidence that the Office of the Revels continued to supply costumes and scenic devices at royal expense. In January 1579 Elizabeth entertained the ambassadors from Alençon (her French suitor) with a masque and barriers. A detailed description of this event is contained in the Revels records, telling first of the entry of six amazons. They wore armour 'gilded within this office', crests on their helmets, long hair hanging down their backs, elaborate kirtles of rich material, and orange buskins, and they carried shields 'with A device painted theron', and javelins in their hands. Someone with a speech for the Queen then entered, accompanied by richly dressed musicians whose elaborate costumes included bows and arrows and 'head peeces of golde Lawne and woemens heare wrethed very faire'. The amazons then danced 'with Lordes in her maiesties presence,' and this was followed by the entry of some knights whose costumes were equally elaborate and are described in equal detail. The knights then danced with some of the court ladies and this was followed by the amazons and knights fighting each other at barriers. Various charges relating to the shields of the amazons and knights are recorded, along with charges for gilding the armour, for the musicians' costumes, for the hire of the amazons' plumes, for head-pieces, for the making of shields and spears, and for 'the translating of certen speaches into Italian'.[46]

Less clear is the evidence concerning the combat at barriers on New Year's Day 1582. The combatants included the Duc d'Anjou, who entered in a pageant in the form of a rock. Among Tilney's records are expenses in the Declared Accounts for 'one fighting at Barriers w[i]th diuerse Devises', but nothing is said about this in the more detailed Audited Accounts.[47] However, we must assume that the Office of the Revels was put at the service of the Duc d'Anjou and his fellow challengers. On the other hand, for the annual Accession Day tournaments, and for the tournaments that followed the proclamation of challenges by such individuals as the Earl of Arundel, Sir Philip Sidney, Sir Henry Lee, the Earl of Essex, and the Earl of Cumber-

26 *Elizabeth I accompanied by Fame. The horse-drawn triumphal chariot may be similar to the type of chariot in which many English tournament participants entered the tiltyard.*

land, I am inclined to believe that the Revels officers may not have been obliged in any way to supply costumes or scenic devices at royal expense, though they were present and received their customary fees for attendance. This certainly would have been consistent with Elizabeth's general policies. It fits too with the occasional statements by contemporary observers that private individuals had borne the entire costs of a tournament. For example, in 1565 at the tournament for the marriage of the Earl of Warwick, the defenders 'did furnish themselves' and thereby invoked the Earl of Leicester's generosity when some of them incurred further expenses.[48] Similarly, in November 1580 Henri III was informed by his ambassador in England that the Earl of Arundel had paid for the considerable costs of the event ('*a fait toute la despence qui est fort grande*').[49]

Even more significant, perhaps, is the fact that the annual cost of the Office of the Revels, which in 1571–3 had amounted to about £1500 a year, decreased thereafter. In 1573–4, for example, expenses were about £670, in 1574–5 about £580, and from then

on no more than £250 to £350.[50] Some of the reduction is due to the fact that expenses were assigned to other departments, as in the case of a banqueting house constructed in 1581, but it seems none the less certain that Henry VIII's easy liberality in fitting out his courtiers was by now a distant memory. Those interested in catching the eye of the Queen by their appearance in the tiltyard would have to do so largely at their own expense in so far as costumes and even scenic devices were concerned (Fig. 26).

In James I's reign, under the continuing Mastership of Tilney and of Sir George Buck (deputy 1603–10 and Master 1610–22), the involvement of the Office of the Revels in tournaments remained unchanged. Both Masters regularly made expense claims for the attendance of themselves and their men at tournaments, and the Declared Accounts regularly refer to the responsibility of the Office for the 'furnishing making and setting forthe of sondry plaies comedies ffeates of activitie Maskes and tryvmphes at Tylte',[51] but precise details are lacking. Unfortunately, the two surviving Audited Accounts of James I's reign, though fairly detailed about many other activities of the Office of the Revels, do no more than mention the customary three days attendance 'at Triumphe att Tilt' of the Revels officers, and they leave us none the wiser as to whether very much in the way of government expenditure on tournaments was channelled through this particular government department. One would probably be correct in assuming, however, that the role of the Office at tournaments remained small.

This view receives some support from the fact that the Office of the Revels appears to have played no major part in events for which government payments are well documented. For Prince Henry's barriers in 1610, for example, the dancers, musicians and actors, and the actors' beards and Spanish leather boots were paid for by the Exchequer, which forwarded the money (£247 8s.) to Thomas Bowker to be disbursed among the various parties involved.[52] With regard to other grants of money related to 'diverse sortes of perles, Silkes and other necessaries' worth some £1986 9s. 7d.,[53] there is also no mention of the Office of the Revels. When an even more startling and extravagant exercise of this kind occurred eleven years later at Prince Charles' first entry into the tiltyard, the total expenses of some £6467 were handled by Charles' Master of the Wardrobe, even though they included long lists of the expensive materials used for costumes, horse trappings, and the decorative items in the Prince's pavilion.[54] For his entry two years later there exists a similar account from the Master of the Wardrobe amounting to £3352,[55] and again the Office of the Revels is not involved.

Armour and weapons were among the most costly items connected with tournaments. No single aspect of a knight's appearance, other than his horse perhaps, could more enhance his prestige than a finely-crafted, beautifully decorated suit of plate armour with fine weapons to accompany it. Princes and great lords often gave armour and weapons to each other as marks of special esteem, and no Renaissance prince would be unaware of the immense prestige that might accrue to the prince and country which possessed the necessary facilities and skilled workmen for the production of the finest armour and weapons.

During the fifteenth century, the very best quality armour was considered to come from the renowned Missaglia workshop in Milan, from the south German workshops in Landshut, Innsbruck and Nuremberg, and above all from the Helmschmied workshop in Augsburg. Other less prestigious workshops were to be found in Spain, France, Burgundy and Flanders, and in London there was the Armourers' Company, founded in the fourteenth century and still in existence today. In the sixteenth century, Milan (in particular the workshops of the Negroli and the Pompeo della Chiesa) and south Germany remained the leading and most influential centres, a particularly strong influence being

the court workshop of the Emperor Maximilian at Innsbruck, founded in 1504. Initially, Maximilian's workshop was in the charge of the great Augsburg armourer, Konrad Seusenhofer, its purpose being to provide high-quality armour for himself and his courtiers, together with armour for general use by the Imperial armies.

The year before Maximilian founded the court workshop at Innsbruck, James IV of Scotland had set up an armour mill at Linlithgow. He also brought over thirteen armourers from France.[56] The next Renaissance monarch to set up a royal workshop was Henry VIII in 1515. This was probably out of a desire to rival James, but Henry was also no doubt spurred on in part by his having been unable to reciprocate in kind when the Emperor Maximilian sent him a suit of Seusenhofer armour (the helmet still exists) in 1514. His decision was also probably influenced by the fact that English armourers were unable to make the kind and quality of armour that Henry himself wanted. Indeed, for a century or so before Henry came to the throne, any Englishman who could afford fine armour and weapons had had to import them from abroad.

Henry's founding of the royal workshop must also be seen as a continuation of his father's programme to enhance the image of the English court and nation as sophisticated, magnificent, and independently powerful. That Henry's project would also serve to enhance the prestige of Henry himself was so much to the better. Before 1511 Henry was already regularly employing craftsmen from Italy and Brussels to make armour for him personally,[57] but in 1515 he brought eleven Almains (i.e. German and Dutch) over to

27 *Sir Henry Lee's field armour as depicted in the Almain Armourer's Album. The armour shown was apparently made abroad, but the drawing is included in the Album because the Royal Workshops at Greenwich made additional pieces to be worn when jousting.*

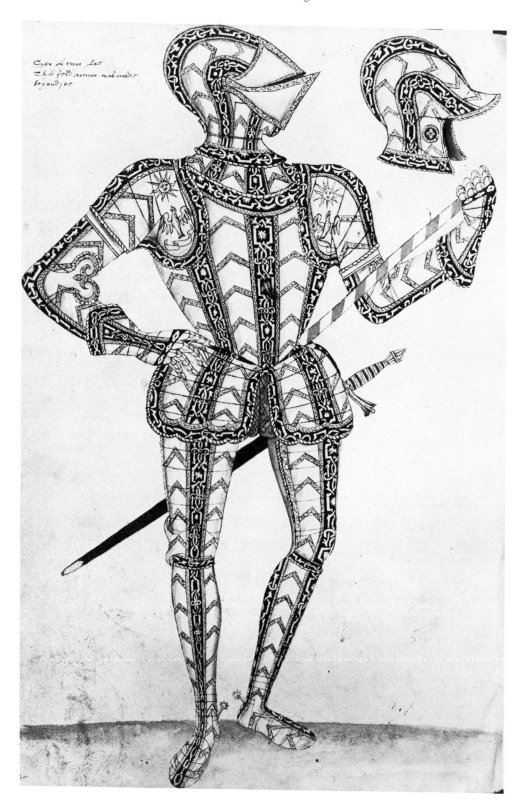

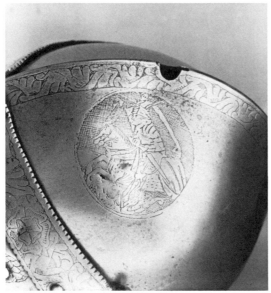

28   *The helmet of Henry VIII's tonlet armour*
(C. 1520) for foot combat (RIGHT) was decorated
with the Virgin and Child (TOP) and St George
(ABOVE) etched on the top. It is typical of one
method used by armourers to enrich their work with
symbolic detail. The helmet is Milanese but the
remainder of the armour was probably made at the
Royal Workshops at Greenwich.

England to work under a master-craftsman named Martin van Royne. Henry installed them all at Greenwich Palace, and there they were commissioned to make armour for Henry and those courtiers who had received the necessary royal warrant and who were wealthy enough to pay the high costs. To give them a suitable workshop, Henry had the Office of the Works add a massive new block with two distinctive-looking towers to the palace in 1516–8, at a total cost of some £1900 (see Fig. 52).[58]

The Greenwich workshops were maintained by successive monarchs throughout the Tudor and Jacobean era. A considerable amount of the high quality armour they produced still survives in the Tower of London Armouries, Windsor Castle, the Metropolitan Museum (New York), and elsewhere. What we can learn from the surviving armour is supplemented by the contents of the beautiful manuscript 'Almain Armourer's Album', thought to be by the German armourer Jacob Halder, who was master-workman from 1576 until 1607 (Fig. 27).[59] The album contains elaborate coloured drawings of twenty-nine Greenwich armours and their extra pieces, all produced in the latter half of the sixteenth century. The respective owners are all identified and some of the armour still survives, its original glory somewhat lessened by the ravages of time.

Such suits were extremely costly, more so because they were frequently gilded and etched (Figs 28 and 35), as the 'Almain Armourer's Album' shows (Figs 29 and 30). Details of actual costs are hard to come by. In 1518 the cost of three complete suits of armour with the extra pieces necessary for tilting, thirteen crinets (armour for a horse's neck) and three shaffrons (armour for a horse's head) was fifty pounds, but by the early seventeenth century, a Greenwich armour might cost between three and four hundred pounds. That made for Prince Henry under the supervision of the master craftsman William Pickering, for example, cost the Exchequer £340.[60] This would have been no

29 *Sir Henry Lee's tilt close helmet (c. 1580) was made in the Royal Workshops at Greenwich. Its decorative effects are typical of the fine workmanship of the Greenwich armourers.*

mean expense for a private individual and it provides us with some sense of the liberality involved when Elizabeth gave her warrant for the making of an armour for Christopher Hatton in 1564 and another for an armour for Richard Brown in 1603, 'complete as for the tilt as for the field; he to pay only the cost of the material'.[61]

Armour was so expensive because it had to be tailor made to the shape and size of its owner, because only the finest and strongest of metals could be used (English metal was consistently rejected), and because of the need for articulated joints, each a masterpiece of design and craft (Fig. 31). There was also the need to provide a stylish, decorative look that would enhance the prestige of the owner without jeopardizing his safety, and, in the case of a garniture (a large set of armour pieces alternated according to the nature of the combat), to supply a large number of extra

78

The Earle of Cumberland

30 *The Earl of Cumberland's armour. One of Cumberland's tournament armours was shown in the Almain Armourer's Album (*LEFT*). It is decorated with white and gilt bands with Tudor roses, annulets, fleurs-de-lis, and the letter 'E' (for Elizabeth) between them. The armour itself still survives and the breastplate is shown above (?1590). Cumberland succeeded Sir Henry Lee as Queen's Champion in 1590 and the armour may have been a gift from Elizabeth on this occasion. Attached to the right side of the breastplate is a lance rest.*

pieces. These would include the special gauntlets, additional breast plates, and protective helmets for use in jousting, the locking gauntlet used in tourneys, and various other pieces used for foot combats. In addition, it was necessary to provide protection for that most precious of possessions, the knight's horse. Horses routinely wore a shaffron or chanfron (Fig. 32), a crinet or crinière, and, when appropriate, armour plate to protect chest, crupper and flanks.

While the Greenwich armour workshops were responsible for making such premium quality products, there was throughout the Tudor and Jacobean periods a small state department responsible for the storage, maintenance and provision of weapons and armour required by the royal armies and for tournaments. The Office of the Armoury, as it still is, was based in the Tower of London. During the Middle Ages matters to do with armour and weapons were the responsibility of various different government offices, but the fully independent Office of the Armoury eventually came into being early in the fifteenth century.[62] In addition to the store of armour and weapons at the Tower and various other buildings in London, the Master of the Armoury was responsible for small supplies of armour at Whitehall, Windsor, Hampton Court, and above all Greenwich, where it became the custom to store some of the finer and more valuable pieces of workmanship in the so-called Green Gallery and in the Great Chamber. The chief responsibility of the Office of the Armoury was, of course, to have a sufficient quantity of armour

31   Henry VIII's armour for foot combat (c. 1520). This unfinished Greenwich armour may well have been the one that Henry had intended to wear at the Field of Cloth of Gold in 1520, but could not use because the French requested a last-minute change in the rules. The plates protect every part of the body and weigh 94 lb; they fix the King's height at 6 ft 2 in.

and weapons in store to fit out an army in time of war. However, various inventories made of the available armour and weapons make clear that the Master of the Armoury also played a vital role in the smooth running of any tournament. Courtiers seem to have kept their best armour in his stores, perhaps because it could then be properly maintained by the Almain armourers, and it also fell to the Master to supply tilt staves, coronels, swords, pikes for barriers, and vamplates (the conical shields attached to the handles of tilting staves) (Fig. 33).

Henry VII's Master of the Armoury, Sir Richard Guildford (1485–1506), who had supervised the coronation tournaments of both Henry and his Queen in 1485 and 1487, was paid £9 6s. by the Treasurer of the Chamber in 1492 for providing 'speres, sperehedes and vamplats' for the tournament held by Henry at Sheen to test the abilities of his knights in preparation for the planned military campaign in France.[63] We know, too, that between 1500 and 1502 the Armoury supplied weapons that had to be transported to numerous places for tournaments, and in 1506 Sir Edward Guildford, the new Master of the Armoury, supplied spear staves for a tournament at Richmond at a cost of £20 6s. 8d.[64] In February 1520 William Hayward was paid £34 15s. for supplying weapons for Henry VIII's Shrovetide jousting at Greenwich, but when the Field of Cloth of Gold tournament took place that June, the Office of the Armoury and the Greenwich workshops were clearly unable to cope on their own with Henry's needs. It was necessary to purchase 2000 mornes ((the blunted heads for tilting lances), 2000 burres (the rings on lances just behind the plate for the hand), and 1000 vamplates from Flanders. One thousand Milan swords were also purchased, along with 600 two-handed swords, and 100 heavy swords for the tourney. From England, however, came 1500 spear staves from the Tower Armoury, a complete armour mill from Greenwich together with the horses to work it, and four forges. Altogether

32 *A shaffron (or chanfron) provided crucial protection for the front of a horse's head. Occasionally a horse's eyes were also completely covered. This example (c. 1575) is from the Greenwich armour made for the Earl of Leicester. The Dudley family bear and ragged staff provide the chief decorative motifs.*

there were thirty-eight wagon loads of armoury material, and at the tournament ground itself the English knights were provided with two master armourers and twenty-four armourers. The costs were understandably enormous, swords and parts of armour alone amounting to some £1000.[65]

Later important tournaments in the Tudor and Jacobean period would also require a special effort from the Armouries, though never on such a vast scale. For Elizabeth's coronation there are records of the expenses relating to supplies drawn from Greenwich and other armouries. These amounted to some £57 for 400 tilt staves, 100 swords, 100 'punching' or puncheon staves (spears for foot combats), 300 new mornes, and the cleaning of 200 vamplates.[66] For James I's coronation tournament the armoury expenses were £181 11s. for 788 tilting staves, 200 pikes, 200 swords for barriers, 69 vamplates, 1000 coronels, and 600 burres; for the tilting and running at the ring when his brother-in-law, the King of Denmark, visited in 1606 the costs for a similar assortment of weapons supplied by Sir Henry Lee, the Master of the Armoury, were £227 16s.[67] Four years later, for Prince Henry's barriers in January 1610, Thomas Lincoln, Yeoman of the Armoury at Greenwich, was paid £81 9s. 6d. for pikes, staves and other materials supplied out of his store.[68]

An indication of the availability of such supplies is to be found in the various surviving inventories ('remains') made by the Office of the Armoury. These show, for example, that in 1561 James Fuller, Yeoman of the Armoury at Greenwich, had in his charge the following tournament equipment 'to be used att such tymes as it shall please [her] Majestie to have any Tryumphes att Tylte': 250 vamplates, 50 tilt staves, 6 'parting' staves, 46 punching staves, 200 burres, 50 counter-burres, 250 mornes, and 9 blunted swords.[69] One of the more detailed inventories, that of June 1611, has a similar list for Greenwich, but also includes an inventory of the Westminster Staffhouse, a building in or close to the White-

hall tiltyard. Here were stored 220 pikes for barriers, 131 tiltstaves with burres and coronels, 85 swords for barriers,[70] 17 vamplates, and 6 parting staves.

The inventories also contain details about armours held in store, which were often kept there long after the owner had died. The 1611 inventory, for example, records that the Earl of Leicester's tilting armour was kept in the Green Gallery at Greenwich 'compleate graven w[i]th the ragged staff . . . the horse having a steel sadle and foreparte of a barde plaine a Crynit and shaffron p[ar]cell guilte and graven w[i]th a hinderparte for a horse made of plates of steele and a bridle'. Other tilt armours included those of the King and Prince Henry, Lord Kildare, Sir Thomas Challoner, and Fulke Greville. A different inventory refers in addition to the 'Great Launces' that are said to have been used by Henry VIII and Charles Brandon. These may still be seen in the Tower Armouries, as can some of the armour listed in the inventories (including that of Leicester). The armour of Sir John Smythe (*c.* 1585) shown in Figure 34 is a typical example.

The joint responsibilities of the Greenwich workshops and the Office of the Armoury in manufacturing, maintaining, storing, and supplying armour and weapons for tournaments were thus considerable, offering yet further proof of the willingness of successive Tudor and Jacobean governments to invest both men and money in tournament spectacles. The other all-important factors in staging tournaments were the knights and their horses.

Throughout the Middle Ages, a knight was by definition expected to be able to supply his own horses. His most important horse was his destrier or great horse, a strong and heavy stallion bred to carry (in late medieval times) the knight, the knight's plate armour and weapons, a heavy saddle, and the horse's protective armour, a combined weight of about 450 lb. Such a horse was ridden only in battle or at tournaments. At other times, such as when a knight was travelling, the horse was

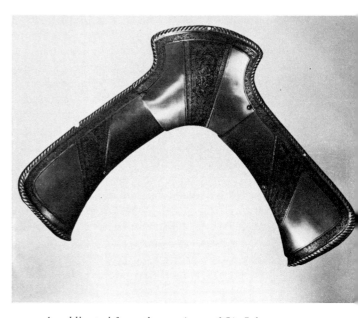

33   Vamplates were fitted to lances to provide protection for hand and arm. This example (c. 1580) from the Greenwich workshops was probably part of an armour made for Sir Christopher Hatton.

34   A saddle steel from the garniture of Sir John Smythe (c. 1585). Saddle steels provided essential protection for a knight's groin area. Smythe's armour is included in the Almain Armourer's Album, but was not intended for use in tournaments.

led by a squire, and it has been argued by some that the term 'destrier' derives from the fact that the squire customarily led the horse on the right-hand side of the knight. Such horses did not trot, since the extra weight of armour would have been too uncomfortable. Instead, destriers were trained to 'run' so that their riders could sit with legs straight and stirrups extended, a technique that permitted maximum control of the lance in jousting and maximum grip on the horse's back, which did not rise and fall as it would have done if the horse trotted. At a tournament, movement along the tilt may not have been very swift, but the power and weight involved as two riders approached each other at a combined speed of about 50 mph with that force directed at each other through the extended length of their lances must have been very impressive.

During the Renaissance, the demands made on knights taking part in tournaments increased. Apart from the destrier, it was also necessary to possess a courser, a large powerful horse bred and built to give more speed than the destrier and ideal for tourneys, and increasingly a knight needed to be able to demonstrate his mastery of the new Italian equestrian arts. Thus, to the image of martial power (implicit in the figure of the armed men of knightly status in combat in the lists) was added the equally elitist image of the skilled rider of a Spanish or Neapolitan horse, so in control of his mount that it could perform a choreographed sequence of charges, halts, leaps and turns.[71] The art of 'managed' riding was quite in keeping with the tournament as spectacle propaganda, for it was a living rhetorical device, designed to impress the superior strength and governing abilities of the rider upon the pedestrian onlooker.[72]

It is not surprising that, among the Tudors,

it was Henry VIII who first responded to the new Italian equestrian arts and the need to improve the breeding of English horses, a concern in line with other attempts to bolster his prestige. Henry was the pupil of Robert Alexander (a disciple of Federico Grisone and of the Neapolitan, Pignatelli), and he could perform extremely well in the new forms of horsemanship, as he proved in the July 1517 tournament: 'Between the courses, the King and the pages, and other cavaliers, performed marvellous feats, mounted on magnificent horses, which they made jump and execute other arts of horsemanship.'[73] Yet when it came to finding suitable horses, Henry was fully aware that the English native stock could not compete with what was available in Europe. Throughout his reign, Henry was continually acquiring horses from abroad. In 1514, for example, his representative Sir Thomas Cheney obtained ten Neapolitan horses for him, and in preparation for the Field of Cloth of Gold a widespread and vigorous search for Italian horses was made by Henry's agents. Determined to build up the size and quality of native stock, Henry enacted a series of laws during the 1530s to encourage better breeding methods. He also created a stud and employed eight Italian grooms in the royal stables, all experts from a country renowned at the time for its breeding of horses.[74]

The officer in the Tudor and Jacobean era responsible for the provision of horses for the monarch and his/her family was the Master of the Horse. Henry VII's officer was Thomas Brandon, who was apparently not a particularly active figure,[75] but during Henry VIII's reign three of his officers—Sir Thomas Knyvet (1510–1512), (?)Charles Brandon (1512–1515) and Sir Nicholas Carew (1522–1539)—were themselves excellent horsemen and constantly appeared in tournaments with Henry. It appears that their involvement did much to encourage Henry in his new breeding policies. None the less, following Henry's reign the efficiency of the royal stables and native breeding generally appears for a time to have declined.[76] Particularly harmful was the poor maintenance of the royal studs and the lack of money to make purchases abroad, but all this changed with Elizabeth's appointment of Robert Dudley (the future Earl of Leicester) to the Mastership. Dudley was an expert in managed riding and cared greatly about horses. On Elizabeth's instructions he did much to improve the royal studs, and further improvements then followed during the Mastership of Leicester's successor, the Earl of Essex (1590–1601). Leicester also brought Claudio Corte to England, an Italian expert and author of a well-known treatise on horsemanship, and in 1576 he commissioned another Italian, Prospero d'Osma, to report to him on the condition of the royal studs.

By the time of Essex' appointment, the Master of the Horse had achieved a considerable status requiring significant expenditure by the crown. The appointment, like that of other Masters, was by patent and carried in this instance an annual fee of 1000 marks (or £666 13s. 4d.), a salary that put him well ahead of many other officers of the household. The total cost of wages for his various officers, from chief avener (£40 per annum) to yeoman bit-makers (4d per diem), amounted to £2100 without provision for all the other many expenses involved in equipping and feeding the royal horses.[77] Though Elizabeth ordered rigorous economies in her household towards the end of her reign, her successor, James I, an avid hunter (albeit a timid jouster), tended to spare no expense in many departments of the royal estate, least of all in the matter of horses. Under the management of the two Masters of his reign, the Earl of Worcester and particularly the Duke of Buckingham, England's wealth in horses notably increased. The Whitehall tiltyard on tournament days must have reflected this, and though tilting skills may well have been in decline at this time, the riding of fine horses retained its political significance as an image of governance and power. The work of the royal stables and studs, so lavishly funded by James, continued to ensure, at least for a while, that tiltyard spectacles could be furnished with appropriate animals.

Bearing in mind what was involved in tournaments, it is hardly surprising that the participants were largely confined to men drawn from court circles. Since medieval times, only those of gentlemanly status could take part, and they had to be able to furnish themselves with the necessary arms, horses and retinue (see p. 61). They also needed to be physically fit and to command a modicum of the necessary skills in arms and horsemanship.

From the time that Henry VIII founded the order of Gentleman Pensioners in 1509 as a kind of personal bodyguard, there was a source of potential participants within the court. As part of their terms of appointment, the Pensioners had in any case to provide their own arms and equip themselves and their attendants. Significantly, too, each man had 'to have three greate Horses'.[78] However, on only one occasion, so far as I can determine, did the Gentlemen Pensioners ever provide almost all the combatants for a tournament. This happened at the very beginning of Queen Elizabeth's reign on 10 July 1559 when a tournament was held in the park (not the tiltyard) at Greenwich and the Pensioners fought with lances and swords against three challengers (Lord Ormond, Sir John Perrot, and Mr North).[79] For the reigns of Elizabeth and James, fairly full rolls of Pensioners' names exist,[80] and a comparison with the surviving tilting lists shows that each tournament would commonly include a number of Pensioners from the available fifty. In addition, there were usually a small number of other men who were neither of the nobility nor Pensioners. Participants of this kind, as well as those drawn from among the Pensioners, appear to have decreased during James I's reign. At the same time the proportion of high-ranking nobility who participated increased, though generally speaking the total number of participants in most Jacobean tournaments was fewer than in previous reigns, a sign perhaps of a lessening of interest, of skill and of the willingness or ability

to expend the necessary funds.

There was, then, no particularly consistent pattern regarding those who participated in Tudor and Jacobean tournaments, and certainly, in contrast to what has on occasion been suggested, no evidence that participants belonged to some special knightly order. All that was required, it appears, was social rank, connection at court, martial skills, and, as will be increasingly clear from what follows, a well-filled purse. However, the tournaments of James' reign include one radical departure from this general picture and, as a result, James must probably be credited with introducing the first professional sportsmen in what had hitherto been a kingdom of amateurs. All the surviving tilting lists of James' reign contain the names of the two Zinzan brothers, Henry and Sir Sigismond (often also known by the surname 'Alexander'), the names usually written towards the bottom of the lists in a manner suggesting the inferior social status of the two men.[81] The father of Henry and Sigismond Zinzan, Sir Robert, seems to have been employed in the royal stables during Elizabeth's reign, and he participated in tournaments regularly between 1565 and 1591.[82] His two sons followed in his footsteps and first appeared at tournaments, singly or together, in the final years of Elizabeth's reign between 1598 and 1602. Though it is possible that Sir Robert and his sons were paid for their services during Elizabeth's reign, there is no proof of it. However, beginning at least as early as 1610, Henry and Sir Sigismond were paid £100 (£50 each) to equip themselves every time they participated. The money was paid as a free gift for which they did not have to account, and the officers of the Exchequer were even expected to deliver it to them. However, it seems probable that the money reflects the fact that these two professionals had some role to play in organizing the tilts and that they acted as practice partners for the royal family. This may explain why, after twenty-seven years of tiltyard appearances (surely a record), Henry Zinzan sought royal relief because of 'long service and extreme hurts he has received by Prince Henry and His Majesty'.[83]

Something has already been said about the manner in which private individuals such as the Earl of Leicester, the Earl of Arundel, Lord Windsor (Fig. 35), Sir Philip Sidney and Sir Fulke Greville appear to have paid a large part of the costs of certain tournaments during Elizabeth's reign. We know too that there were a number of privately sponsored tournaments during Henry VII's reign.[84] Among the best known was that at Kennington in May 1507 at which Charles Brandon, Thomas Knyvet, Giles Chapel and William Hussy challenged all comers. Another was the extravaganza involving a tournament and multiple feasts held by Sir Rhys ap Thomas at Carew Castle the same year in celebration of his receiving the Order of the Garter, a grandiose exercise in self-aggrandisement involving hundreds of guests and their retainers.[85] The traditional expenses incurred by individuals for heralds' fees, horses, armour and weapons have also been mentioned, though, as we saw, apart from heralds' fees, these other expenses were often absorbed by the crown, particularly during the early Tudor period. A key change, however, occurred during Elizabeth's reign as private individuals began to bear an increasingly larger part of tournament costs. What these costs were is best determined by considering what a participant would have to do to prepare himself for a tournament.

Typically, a knight would have to spend some time practising his martial skills. The usual place for this, perhaps because it offered a degree of privacy, was the tiltyard at Greenwich, about which we shall be hearing more in the next chapter. A German visitor to Greenwich on 11 November 1584 recorded in his travel diary that he had watched English knights practising for the forthcoming Accession Day tournament, and another foreign visitor, fourteen years later, noted similar activities.[86] We know too that the Earl of Essex spent a week practising there in

preparation for the tournament at Windsor in 1593. Lord Herbert of Cardiff practised there in 1600, and in March 1605 Sir Dudley Carleton wrote to Sir Ralph Winwood of how there was much practising at Greenwich for the forthcoming tournament.[87] Time so spent could be expensive as is evident from Essex' household account books which record that he required £74 10s. to cover the costs of his diet and charges for one practice period.[88]

Even before going off to Greenwich, a tournament participant in Elizabeth's or James' reigns might have many decisions to make. He would have to decide upon a theme for his entry into the tiltyard, and the costumes for himself, his pages, his servants, his lance bearers, his armourers, his trumpeters, his grooms, and any actors or musicians he had hired. His horses would also require caparisons to match his own costume. He would have to compose an impresa (or have someone do this for him) and have it painted on a shield, and, if he planned to present a speech or some form of miniature drama involving actors, he or someone else would have to prepare the necessary text. The combined cost of all these items could be considerable; yet individuals in both Elizabeth's and James' reigns appear to have readily invested the necessary money in order to compliment their sovereign and perhaps in return earn esteem and even favour. The Earl of Essex, for example, spent over £80 on his preparations for one Accession Day tournament. His costs, according to the badly-damaged section of the accounts, included various sums for footmen's hats, 'necessaries' from Lady Rich's tailor, staves and lances, and armour for the combat at barriers.[89] For the 1594

35 Portrait of Henry Windsor, 5th Baron Windsor, by an unknown artist (1588). Windsor was a participant in tournaments in 1597 and 1598 and the portrait shows him in a German armour with etched decoration. Windsor's impresa is shown in the top left and the unicorn motif matches that on his armour.

Accession Day tournament, Essex brought 'certeine schollers' from Oxford and paid for their costumes so that they could act in his device, and the following year he again hired university scholars to act in a tiltyard device (see Chapter 7), the text of which may have been written by himself or by Francis Bacon.[90]

Employing the services of a skilled author was not uncommon. In 1601, for example, Sir Robert Cecil invited Sir John Davies to write an introductory speech for a combat at barriers, and in October of the previous year Rowland White wrote to Sir Robert Sidney explaining that Lord Herbert of Cardiff (the future Earl of Pembroke) was intending to make his first appearance in a tournament. White feared that Sidney's help was needed since without it Lord Herbert's tutor, Hugh Sanford, might well produce some unsuitable 'pedantike Invention',[91] a phrase which probably refers to both impresa and accompanying speech or speeches. Though Sir Robert Sidney may have given freely of his services, such would not have been the case when Ben Jonson supplied a sixteen-line poem to accompany the entries of Sir Robert and Sir Henry Rich in 1613. Ben Jonson would also have charged for the texts he wrote for the barriers at the marriage of the Earl of Essex and Frances Howard in 1606, and for *A Challenge for Tilt at a Marriage* which was written to celebrate the marriage of the Earl of Somerset and Frances Howard in 1613. The writing of impresas too might be contracted out, as we know from the fact that Francis Manners, the Earl of Rutland, paid Shakespeare forty-four shillings in gold for the composition of an impresa in 1613, Richard Burbage receiving the same amount for painting the impresa onto Rutland's shield.[92]

It is this same Earl of Rutland who has left us the clearest indication of the kinds of expenses that a private individual could incur. His surviving account books provide a unique record of tournament expenses, though just how representative these are is hard to say, since expenses during the Jacobean period seem generally to have climbed, while Rutland himself was something of a lavish spender and hence not necessarily typical. The first surviving account, that for the Accession Day tournament of 1613, includes, as already indicated, payments for his impresa, but it also lists costs of £3 16s. for the painting of twelve tilt staves, four vamplates, and seven puncheon staves. The following year there are payments to an armourer, a painter, a saddler, a bit-maker, a hatter and a cutler, together with further expenses relating to tilting staves, the trumpeter's uniform, and the ceremonial chariot in which Rutland entered the tiltyard. The full total came to about £50.[93] Rutland did not participate in 1615, but in March 1616 he was back in the tiltyard, and his expenses were yet higher:[94]

Paid to Samuel, goldsmith, for 24 yardes and 3/4 of watchet silver velvet for 2 caparaisons, at 25s the yarde, the soom of £30 18s. 9d.

Paid for tiltinge staffes and tronchions, £3 14s. 9d.

Paid to 2 trompetes for there attendance the tyme of tiltinge, £10.

Paid for watchet velvet to cover a booke presented, with charg of binding, 13s. 6d.

Paid given Richard Burbidg for my Lorde's shelde and for the embleance, £4 18s.

Paid the feather maker for feathers for my Lorde's plume, for feathers for pages and groomes, appearinge by bill, £19.

Paid Edward Cropplie, silkman, upon full payment of a bill of particulers, for silver and golde fringe lace and other thinges used for the tilting, £53 15s. 4d.

Paid Richard Hodgskins, my Lorde's tailor, for making apparell for my Lorde's pages and groomes uppon this occazion, £29.

Paid given as reward to my Lorde's armorer for attendance, £1 10s.

The total for all these items was £153 10s. 4d. Four years later, Rutland was still an active participant and was involved in Prince Charles' first Accession Day tournament on 24 March, and it would appear that he joined with three other knights in the presentation of an allegorical device involving a lady. Rutland's quarter share for this and for other 'giftes and rewardes' came to £9 14s. In addition, his accounts list further payments relating to tilting staves, his armourer, a painter, and an embroiderer. These total £28 19s. 6d,[95] a very modest sum in comparison to the previous year and to the sum of almost £6500 that was spent by the Exchequer on behalf of Prince Charles.

Expenses might also be incurred for additional entertainment. In 1594 Essex preceded his tiltyard entry on 17 November with some kind of preliminary entertainment the day before. His expenses for this included the cost of 'white taffeta to fould the christall in delivered to her Majestie'.[96] Presumably the 'christall' was a gift to Elizabeth and as such was intended both to compliment the Queen and to elicit her favour for the giver. At this period in his ill-fated career Essex was doing all in his power to persuade Elizabeth to grant him a number of requests and he no doubt considered the opportunity to present her with an expensive gift well worth the financial cost.

A second example of the presentation of gifts dates from the year before. Sir Robert Cary, a young relative of the Queen, having married a widow who had little money to her name, subsequently found himself in disgrace with Elizabeth because he had married without her permission. His response was to appear incognito at the Accession Day tournament as 'Sir Unknown'. He was, so he explains in his memoirs, 'the forsaken Knight that had vowed solitariness, but hearing of the great triumph thought to honour my mistress with my best service'.[97] To sweeten

things a little more, Cary also 'prepared a present for her Majesty, which with my caparisons cost me above four hundred pounds'. Yet Cary's income was but £100 a year, and in 1593 he already had debts of £1000! Though she continued to pretend that she did not know that Cary had returned to court, Elizabeth was duly placated, and after a short time she entrusted him with a mission to the King of Scotland. Explaining to Cary's father what she wanted, she said, 'I hear your fine son that has lately married so worthily, is hereabouts; send him if you will to know the King's pleasure'.[98] Thus, expensive gifts, like other lavish expenditure by individuals, obviously did on occasion bring about the intended reciprocal reward.

*   *   *

The organization and financing of tournaments were thus complex and expensive matters requiring the labour, energy and funds of government offices and, increasingly, of private individuals. The scale and frequency of tournaments during most of the Tudor and Jacobean periods is, as I have suggested earlier, an indication of the importance that successive monarchs attached to them. The full cost and the amount of manpower involved in the preparation of every detail, from the construction and maintenance of the tiltyard itself to the livery and diet of the lowliest attendant, show clearly that tournament expenses far surpassed all other forms of pageantry and spectacle (including the Jacobean masques). What follows in the remainder of this book will, I hope, emphasize this point yet further.

III

Such a Noble Theatre

HE MICROCOSM OF the realm provided by a crowded tiltyard on a tournament day was in itself a potent instrument of royal propaganda, and the great tournaments held before the north facade of Westminster Palace or those in Henry VIII's specially built tiltyard at Whitehall, set as they were amid impressive buildings, were a means of underlining the prestige of the crown. The provision and maintenance of that tiltyard setting, along with the costly events it served to display, were all part of a serious and far-reaching purpose.

Few if any, public occasions can have matched the tournament for sheer size and splendour. At any major Tudor tournament, for example, thousands of spectators packed themselves in double-tiered viewing stands around a rectangular area approximately the size of a soccer pitch or an American football field. One man who went to Westminster in 1501 to see the tournament celebrating the marriage of Katherine of Aragon and Prince Arthur was so struck by the sight of the vast numbers of spectators that he remarked that there 'was nothing to the eye but only visages and faces without appearances of their bodyes'. Then there is the report that 50,000 people attended a tournament at Greenwich in 1517; however, a more realistic estimate of the kinds of numbers involved is probably the

figure of 12,000 mentioned in a proposal of 1622 to build an arena in London for 'exercise of Tilts, Turney, course of Field, Barriers, Running at ring and other martiall and manly exercises'.[1]

Events of this nature lasted for several days in succession. Spectators were charged an entrance fee of a shilling and must have returned each day to stand for hour after hour from late morning to dusk. Upon arrival, they first had to wait for the appearance of the nobility and the monarch at about midday or an hour or two later, one o'clock being one of the most commonly selected times. During this time spectators would have had ample opportunity to observe the features of the tiltyard. Apart from the crowds and the stands (those for royalty, the nobility and special guests sumptuously bedecked with tapestries), there was the tilt barrier, about 100 yards long and six feet high, and the care-

36 Joust between Sir John Astley and Pierre de Masse in 1438. The wooden tilt barrier is about four feet high, and the combatants are using sharp lances. Astley is in the foreground. Leaning vertically against one of the buildings are spare tilting lances with sharp heads, vamplates, and spiked burres. By pressing the spikes on the burres into a wooden block, the lance could be held steady in a rest.

fully prepared surface of the combat area, free from debris and potholes and, if paved, well-sanded to give the horses a good footing. Around this area were fences, six to seven feet in height, painted (in Queen Elizabeth's reign, at least) black and white and perhaps decorated with some heraldic motif. Guards were placed at intervals along the fences to ensure that nobody, whether out of misguided enthusiasm or a desire to get closer to the action, encroached upon the combat area.

At one or both ends of most tiltyards, gates were marked where the challengers and answerers, their retainers, spare horses, and moving pageants would eventually enter. Like the tunnels leading into many modern arenas, these gates offered a point towards which expectant eyes would turn with increasing frequency as the magic moment of the entry of the first challenger approached. Before the trumpeters signalled this, however, the attention of all would be directed towards a pictorial treat of another kind. Foreign ambassadors and their retinues, the tournament judges, the nobility, and the royal family all made their entrances in ascending order of precedence and dressed in finery befitting their respective ranks. When all were finally present, something approaching a cross-section of the entire nation was visible at a glance. A key part of the experience of attending a tournament was looking at the élite in the audience, and the resources of the crown that had been invested in setting up an appropriate venue would have their desired effect even before the spectacle started.

The central feature of any tiltyard on the first day of a tournament, which by convention was assigned to the jousting, was the tilt itself. Most tilts were made of wood, but for a time the one at Greenwich appears to have been made of canvas.[2] Yet even at Greenwich the tilt had become a permanent wooden fixture 150 yards long by 1558, when Anthonis van den Wyngaerde, an Antwerp artist in the employ of Philip II of Spain, drew the Palace as seen from the River Thames (see Fig. 52).[3]

We know that the one at Whitehall was approximately 107 yards long,[4] whereas that built much earlier for the Field of Cloth of Gold in 1520 was a shorter eighty-yard structure.[5] As various English illustrations show, most tilts were about six feet high, on a level with a horse's ears or the top of a man's hat (see Figs 36, 37 and 42).

Some tilts (see Fig. 38), including that at Whitehall (see Fig. 39), appear to have had an angled section at either end. This addition to the barrier, which I have never seen explained, may have been designed to prevent a horse from swerving to the wrong side as it approached the tilt end on. In the same way that the knight's vision was severely limited by his jousting helmet, that of the horse was sometimes limited by the use of a shaffron with metal flanges to protect the eyes. The projection at the far end of the tilt barrier, which would in part have stretched across a rider's path, would have had the effect of turning his horse away from the line of the tilt once it approached the end of its run. If space at the end of the tiltyard was limited, this would have been a helpful feature if rider and horse were to avoid running into the palisades around the lists. For a knight encumbered by a twelve-foot lance in his right hand, and with his left hand encased in a manifer and the control of his horse possibly threatened or lost after making contact with his opponent, some help in turning his horse would no doubt have provided a welcome measure of safety.

When opponents in any physical competition face each other outdoors, the position of the sun or the direction of the wind may tend to favour one side at the expense of the other, hence the systems created for the assigning

37 *In this illumination Sir John Astley and an unidentified opponent have both broken their rebated lances dramatically before the lady of the tournament. Astley is in the foreground and the wooden tilt barrier would appear to be about five feet high. Each knight wears a fanciful crest, typical of tournament costume.*

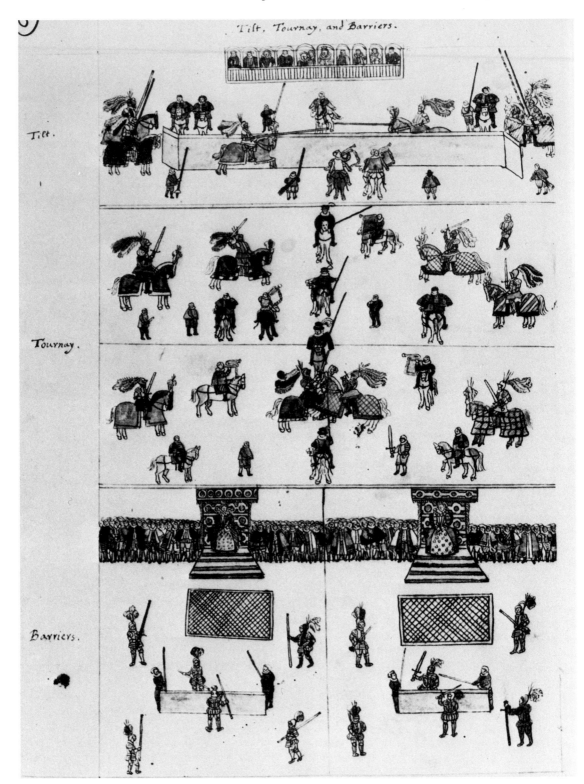

LEFT AND ABOVE

38   This unique illuminated drawing of an Elizabethan tournament shows Queen Elizabeth watching first the jousting, then the tourney. The combat at barriers appears to be an indoor event. The drawing of the tilt barrier is of particular interest since it is shown having angled ends, a feature recorded in a number of maps of Westminster. Mounted trumpeters and heralds are shown in the tiltyard for both joust and tourney. The knights' pages, who hold spare weapons, are on foot. Other knights awaiting their turn are also shown to left and right. The detail (ABOVE) shows the wire grill at the rear which was placed in front of the Queen to protect her from flying pieces of broken weapons.

and exchanging of ends in such sports as football, rugby and tennis. In jousting a degree of equality may have been created if each rider rode successive courses in opposite directions along the tilt. In this way the effects of an adverse wind or a blinding sun would be shared equally. While there is no evidence that this practice was actually employed, there is some evidence that attempts may have been made where possible to place tilts upon an east-west axis so that the sun would favour neither combatant. Certainly the rules for trials by combat as set down by Thomas, Duke of Gloucester, in the time of Richard II, place one combatant at the east end of the lists and the other at the west.

The choice of an east-west axis for the tilt at tournaments, however, was probably conditioned not so much to aid combatants as to place the most important spectators (royalty and the nobility) in the most advantageous viewing position with their backs to the sun. The royal stand would also be as near as possible to the centre of the tilt, the best place from which to observe what was going on. Once again, the physical arrangements in the tiltyard must be seen as having an important symbolic significance, royalty being given the place of pre-eminence as befitted those of

39 *Elizabethan maps of London and Westminster. Frans Hogenberg's map of 1572 (ABOVE) shows the walled city of London with Westminster to the left, around the bend in the River Thames. The long, narrow tiltyard, with its tilt barrier (angled at each end), runs north-south parallel to the long street and its site is now covered by the government buildings of Whitehall. John Norden's map of Westminster of 1595 (ABOVE RIGHT) shows the King's Bridge, the entrance from the river to the old Palace of Westminster, and the Privy Stairs, the royal entrance to Henry VIII's new Whitehall Palace. Henry's tiltyard is slightly to the left of the centre of the map and is marked with an 'N'.*

highest rank and status. For the jousts between Lord Scales and the Bastard of Burgundy in 1467 at Smithfield, the King's stand was erected on the south side of the lists, the challenger and defendant facing each other at east and west (the King's right and left respectively).[6] The tournaments at Westminster in front of the north door of Westminster Hall were also set up this way, the royal stand being on the south side of the yard, stands for the mayor and other civic dignitaries on the north side, and the tilt on an east-west axis.[7] Again the challengers took the east end on the King's right. Significantly, when Henry VIII's commissioners drew up a design for the tiltyard at the Field of Cloth of Gold, they placed it on an east-west axis with the royal gallery facing north.[8]

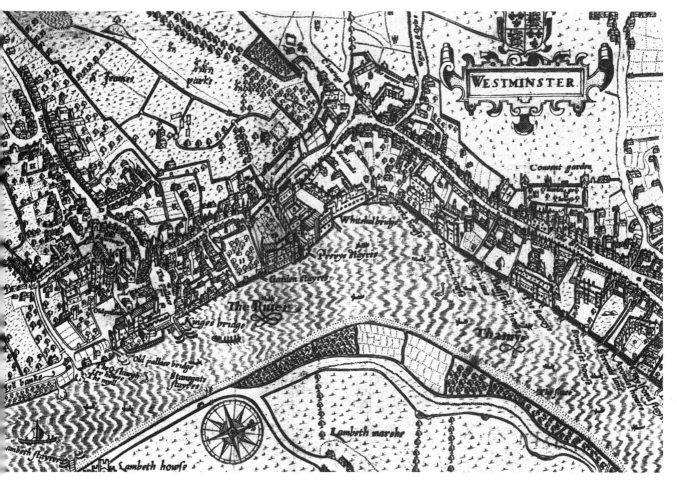

Immediately in front of the most privileged viewers at tournaments there was usually space for the erection of another type of barrier designed as a safety feature for use in foot combats (Fig. 40). Just as mounted knights at the tilt completed an agreed number of courses (generally six), those who fought on foot, usually at a later stage in the tournament, were separated by a barrier and fought a predetermined number of pushes with a pike and strokes with a sword. The presence of the barrier added to the safety of each participant by ensuring a certain distance between the combatants. There were also rules that forbade any blows being delivered beneath the barrier or below an opponent's girdle, a point reflected in the general practice of not bothering with leg-armour when fighting on foot,

something which explains why the Earl of Sussex is able to show off his shapely legs in the portrait depicting him dressed for a foot combat (see Fig. 71). A typical barrier for foot combats was described in the account of the tournament to welcome Katherine of Aragon in 1501: 'a certaine barrier which was sett over thwart the place before the Kinges stage being of the middle height of a man made stedfast and in Bayles on each end of the Barrier sett vpright and tyed together in the toppes with Cordes.'[9]

The palisades enclosing the rectangle within which the tilt barrier stood were probably at least 123 yards in length to accommodate the tilt and to allow for sufficient space at either end for mounting blocks and for riders to prepare themselves before begin-

ning a course against an opponent.[10] An illustration of jousting in a College of Arms manuscript (see Fig. 48) clearly shows the mounting steps or horse blocks at each end of the tilt and, standing on those at the left with his hammer in his hand, the all-important armourer, who has just assisted his knight to arm.[11]

Apart from providing space for horse-blocks, the area of the lists at either end of the tilt barrier might also have to accommodate various scenic devices, spare weapons and horses, and those waiting their turn to fight. Since each participant in a joust might require a new stave for every course, dozens of staves might be required for a day's jousting. Some 327 staves are recorded as having been broken at the Field of Cloth of Gold, and for this same tournament—admittedly an especially grand affair—the English participants took along as many as 2000. Obviously the storage of staves could be a problem. In the 1501 Westminster tournament this difficulty was solved by storing them beneath the royal gallery,[12] but another solution was to stack the staves vertically. This is the method shown in Figure 48, in which unused staves are depicted standing on their butts at either end of the tilt barrier.

A mast or frame was required to support them in this position and one of these may

40 *Foot combat at barriers with staves. This drawing, which accompanies the 1554 challenge of Lord Strange and various Spanish noblemen, illustrates one means of constructing a barrier and its approximate height in relation to the combatants.*

be what is depicted on the left side of the drawing, slightly to the right of the stack of staves. Evidence that such frames were used occurs in the Works Office accounts for the year 1594 to 1595 where a payment is recorded for 'makeinge a frame to houlde vp the runing staves' at Whitehall, and some such frame must have been used at Whitehall in January 1581 when the Earl of Oxford sat beneath a golden tree, beside which 'stood' twelve golden tilting staves.[13] A similar purpose seems to have been served by the 'mast for a great spear or two spears' provided by the Revels Office for the tournament at Greenwich in July 1517.[14] At Whitehall there was a 'spearehowse' in the tiltyard, but I suspect that this building was not used during tournaments and was designed to store staves between tournaments. From all this it is clear that the space at either end of the tiltyard could be quite cluttered, especially when room was also needed for pavilions in which the knights could arm themselves or rest from their endeavours, but I shall have more to say of these in a moment.

The width of the jousting area (about eighty yards) would have been less than the length. But where the tilt barrier was a permanent fixture sufficient space would still be required between the tilt and the fence in front of the royal gallery for tourneying and for combats on foot. At some tournaments, such as that at Westminster in 1501, the tilt was removed after the jousting was over to make ready for the tourney and the barriers. At the later Whitehall and Greenwich tiltyards, however, the tilt would remain in place until the next tournament.

The prime purpose of the fence erected around the combat area was, of course, to protect participants in a tournament from the crowds and vice versa. One commentator observed that its function was to prevent spectators 'wandring amonge the speares horses and Coursers aswell for the ease and regard of their hurt'.[15] For the combat between Lord Scales and the Bastard of Burgundy at Smithfield in 1467, the fencing was seven and a half feet high. Each bar was three and a half inches thick and five inches broad.[16] The same measures were used for the tournament at Westminster in 1501, while plans for the Cloth of Gold tournament included fencing, a ditch, and a rampart, though these were in part designed to provide security for those invited to attend the event, King Francis being particularly concerned about unwanted infiltrators. Almost a hundred years later in February 1613, King James I, his son Prince Charles, and James' new son-in-law the Count Palatine, as part of the celebration of the marriage of James' daughter Elizabeth, ran at ring before 'many thousand beholders' at Whitehall, a novel public spectacle that made it more than ever necessary to place guards around the tiltyard fence: 'First, about the rayles or lists in the Tylt-yard, adjoyning to White Hall, were placed many Herolds at Armes, to beautifie the honourable atchiefements of these knightly Potentates, and withall, the Knight

marshall of England, and his seruants, all in new liueries with their staues of office, to abate the too forward vnruliness of many disordered people, which otherwise would haue much troubled the Turnaments, and as an ayde vnto them, many of his Highnes Yeomen of the Guard were attendant in the lists, and withall, most of the Kings Trumpetters in their rich imbrothered coates, the pentioners and Knights of his graces household with their guilded Pole-axes, guarding as it were in a round, the King with his Knightly followers.'[17]

Two fences were often erected around the tilting area as a further precaution, only authorized persons such as the heralds being permitted to enter the space between. The two fences were about five to eight feet apart. John Stow describes such an arrangement in his account of the 1467 Smithfield tournament. In length, he says, the lists were '120 Taylors yardes, and 10. foote, and in breadth 80. yardes, and 20. foote, double barred, 5. foote betweene the barres'.[18] René of Anjou's well-known *Livre des Tournois* contains a clear illustration of such double fencing at a tournament in about 1450 (see Fig. 41). Trials by combat had traditionally used such double fences, and this was still the general arrangement at the time of Queen Elizabeth, as can be seen from a diagram giving details for the trial by combat planned to take place in Tuthill Fields in 1571.[19]

Knowing the length of the fences allows us to visualize the size of the tournament area. Though the measurements are widely disparate, Stow's '120 Taylor's yardes, and 10. foote' by '80 yardes, and 20 foote' and the 300 yards by 296 feet for the Field of Cloth of Gold tournament are the most precise surviving indications of what was considered an appropriate size for the combat area.[20] René's instruction that the fences ought to be one quarter longer than wide, the height of a man, made of strong wood with two cross bars, the lower at knee height, with an inner fence (with only a single bar) providing a clear area four paces wide to protect the knights'

attendants and to guard the participants from the press of spectators, makes clear that English arrangements were quite in harmony with those employed elsewhere.[21]

Viewing stands were essential because of the height of the palisades around the lists and the tilt barrier itself. At ground level the tilt barrier obscured the lower part of the rider on the far side and much of his horse. This problem has caused a modern exponent of jousting to lower his tilt to four feet six inches and to leave it partially unblocked so that spectators can see both over it and through it, a departure from the practices of 500 years or more that has added to the difficulties of any modern 'knight' who attempts the exacting art of jousting.[22] However, in Tudor and Stuart tiltyards, as elsewhere in Europe, the

41   This illustration from René of Anjou's Le Livre des Tournois *shows a French tourney* c. *1450, an example of the earlier form where groups of knights fought each other. Once the dividing ropes were cut by the two men with axes, the knights would charge each other. The combat area is enclosed by double fences and the guards standing inside are to keep participants and spectators apart. The characteristic raised viewing stands, like the double fences, were a feature of many English tournaments.*

solution to problems of visibility was to raise the viewpoint of the spectators so that they would be able to see as much as possible of both riders. For the tournament judges, of course, this must have been a necessity.

The Office of Works constructed what the account books usually refer to as 'scaffolds' or 'standings', which were stands built vertically over open scaffolding and containing two roofed viewing levels, one above the other.[23] Such stands took up the minimum of space and were not too complex to construct, but they were among the most important and visible signs of government expenditure. Moreover, they cannot have been particularly cheap since, however easy they may have been to put together, they had to be 'well builded and planked'.[24] If they were poorly constructed and too many people tried to crowd into them, there was always the possibility of a disaster. Just such a calamity occurred at Henry VII's coronation, but the problem was by then already familiar. Edward III had ordered a royal gallery of stone to be built in Cheapside alongside the church of St Mary Bow for watching 'Iustinges and other shewes' because in 1331 the upper storey of a wooden stand, 'in which the Ladies were placed, brake in sunder, wherby they were with some shame forced to fall downe, by reason whereof ye knights and such as were vnderneath were grieuously hurt'.[25] Two and a half centuries after this accident, wooden stands were still risky. The festivities of a tournament at Whitehall in January 1581 were sadly marred when 'through the great concourse of people thither repairing, manie of the beholders, as well men as women, were sore hurt, some maimed, and some killed, by falling of the scaffolds ouercharged'.[26]

The responsibility for building viewing stands was in the hands of the royal household, but Tudor records concerning such temporary structures before the reign of Elizabeth are very sparse. A fair amount can be gleaned from Henry VIII's Office of Works accounts about the building of permanent stone or masonry viewing places adjacent to the Greenwich, Hampton Court and Whitehall tiltyards, but we know very little about the temporary wooden royal galleries erected at Westminster and the wooden viewing stands for other spectators at Westminster

and elsewhere between 1485 and 1580. However, we do know that there was a stand for Henry VII, his Queen, his son Arthur, his daughter-in-law Katherine, and 'all ther nobles & estates' on the south side of the tiltyard at the 1501 Westminster tournament. We also know that 'ther was another Stage for the Maior of Lond[on], the Sheriffe, Aldermen and worshipfull of the Craftes and in all the Circuit of this field of warre by and vpon the walles were double stages very thicke and many well builded and planked for the honest and Comon people'.[27] This tournament in celebration of the wedding of Prince Arthur and Katherine of Aragon was an especially grand state occasion, but other such events may not have required much less in the way of viewing stands.

The siting of viewing stands was especially important, as already explained. An undated document that probably refers to one of the Westminster tournaments between 1485 and 1512 describes the arrangement of the 'standing scaffolds in the Kings Palace of westminster att his iusts'.[28] On the south side of the lists was the king's 'stage'; on the king's right all the earls, barons and knights for whom there was no room in the royal stand; beyond them the 'Iudges, sarieants & ho[nor]able learned men as the said iudges will take to them'; and next to them 'all the dutchesses woomen, the Countesses, Baronesses & ladies of the Court woomen'. To the left of the king was the queen and (though they are not mentioned explicitly) the ladies of the court; to their left 'all the strange ladies and gentle wo[men] yt be not of the Court'; next to them 'all the marchant wives of the Citty of London, w[hi]ch be of worshyppe'; and next to them 'all other honest woomen'. On the north side of the tournament ground, directly opposite the King, were the Mayor London, the City Aldermen, and the 'Councell of the Citty, & such as he will take to him'; to their right were 'all the gentlemen of the Innes of Court'; and next to them the 'Companies of the Citty'. To the left of the Mayor were merchants and 'strangers'.

The social and sexual hierarchy was clearly the determining factor in this arrangement, but what is notable is that stands were available for those who attended such events, whatever their social rank. The records of the Inns of Court, for example, show that in 1494 the members paid £4 12s. od. 'for the stage at the Jousts',[29] and in 1501 the Middle Temple members took a similar levy, recorded on this occasion as 12d. a head (later the levy rose to 20d.), to pay for their stand.[30] Other records from these two Inns and the Inner Temple establish a similar pattern for Henry VIII's tournaments of 1509, 1511, and 1533, and for the coronation tournament of Edward VI in 1547.[31]

Important state tournaments from the time of Henry VII were clearly public events that required the construction of viewing stands (Fig. 42) for which spectators might have to pay, and this pattern certainly continued during the reigns of Elizabeth and James. A German visitor (von Wedel) in 1584, for example, commenting on arrangements at the Whitehall tiltyard, said that anybody could get a place in a stand by paying 12d. and that many thousands of spectators, both men and women, paid for such places.[32] Three years earlier a French visitor had mentioned the viewing stands 'erected for the numerous spectators' on 'both sides, and at either end' of the lists at Whitehall, and in an undated source (probably also from the 1580s) it is implied that anyone can go to Whitehall to see the tournaments 'for the spence of a few pence'.[33] Towards the end of King James' reign in 1620, the entry fee to the public stands was still only one shilling. Edward Alleyn, the theatre manager and founder of Dulwich College, recorded in his diary on 24 March of that year that he 'rode to see the tilting: paid for a standing 0.1.0'.[34] Admittedly, twelve pence was no small sum for many pockets, since it represented approximately half or three-quarters of a journeyman's daily wage (about 16d a day in the early seventeenth century). Yet even this high price apparently did not deter those citizens who

wanted to attend, a phenomenon for which there are a number of modern parallels.[35] Just how the money received from the thousands of paying spectators found its way back (as it presumably did) into the Exchequer is not clear, but there must have been considerable sums involved that would have partly offset some of the initial costs.[36]

More detailed information about viewing stands is to be found in the account books of the Office of Works during the reigns of Elizabeth and James. In the early years of Elizabeth's reign, the accounts are so arranged that it is not possible to tell what specific work was carried out in the tiltyards, but by the late 1570s the accounts are more specific. It is possible to deduce, for example, that there were probably no wooden viewing stands used at Greenwich and Hampton Court and that those at Whitehall were permanent fixtures. At Greenwich the permanent gallery, built by Henry VIII alongside the tiltyard as part of the palace, was considered adequate for the tournaments held there. It provided accommodation for the monarch and the nobility, together with any important foreigners, but commoners presumably did the best they could around the perimeter of the remainder of the lists. The only relevant reference to viewing stands at Hampton Court in the accounts appears to refer to an event not held in the tiltyard itself.[37] At Whitehall, on the other hand, the stands appear to have been permanent in the sense that they were not removed at the end of each tournament, unlike the judgehouse and the staging beneath the royal gallery.

However, not all the stands were alike. Even if constructed along similar lines, they might differ considerably in appearance because of the manner in which they were decorated and furnished. Those for the citizenry might be very plain, but those for royalty and the nobility, for ambassadors, and for important foreign visitors were sumptuously fitted out with rich hangings, tapestries and cushions. Such stands were part of the general spectacle of a tournament, and

42 Henry VIII in the Palace Yard at Westminster during the tournament in February 1511 to celebrate the birth of a prince. The King is riding from his pavilion on the left and has just shattered his lance against his opponent's helm. In the background is Queen Katherine's elaborate specially-built viewing stand, its roof and columns decorated with the royal badges (fleurs-de-lis, portcullis, red roses) and the Tudor colours of green and white. The interior is richly decorated. The gentlemen to the Queen's right lean on tapestry cushions, and the Queen sits beneath a gold canopy. She and the woman with her (? Princess Mary) lean upon cushions of blue cloth of gold.

in the case of those for ambassadors and foreign visitors, they were an effective and diplomatic means of demonstrating the provider's magnificence in a manner likely to be reported in despatches to other European monarchs. The nature of the furnishings provided in an ambassador's viewing stand, like the location of the stand itself in relation to the royal stand, was a clear indication of that official's political and social status. Hence the elaborate and detailed descriptions that ambassadors gave in their despatches were more than just entertaining gossip. This is also the reason why many accounts of tournaments

seem as much concerned with the colourful furnishings as with the events within the lists. Indirectly, of course, such descriptions provide evidence that the government expenditure involved was fully justified in so far as it succeeded in enhancing the prestige of the ruler in question.

The hangings and furniture supplied for these and other such well-appointed stands were very costly, as can be inferred from the special measures taken to protect them from vandalism, theft and the weather. At Henry VII's coronation tournament at Westminster, for example, nine men were paid thirty shillings for 'iiij nightes waching [. . .] for thapparellyng,' and four men were paid solely to watch over 'the stuffe w[ith]in the Kinges stonding'.[38] During the reigns of Elizabeth and James, the Office of Works regularly made such payments for groups of men to watch over the stands in the Whitehall tiltyard. Since the royal gallery was part of the palace, which had its own guards, its furnishings were not a concern, but the palace guards would not have been responsible for those in other viewing stands and the judge-house.[39] The accounts record many such payments, and we can assume that 'watching' the stands was a standard task for the employees of the Office of Works.

The Office of Works constructed the viewing stands and took responsibility for their overnight protection, but it was the Office of the Treasurer of the Chamber which was responsible for 'apparelling' and making them ready, or, as we would say, decorating and furnishing them. During the reigns of Elizabeth and James this task was usually supervised by a gentleman usher, whose assistants consisted of one yeoman usher, three yeomen, two grooms of the Chamber, two grooms of the Wardrobe, and one groom porter. Their full responsibilities at a tournament involved preparing the royal gallery, the judgehouse, any specially erected stands, rooms or windows around the tiltyard used by ambassadors, and on three occasions the pavilion erected in the Whitehall tiltyard for Prince Charles. Whatever was done must have followed a set formula and the accounts are, as a result, tantalizingly sparse in their details, the phrase 'making ready' being used to describe what must have been a whole variety of jobs. It would appear that these tasks included the furnishing of the monarch's place in the royal gallery at Whitehall (Fig. 43) with the 'hanginge of a state',[40] and the use of hangings or tapestries to divide the gallery into separate compartments. The partitions provided further comfort and a further show of magnificence, but they were also a means of establishing an order of precedence among the spectators as well as a means of segregating the sexes.[41]

Not surprisingly, foreign ambassadors admitted to the royal gallery vied with each other in being in a 'room' or 'compartment' as close as possible to the monarch, and if possible on his or her right side. In 1565, for example, the Spanish ambassador described his attendance at a Twelfth Night joust and in doing so gives us a glimpse of the nature of the interior arrangements in the gallery at Whitehall: 'Secretary Cecil and the Chamberlain put me in the gallery from which the Queen generally sees the feasts. There were three or four compartments divided by cloths, and they took me into the one adjoining that of the Queen and adorned in the same

way as hers. Soon afterwards the Queen came and entered the compartment where I was, calling me to her. I was with her at the window until the entry and a good number of the jousters had run.'[42] Unfortunately the ambassador does not say how his section of the gallery was 'adorned', but we may assume it was hung with hangings or tapestries, and also that some such cloth was hung out over the window sill to provide a suitable leaning place and to make a colourful spectacle for the spectators in the other stands.

Fifty years or so later the same kind of arrangements seem to have been in use. In 1618 the Russian ambassadors were taken to the tiltyard gallery at Whitehall 'where in the first Window next that entrance were placed for them two Stooles, and a Carpet to leane on, the Travers drawn between them and the King, whom after the Tylting they were admitted to see and salute'.[43] The ambassadors' retainers on this occasion were not granted such good accommodation. None the less they had a viewing stand of their own near the royal gallery, built by the Office of Works and 'apparelled' by the Office of the Chamber: 'Their Followers of all conditions (excepting their Interpreter for their use) were bestowed on a Scaffold ordained only for them next the entrance into the Tylt-yard on the Kings left hand, where three or four of the better sort of them had a leaning Carpet laid before them, and Seats to sit on, the rest had a Seate or two, and so took as they could their best commodities.'[44] Clearly a seat provided by the Office of the Chamber was a sign of favour and prestige, it being assumed that most spectators would stand. This explains why a description of the arrangements for ambassadors at the 1621 Accession Day tournament specifically mentioned that the Polish ambassador found 'the French, Venetian, and Savoy Ambassadors [. . .] seated' when he came to take his place at the Whitehall tiltyard 'on their and his appointed stand, hung and covered with tapistrie'.[45]

Occasionally, rather than being placed in viewing stands, ambassadors at Whitehall

43 *Queen Elizabeth watching two knights jousting from the window of the viewing gallery at the Whitehall tiltyard. Members of her court stand at other windows to either side of her. The drawing is not a faithful rendition of the Whitehall tiltyard since her window faced up the length of the barrier, rather than being opposite its centre.*

tournaments were accommodated in the windows of the houses adjoining the tiltyard. For example, the six Commissioners of the States General and the Ambassador Ordinary in 1621 were placed in Lady Walsingham's house in a 'Chamber next the Gate, at the lower end of the Tyltyard' (i.e. the end farthest away from the royal gallery, which was at the 'upper' end).[46] These dignitaries were less favoured than the other ambassadors (partly because they did not represent monarchs). The year before, the French ambassador had been assigned a position 'in the first Window of the Duke of *Lenox* his Lodging over the great Gate next without the Tilt-yard East-ward'.[47] On both occasions the Chamber accounts record payments for the work done in 'making ready' these viewing places, work that was probably little different from what was involved in making ready a separate viewing stand.[48]

As has already been made clear, the positioning and furnishing of viewing stands and viewing windows, and a person's position within the royal gallery if admitted were matters of considerable consequence in diplomatic circles. In despair at ever satisfying everyone involved, James I even ceased inviting any ambassadors to tournaments for a period. The endless ambassadorial squabbles over precedence were copiously illustrated in diplomatic despatches and the memoirs of Sir John Finet, who was the Master of Ceremonies from 1612, an office that was part of commoners in their own stands.

Throughout Tudor and Stuart history no other type of occasion provided a more complete public manifestation to monarch and commoner alike of the totality of the political structure. Even when the monarch appeared in Parliament, which included members of the Church and judiciary (admittedly missing from the tiltyard), the commons were represented by only a limited number of men. Furthermore, royal appearances in Parliament were not 'public' in the way that tournaments were. Only the tiltyard encompassed the entire image of the commonweal, an image made clear by the arrangement of the viewing stands. Built to assist their occupants to see the activities in the lists, they also offered the greater spectacle of a nation in microcosm. Little wonder, then, that Elizabeth and James each chose the tournament as the chief medium for the annual celebration of their respective accessions.

Another feature of a tiltyard that would be obvious to any visitor was the gate or gates providing participants with access to the combat area. In theory that of the challenger would be to the monarch's right and that of the answerer to the left, the adversaries then having their own identifiable symbolic 'ends'. However, in practice challengers and answerers at the English tournaments often entered through the same gate, processed around the lists, and then took up their positions at opposite ends, though in the special circumstances involved in the meeting of Henry VIII and Francis I at the Field of Cloth of Gold it was thought imperative to provide

44   *The pageant device (1609) that Inigo Jones designed for Richard Preston, Lord Dingwall, for his grand entry into the tiltyard. Unfortunately, the device was so slow and cumbersome that it did not arrive until after the tournament had already begun. The motto at the foot of Jones' drawing is probably Preston's impresa for the occasion.*

of the Lord Chamberlain's department. The office had been instituted by James I in order to take care of ambassadors and the many problems created by their concern over precedence and etiquette. The many disputes of this kind are a further reminder that the staging of a tournament was both a calculated display of magnificence and a powerful demonstration, both literally and figuratively, of the hierarchical structure of the body politic, from the single figure of royalty in the most central and most lavishly-appointed viewing place, flanked by the ranks of the nobility and civic officials, to the thousands

45   *This map, attributed to Ralph Agas, shows the Whitehall tiltyard, the Holbein Gate and the Palace buildings between the Holbein Gate and the river. At the foot of the tiltyard was the royal viewing gallery which was approached by a gallery running through the Holbein Gate above the street. Curiously, no gate into the tiltyard for tournament participants is shown.*

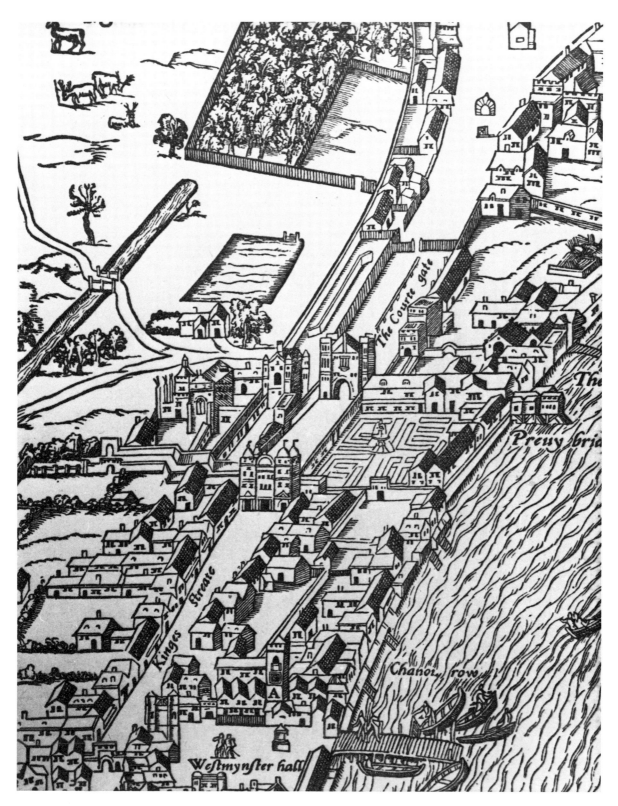

a tournament ground with two gates.

Whether one or two, such gates had to be of a sufficient width and height to accommodate the elaborate pageants that were often included as part of the participants' initial entries into the tiltyard. At the opening of the 1501 Westminster tournament, for example, William Rivers, one of the answerers, entered through the King Street gate 'in his pavylion, in a goodly shippe borne up w[ith] men'. As one witness put it, the ship appeared in the gateway 'w[ith] all man[ner] of tacklyngs and marin[e]rs in her, the which in the seid appierau[n]ce made a great and an houge noyse w[ith] s[er]pentyns, and other gun-[n]eshote'.[49] Nine and a quarter years later, the Revels Office accounts record the building at Blackfriars of the very large forest pageant (26 × 16 × 9 feet in dimension) already mentioned in Chapter 2. Although this pageant entered the Westminster lists from Westminster Hall, it none the less provides some indication of the size that pageants could be and hence of the size of gates required to accommodate them.[50] The Elizabethan and Jacobean pageants at Whitehall also must on occasion have been very large. The Earl of Arundel's pageant in May 1581, for example, was such that a bridge had first to be repaired to bear its weight and the road gravelled to give the horses a footing. Years later in March 1609, Sir Richard Preston's pageant was an elephant with a castle on its back (Fig. 44). The device was apparently so cumbersome that it arrived after the jousting had already begun, and then it caused a delay because it took so long 'creeping about the Tilt-yard'.[51] Presumably such a pageant was both heavy and large, one that would require a suitably high and wide gateway (Fig. 45).

Some Knights entered the lists beneath a portable pavilion supported by their retainers, and these pavilions had a more than decorative function. A knight required some sort of shelter during the lengthy hours of a tournament, especially if the sun was shining and he needed to avoid getting over-heated.

But the chief purpose of a pavilion was to provide some privacy so that he could remove some of his armour until it was his turn for combat. On occasion participants had pavilions already erected in the tiltyard for their use (Fig. 46).

This need for privacy and the consequent ability to make a sudden and dramatic appearance in the field would have been especially attractive to any participating royal prince, and it is not surprising that suitably costly and elaborate pavilions were employed by Henry VIII. He and his three fellow challengers, for example, entered the lists on the second day of the 1511 Westminster tournament beneath portable pavilions. These were no simple utilitarian affairs, as the illustration in the Great Tournament Roll shows (Fig. 64). Those of Henry's three aides were of crimson damask and purple, embroidered in gold with the letters H. and K. [for 'Henry' and 'Katherine']. Henry's was of cloth of gold and purple velvet, also embroidered with golden letters, and surmounted by a golden imperial crown.[52] Each large enough to cover a mounted man, the four pavilions stood in a row in the tiltyard. While one knight was in combat, the doors of his pavilion would be closed, while the other three apparently sat mounted inside with the doors open.[53]

Henry's use of such portable pavilions in the tiltyard was probably modelled on what he had observed at the Westminster tournaments of 1494, when he was created Duke of York, and 1501, at the time of the marriage of Katherine of Aragon to his brother Arthur.[54] But Henry's pavilions were not always of the portable variety. In 1513, following his successful siege of Tournai, he ordered celebratory jousts to be held in the market square where he had erected a tent of cloth of gold 'for the armorie and releue,' and in 1520 at the Field of Cloth of Gold both he and Francis I had pavilions made of wood. For this latter event, the French initially wanted canvas pavilions, but Henry's commissioners had persuaded them that the two Kings should be provided with small

The Combate in SMITHFEILD betwixt the same IOHN DE ASTLEY and Sᴿ PHILIP BOYLE, 30 Ian: An: 1441.

46 *Combat on foot with swords at Smithfield (30 Jan. 1441). The tournament between John Astley and Sir Philip de Boyle, a knight of Aragon, at which de Boyle was killed, was held before Henry VI. The drawing illustrates the separate gates for opposing combatants and the separate arming pavilions.*

wainscot structures 'such as are used in princes' camps in time of war', and these were subsequently erected on either side of one of the two entry gates.[55] Close by, though outside the lists, were two sets of pavilions for the French and English knights where they could arm themselves and rest between appearances in the tiltyard. These pavilions, however, appear to have been of cloth or canvas rather than wood.

Three years before the Cloth of Gold tournament, the Revels accounts mention some canvas stored at Greenwich for use as 'a shed to arm in'.[56] No doubt this canvas 'shed' served the same purpose as the 'tente'

illustrated in the inventory of a fifteenth-century manuscript explaining what a challenger and answerer should have with them in the field (Fig. 47).[57] Following these early references to pavilions and arming sheds, there are, so far as I am aware, only two other such allusions in the records of English tournaments before the period when the sons of James I began to participate publicly in feats of arms. Both examples involved what must have been very considerable expenditure on the part of private individuals, whereas the examples just mentioned all appear to have been paid for by the crown.

In January 1581, the Earl of Oxford appeared in the Whitehall tiltyard as the Knight of the Tree of the Sun in answer to the challenge of Callophisus (the Earl of Arundel) and it appears that he concealed himself in his pavilion before any of the other participants arrived. 'By the tilt', we learn, 'stoode a statelie Tent of Orenge tawny Taffata, curiously imbroydered with Siluer, & pendents on the Pinacles very sightly to

How a man schall be armyd at his ese
when he schal fighte on foote

He schal haue noo schurte up on him but a
dowbelet of ffustean lynyd with satene cutte
full of hoolis. the dowbelet muste be strongeli bounde
there the poyntis muste be sette aboute the greet of the
arme. and the b ste before and behynde and the gusse
tis of mayle muste be sowid vn to the dowbelet in
the bought of the arme. and vndir the arme the ar
mynge poyntis muste be made of fyne twyne suche
as men make stryngis for crossebowes and they

behold'. As the opening ceremonies got under way, 'From forth this Tent came the noble Earle of Oxenford in rich gilt Armour, and sate down vnder a great high Bay-tree, the whole stocke, branches and leaues whereof, were all gilded ouer, that nothing but Gold could be discerned. [. . .] After a solemne sound of most sweet Musique, he mounted on his Courser, verie richly caparasond, whe[n] his page ascending the staires where her Highnesse stood in the window, deliuered to her by speech [his] Oration [. . .]'. After he had finished his tilting 'both the rich Bay-tree, and the beautifull Tent, were by the standers by, torne and rent in more peeces then can be numbred', a not uncommon fate for costumes, scenic devices and other such things at Tudor tournaments.[58] It is just possible that pavilions such as Oxford's were a fairly common sight at Tudor and Jacobean tournaments, but this idea is not supported either by the evidence of surviving descriptions or by the household accounts of even such lavish spenders as the Earl of Essex and the Earl of Rutland. It is more likely that pavilions were a rarity in the tiltyard after Henry VIII's reign.

Nine years after the Earl of Oxford had seen his orange pavilion torn to shreds by spectators, Sir Henry Lee devised a dramatic pageant at the end of the 1590 Accession Day tournament during which he removed his armour and pleaded for the Queen's permission to retire from his role as her Champion. During the pageant, 'the earth as it were opening, there appeared a Pauilion, made of white Taffata, containing eight score elles, being in proportion like vnto the sacred Temple of the Virgins Vestall.[59] The elaborate temple contained burning lamps and an altar upon which were gifts for Queen Elizabeth.

47 *A knight being armed for a foot combat in his pavilion. The fanciful wooden building provided privacy, a place to rest and tend to any wounds and a shelter from hot sun, one of the greatest discomforts for anyone in armour.*

From this description the pavilion would appear to have had little in common with the traditional arming tent. However, in his poem celebrating the event George Peele makes it clear that Lee used the pavilion to disarm himself before making his petition to the Queen:

And in a faire Pavilion hard at hand,
Where holie lightes burnt on the hallowed shrine
To Vertue or to Vesta consecrate,
Having unarm'd his body, head and all,
To his great Mistresse his petition makes . . .[60]

It was rare for an individual to invest so much in a pavilion at Tudor and Stuart tournaments, and on the last occasions when pavilions were used funding was supplied by the crown, as in the earlier examples just cited. This was so, for example, on 6 January 1610, when Prince Henry, James I's eldest son, fought at barriers with six aides against fifty-six defendants in the great Banqueting Hall at Whitehall. The Office of the Works erected to the right of James I's chair of State 'a sumptuous pavilion for the Prince and his associats, from whence, with great bravery and ingenious devices, they descended into the middell of the roome'. At the opposite end of the Banqueting Hall the defendants had 'a very delicat and pleasant place, where in privat manner they and their traine remained, [. . .] from whence in comly order they issued'.[61]

Prince Henry died before he was old enough to take part in a full-scale tournament, but in 1620 Prince Charles made his first appearance in the Whitehall tiltyard. For the convenience of the Prince a special pavilion was pitched close to the royal gallery: 'Next to St James Parke gate was erected a most rich and stately Pauillion of greene, yellowe, and white damaske layde on with broade lace of silver and gold, with a verie deepe vallence of Cloth of Siluer fringed about with a deepe fringe of gold and siluer garnished about with the Princes Armes, and Badges, on the Toppe of it was sett an Eglett in her nest looking vpp at the Sonne with his Motto at it: NEC DEGENER HAERES.'[62]

After the Prince had entered and dismounted from his horse, the same source tells us, he 'went into his pauillion to sett and repose himself whilst the other Tilters were brought in'.[63] The Office of Works accounts show how large this pavilion was—it is described as thirty feet long and ten feet wide 'with twoe paire of staires to the same'.[64] It was supported by six round pillars 'being guilt over with silver' and was decorated with a 'greate Armes w[i]th a Compartment round about yt painted and guilded w[i]th fine gold'. Six small shields were painted and gilded 'on both sides with his Highness ffeathers thereon'.[65] The young prince participated in a tournament the following year, again as part of the annual celebration of his father's accession to the throne, and similar details concerning his pavilion have survived.[66] In 1622 a pavilion for Charles was again made ready, but it was never used because the event was deferred and ultimately cancelled because of the bad weather and the King's ill health.[67]

A suitable viewing stand for the judges of a tournament needed to be close to the point where the combatants would meet, whether on horse or on foot. Special stands, often referred to as judgehouses, were frequently made available and were a further opportunity for a show of costly magnificence.

Two pen and ink drawings in the College of Arms provide the only illustrations of such structures (see Fig. 48). The first is of an elaborate three-storey building situated inside the lists.[68] Five judges sit at an elevated opening a few feet above the level of the fence, which, as we have seen, was usually about six or seven feet high. A door to the left side provides access to and from the combat area. In the storey above the judges are two windows with female spectators, and above them a third storey with gabled lattice windows, but no spectators. On top of the building fly three flags of St George. Another drawing in the same manuscript, possibly representing a trial by combat (Fig. 49),

shows the judgehouse placed between the double fences which surround the almost square area for the combatants.[69] The judgehouse is raised on scaffolds under which are four observers. In the raised first storey sit what appear to be two judges and, as in the other drawing, a door and stairs at the left give access to and from the combat area. In the next storey above sits the King, with two attendants partially visible on either side, and above him is a gabled lattice window but no spectators.

Neither of these drawings can be dated or linked with any particular tiltyard, and we should consequently be cautious about assuming that similar structures were ever used as judgehouses at Tudor and Jacobean tournaments. None the less the second drawing makes it clear that it was feasible to house judges at the best viewing point by accommodating them in some way in the royal viewing stand. Since the judges were always selected from those of high social rank, this would not have posed any great problems of precedence. If, indeed, judges were customarily housed in this way, it would explain why separate judgehouses are virtually never mentioned in surviving records of tournaments, except in the case of the Greenwich and Whitehall tiltyards. At Whitehall, as will be shown later, the peculiar layout of the tiltyard necessitated a separate judgehouse. Subsequently, perhaps, the practices established at Whitehall tournaments were carried over to those tournaments held at Greenwich.

The most important sources of in-

48 *This drawing is contained in an English heraldic manuscript, probably Tudor in origin. A number of details, such as the length of the tilt barrier and the fact that the knights hold their lances in their left hands, are clearly inaccurate, but other features seem to be correct, including the mounting steps at each end of the lists, and the vertical storage of lances.*

33

The ordinances statutes and rules made and jnacted by John Erle of worcestre constable of england, by the kinges comandement at windesore the xxiv daye of may in the vj yere of his noble reigne, to be obserued and kepte jn all maner of Justes of peace Royall, within this realme of England, before his highnes or lieutenant by his comandemet or licence, had fro this tyme foorth, reseruing alwais to the Auens highnes and to the ladies there present, the attribution and gifte of the price, after the maner and forme accostomed, the merrites and demerites attribute according to the articles sollowenge formation concerning judgehouses are the accounts of the Office of Works and those of the Treasurer of the Chamber during the reigns of Elizabeth and James. The latter accounts show that, like the viewing stands prepared for ambassadors, judgehouses were 'apparelled', but nowhere is there any indication of precisely what this involved. We have to assume that the furnishings consisted of tapestries, leaning carpets, seats and perhaps cushions. Certainly the materials used must have been of considerable value, since the Office of Works arranged for the judgehouse to be guarded at night along with any specially prepared viewing stands. From the constant references in the Office of Works accounts to 'setting up', 'Rearing', and 'taking down' the judgehouse we learn that part of it, and perhaps all of it, was not left standing between tournaments at the mercy of thieves and weather. Part of the structure (perhaps the roof) seems to have been made of some non-durable material, such as canvas or cloth. This would certainly explain why there are regular payments to the Wardrobers for 'coveringe the Iudge house against the dayes of Tyltinge'.[70]

The accounts also record payments for 'boordinge the floore' and 'boording the floore and sydes'.[71] It is equally clear that there were wooden stairs giving the judges access to the area within the lists.[72] Such a staircase is shown in the second drawing discussed above, although the elaborate three-storey affair, which was also designed to provide a place for the King, was probably larger than the kind of judgehouse referred to so frequently in the Office of Works accounts. Just what an Elizabethan or Jacobean judgehouse may have looked like is thus to a considerable extent a matter for speculation.

At the 1501 tournament at Westminster there were 'stayres downe to the place of Tournaye for messingers and those by whom it pleased the Kinges highnes to haue his minde and errand done' next to the partition in the royal gallery dividing the King and

Queen.[73] These stairs, it is made clear, were quite separate from the entrance to the stand provided for the royal spectators. Much later such stairs and an accompanying platform-stage below the royal gallery became standard features in the Whitehall tiltyard, and the stage was used during the reigns of Elizabeth and James for the presentation of speeches and impresa shields to the monarch.

Long before, however, it was the practice of those participating in the tournament to approach the monarch. At the 1511 Westminster tournament, for example, a large and elaborate forest pageant entered the tiltyard. It contained the four Challengers and a maiden who had six dozen roses 'wrought [. . .] into a garland'.[74] When the pageant had circled the tilt, it stopped in front of Queen Katherine's viewing stand where the maiden presented her floral wreath and the four knights presented their shields. On the second day, Charles Brandon, one of the answerers, entered through the King's Gate enclosed within a tower and preceded by a jailer holding a great key in his hand. When this pageant arrived in front of the Queen, the jailer unlocked the tower and Brandon emerged on his horse dressed as a pilgrim and carrying a staff to which was attached a letter. This was then 'sent & delyverd unto the Quenys grace, upon the which when she had a whyle lokid, she sent such answer that the prisoner cast ffrom hym hastely his clothyng berd & hat and shewid him sylf In brygth harneys, and fforthwyth smote his horse wyth the sporys and [?went] a lusty pace unto the tyyltes ende'.[75]

During the Elizabethan period, such dramatic interaction between the royal stand and the participants was to grow into a major part of tournament ritual, an opportunity for each individual to have some direct and

49 *A combat on foot with swords from an English heraldic manuscript, probably Tudor in origin. It illustrates the use of double fences and a triple-storeyed judgehouse.*

personal contact with the sovereign, albeit usually through the medium of a page or squire. Not only did it become customary to present a shield displaying an impresa, a personal emblem consisting of picture and motto (see Chapter 5), but speeches and brief dramatic inventions were often performed. In keeping with this development, stairs from the tiltyard to the royal gallery were a necessary provision, and a scaffold (stage) below the royal window was also seen as essential. The following sample entries are typical of those that appear in the Works accounts between 1581 and 1609:

(a) 1581. 'new ffrayminge and settinge vpp a great longe Scaffold vnder the Quenes window in the said Tiltyearde with a great paire of hallpace staires'.

(b) 1594. 'framinge and settinge a Scaffolde or standinge w[i]th a paier of stayers a hallpace and flowre vnder the Queenes windowe towardes ye Tilteyarde'.

(c) 1597. 'setting vp a greate frame w[i]th ij paire of staires a hallpace and a floore boorded w[i]th deales and steppes goinge vpp to the Queene's windowe in the gallerye at the Tilteyearde and takeinge the same downe againe after the Justes and pastimes performed'.[76]

The last statement seems to imply that two sets of stairs went up to the platform from which steps continued to the Queen's window. Evidently, too, the platform was quite large ('a great longe Scaffold'), and it is also clear that steps and platform were removed after each event, no doubt as a security measure.

One of the best descriptions of how stairs and stage were used during a tournament comes from von Wedel's account of the 1585 Accession Day tournament. First he mentions the Queen's room in the gallery from which 'a broad staircase led downwards', and he then goes on to discuss the entry of the knights into the tiltyard: 'When a gentleman with his servant approached the barrier, on horseback or in a carriage, he stopped at the foot of the staircase leading to the queen's room, while one of his servants in pompous attire of a special pattern mounted the steps and addressed the queen in well-composed verses or with a ludicrous speech, making her and her ladies laugh.'[77]

Sometimes, participating knights hired actors and musicians to perform with them or on their behalf. The miraculous appearance of the pavilion-like temple at Lee's 1590 retirement tilt, for example, was accompanied by music sung by 'M Hales her Majesties seruant' as three 'vestall maydens' presented Elizabeth with Lee's gifts.[78] The Queen, understood as the fourth Vestal, is thus brought into the tiny drama as she so frequently was in the course of the many pageants in her honour. The role of stairs and stage in this process is crucial, for they provide the physical bridge between royal window and tiltyard, between monarch and subject, between the one celebrated and those who celebrate. Like the careful placing of viewing stands, the stairs and stage thus had an inherent symbolic purpose that was taken full advantage of during the Elizabethan period. In 1609, however, there was a sudden end to references to stairs and stage in the Office of Works accounts. Were the rituals for which these structures were employed discontinued, and, if so, was there some lessening of the bond between monarch and subject, some distant sign of the Stuart tragedy to come?

‒‒‒‒•‒ *IV* ‒•‒‒‒‒

From Westminster to Whitehall

S MUST BE APPARENT from the previous chapter, the most important Tudor and Jacobean tiltyards were situated at Westminster, Greenwich, Hampton Court and Whitehall. However, between 1485 and 1625 several other locations were on occasion used for tournaments. One of these, Richmond Palace, may for a time have had a permanent tiltyard, but I have found no details concerning it. Henry VII, who completely rebuilt the palace after a fire there in 1497 and changed its name from Shene to Richmond, held several tournaments there, and in January 1510 Henry VIII was at Richmond because of the plague and made a dramatic debut in his first tournament. Disguised as a stranger knight, he arrived in 'the litle Parke' with William Compton, who was also disguised. The light-heartedness of the affair was suddenly curtailed when Compton was severely wounded, and one of the spectators, who knew of Henry's presence, then caused great consternation by crying out 'God save the King!' Henry was immediately forced to remove his disguise in order to prevent a panic.[1]

Later that year, Henry, with Charles Brandon and William Compton (now recovered), challenged all-comers to a tilt and tourney at the palace, and in April 1515 Henry provided the encouragement, financial assistance and weapons for a tilt there 'to encourage all youthe to seke dedes of armes'.[2] The last tournament held at Richmond was for the marriage of Lord Lisle, the Earl of Warwick's son, to Lady Anne, daughter of the Duke of Somerset. There was dinner and dancing, after which 'the King and the Ladies went into two chambers made of boughs, where first he [the king] saw six gentlemen of one side and six of another run the course of the field, twice over'. Then there were 'three masquers of one side and two of another, which ran four courses apiece', and finally 'came the Count Rangone, with three Italians, who ran with all the gentlemen four courses and afterwards fought at tourney'.[3] Had there been a special area laid out as a tiltyard, we should probably have heard about it.

There is even less known about other occasional sites used for Tudor and Jacobean tournaments. William Segar claims in *The Book of Honor and Arms* (1590) that Henry VII held a tournament 'in the Tower of *London*. Anno. 1502'. This may be a reference to the tournament held there in May 1501. No other records concerning tournaments at the Tower after 1485 appear to have survived.[4] Hall notes in his *Chronicle* that, during the first progress of his reign in the summer of 1510, Henry VIII not only practised every day at shooting, singing, composing music, dancing, wrestling, casting of the bar, and playing the recorders, flute, and virginals, but 'whan he came to Okyng [?Okingham, Berks.], there kept both Iustes and Turneys'.[5] Forty years or so later, in July 1551 and again in May 1552, Edward VI participated with horse and lance in some kind of martial exercise (running at ring on the second occasion) at Blackheath, a short ride away from Greenwich, but it does not appear that either event had the formality of a tournament proper.[6]

Three further events are worth noting in this brief survey of tournament locations other than the principal permanent tiltyards. At Shrovetide in either 1554 or 1556, while Princess Elizabeth was under the guardianship of Sir Thomas Pope at Hatfield, Pope arranged an elaborate indoor pageant and masking in the great hall at his own cost. This included a mock tournament involving 'a castell of clothe of gold sett with pomegranates about the battlements' and six knights in rich harness who engaged in tourneying.[7] Again, the event does not really count as a tournament proper, though, along with certain other events, it was significant in exposing the young Elizabeth to the potential of a certain type of tournament pageantry that was later to figure so prominently in the annual tournaments held years later to celebrate her Accession Day.

About thirty years after Sir Thomas Pope had entertained Elizabeth at Hatfield, thereby earning a brusque reprimand from Elizabeth's sister, Queen Mary, Elizabeth (now Queen) was welcomed by Sir Henry Lee to the royal manor of Woodstock. Lee, who was Lieutenant of the manor and park, had already been instrumental in re-establishing the tournament as a major event in the court calendar and had himself participated in several of them in the preceding few years. It was probably unthinkable to him that the Queen's visit to Woodstock during her summer progress in 1575 should not be marked by some form of 'knightly' entertainment. As she approached the manor, she came upon

two mounted knights, Contarenus and Loricus, battling for the honour of their ladies. This 'staged' encounter continued with the arrival of a hermit (Hermetes), who explained the complicated background story of unrequited love, a melange of Greek and chivalric romance. This anticipated the style of Sidney's *Arcadia* and future scenarios for Accession Day tournaments in which Lee, Sidney, and others fought under the names of chivalric personae and continued the imagery and general character of the Woodstock device (see Chapter 6). Elizabeth stayed at Woodstock from 29 August until 3 October, during which time, besides watching the local countrymen run at the quintain (a common game in many villages, involving a kind of tilting against an object attached to a wooden post), she appears to have been entertained by jousting.[8] However, apart from the survival of a draft of a challenge for these jousts no further information about them is known.[9] As for any arrangements that Lee may have made for a tiltyard at Woodstock, the records of the period remain silent.

Apart from these examples of tournaments on sites other than Westminster, Greenwich, Hampton Court or Whitehall, there was also an occasion in 1593 when, because of an outbreak of the plague in London, the court took refuge at Windsor in August and the annual Accession Day tournament was held there on 17 November. By November the number of deaths in London had been decreasing for some time, but it was clearly still unsafe for the court to return to Whitehall for what had come to be the biggest public spectacle of the calendar. A viewing stand was hastily erected and made ready at Windsor. The surviving heralds' score cheques record that some sixteen participants took part in the 'Course att ffeilde'.[10] These included the Earl of Essex, who, as already mentioned, had been practising hard in preparation, the Earl of Cumberland (the Queen's Champion), who entered as a seaman returned from a long voyage on a pageant car representing Pendragon Castle, and Sir Robert Cary, who had been temporarily out of favour and now entered disguised as an unknown knight to woo his way back into Elizabeth's good graces by presenting her with an expensive gift. Pageantry, dramatic *mises-en-scène*, lavish expenditure (both Essex and Cary are known to have spent a great deal), and covert political lobbying were all present to the customary degree. But for the unusual location, this event would superficially appear to have been like any other full-scale tournament held at Whitehall in the 1590s.

Long before, Edward III had held a Round Table at Windsor for 'hastiludes' and jousting, and Richard II and Henry IV had also held tournaments there. Given the long-standing connection between Windsor and the chivalric institution of the Order of the Garter, with its various Arthurian connotations, it is surprising that Windsor Castle was not used at other times for tournaments. However, what Windsor lacked was easy access for the London multitudes. Elizabeth had already moved the annual Grand Feast at Windsor to Whitehall as part of her deliberate development of the annual St George's Day ceremonies into great public spectacles.[11] Likewise, the annual Accession Day tilts were developed through the 1580s and 1590s as major court spectacles at which the presence of as many onlookers as possible was considered of some political consequence. For this reason, Whitehall, the closest residence of the court to the City of London in Elizabethan times, would obviously always be the first choice of location.

At the time of Henry VII's accession in 1485, the principal royal residence was the Palace of Westminster, a rambling heterogeneous collection of buildings in the neighbourhood of Westminster Abbey. The most prominent of the Palace buildings was undoubtedly Westminster Hall. This had been originally built by William Rufus, but it was altered and supplied with its famous hammerbeam roof by Richard II between 1394 and 1400. The courts of Common Law were held here and on occasion important

state trials, such as those of Sir Thomas More, Anne Boleyn, the Earl of Essex, and the Earl of Somerset.

However, in addition to its associations with the law, the hall also had a long connection with a less sombre side of court life. From the time of Richard II the records of banquets and coronation feasts there regularly enliven the pages of the chronicles. The coronation feasts, which only ceased when Queen Victoria came to the throne, traditionally occurred on the day of the coronation itself and were accompanied by the ritual entry of the royal champion on horseback. The champion would throw down his gauntlet and challenge anyone unwilling to accept the newly-crowned monarch as rightful ruler. The following day, or shortly thereafter, the festivities would continue with a tournament.

The coronations of Henry VII, Henry VIII, Anne Boleyn, Anne of Cleves, Edward VI, and Queen Elizabeth were all celebrated by such tournaments. Whether there was initially some connection between the ritual appearance of the champion in Westminster Hall and the tournament that followed is not fully clear, but what is certain is that the tournament ground for the coronation festivities of Henry VII and Henry VIII was just outside the north door of the Hall in the open area known as New Palace Yard, the north front of the Hall providing an entrance way into the lists for the challengers. (This large area had been confusingly referred to as 'new' ever since the eleventh century when Westminster Hall was built as the King's new palace to replace the old palace of Edward the Confessor.)

Westminster Hall now fronts upon a very much smaller New Palace Yard, but even so it is helpful in reconstructing the site of the tournaments held at Westminster before 1512, the year that a great fire destroyed much of the Palace and rendered it virtually uninhabitable. Between the time of Henry VII's accession and the 1512 fire, at least five tournaments were held in the yard. Two of these five tournaments were for coronations (1485 and 1509), and the remaining three were to celebrate the creation of Prince Henry as Duke of York in 1494, the marriage of Prince Arthur to Katherine of Aragon in 1501, and the birth of the short-lived Prince Henry (son of Henry VIII) in 1511. All were tournaments on a grand and lavish scale, and New Palace Yard, with the great north end of Westminster Hall as its most striking visual feature, provided an appropriate setting, fully in keeping with the early Tudors' clear desire to project an appropriate image of royal splendour.

Unfortunately the Works Office accounts give few details about what was done at Westminster to prepare for the first two of these events. The account of Thomas Warley, Clerk of the King's Works, does survive for the period April 1500 to March 1502, however, and it tells us that over £250 was spent to set up the viewing stands and to decorate the north front of Westminster Hall in preparation for the tournament to celebrate the marriage of Prince Arthur and Katherine of Aragon.[12] The viewing stands were only part of the general transformation of the yard. There were to be new doors for the hall; the

BELOW

50   Van den Wyngaerde's view of Westminster (c. 1544–5). The drawing shows New Palace Yard, approached from one end by the King's Bridge for those coming by water and entered from the other through a large gate. The long roof between Westminster Abbey (the large building at the rear) and the river bank is Westminster Hall, the north front of which faces out into New Palace Yard, site of most of the important early Tudor tournaments before the devastating fire of 1512.

BELOW RIGHT

51   New Palace Yard, Westminster, by Wenceslaus Hollar (1640). To the left is the imposing north front of Westminster Hall. At the far end is the great gate used by some tournament participants as an entry gate. To the right is the clock tower containing a large bell that was known as 'Edward of Westminster', the predecessor of the modern Big Ben. In the foreground is the conduit. At some tournaments special plumbing allowed its spouts to provide a choice of wine for spectators.

bosses of its porch were to be painted and gilded with portcullisses, flowers, roses and stars; there was to be new stained glass in the great window at the north end; and two lions supporting a great red rose and an imperial crown over the door. Although the accounts connected with Henry VIII's coronation do not exist and other records for Westminster before 1512 lack the kind of details just described, it is very likely that, for such important state occasions as all the Tudor Westminster tournaments were, equal care would have been taken to ensure that the palace buildings were at their best.

In spite of the paucity of such official records, it is none the less possible to obtain a fairly clear idea of the general layout of the site of the Westminster tournaments from various other sources. Paramount among these is Anthony van den Wyngaerde's panorama (*c.* 1544–5), part of which shows the Palace of Westminster as seen from the east (see Fig. 50). Jutting out into the river is the King's Bridge or landing stage, the main entrance to the palace for anyone coming from Greenwich, London, Richmond, or Hampton Court. The bridge is flanked by tall

posts and these were surmounted by figures of heraldic beasts, together with those of Guy of Warwick and his legendary adversary, the Dane Colbrand; for the 1501 celebrations these posts were repaired and repainted. Those coming by river entered New Palace Yard through a large gate in a high wall facing the King's Bridge.[13]

Van den Wyngaerde's drawing, the earliest of several visual sources, shows the north end of Westminster Hall, flanked by two towers and a series of other buildings on the left side of the yard as one entered from the King's Bridge. We know from John Stow (*c.* 1525–1605), the great antiquary, topographer and chronicler, that there was a large chamber housing the Court of the Exchequer to the right (west) of the Hall doorway, which was reached by a stairway ascending from the entrance to the Hall. On the left (east), also reached by a stairway, was the Office of the Receipt of the Exchequer and the Star Chamber.[14] In 1501 the royal family entered their viewing stand 'through West[inster] hall by the chequor chamber'.[15] Since the Hall doorway is situated somewhat towards the southeast corner of the yard, we can probably

Sala Regalis cum Curia West-monastery, *vulgo* Westminster hall.

assume that the royal viewing stand was placed on the west side of the Hall, which means it would be more or less level with the centre of the tilt barrier. The royal entry was thus through the chamber housing the Court of the Exchequer.

To the right of the Water Gate on the north side of the yard were two further important features, both of which Stow mentions: 'The sayd Pallace, before the entrie thereunto, hath a large Court, and in the same a Tower of stone, containing a clocke, which striketh euery houre on a great Bell, to bee heard into the Hall in sitting time of the Courts [. . .] By this Tower standeth a fountaine, which at Coronations and great triumphes is made to runne with wine out of diuers spoutes.'[16] The clock tower contained a bell weighing over four tons. Known affectionately as Edward of Westminster, it was the predecessor of Big Ben. Erected between 1365 and 1367, and built of ragstone, the clock tower with its square design and pyramid roof are clearly shown in van den Wyngaerde's drawing and in the much later engraving of New Palace Yard by Wenceslaus Hollar (see Fig. 51).

The other feature mentioned by Stow was the Great Conduit, built in 1443–4 and probably incorporating some fragments from a twelfth-century fountain from a different site. The Great Conduit had an octagonal stone base and was approximately forty-five feet to the finial of its cupola.[17] It stood directly on a line with the clock tower and the front of Westminster Hall on the north side of the yard. It is clearly seen in Hollar's engraving, but, as excavations in 1972–4 showed, Hollar's positioning was somewhat inaccurate.[18]

At the coronation tournament of Henry VIII in June 1509 the Great Conduit was transformed into a castle-like fountain described by Hall in some detail 'in thesaied Palaice, was made a curious Fountaine, and ouer it a Castle: on the toppe thereof, a greate Croune Emperiall, all the imbattelyng with Roses, Pomegranetes gilded: and vnder and aboute thesaied Castle, a curious Vine, the leaues and grapes thereof, gilded with fine

Golde, the walles of the same Castle coloured, White and Grene losengis. And in euery losenge, either a Rose or Pomegranet, or a Sheffe of Arrowes, or els. H. and. K. gilded with fine Gold, with certain Arches or Turrettes gilded, to suport thesame Castle. And the targettes of the armes, of the defendauntes, appointed for thesaied Iustes, there vpon sumpteously set. And out at seuerall places, of thesame Castle, aswell the daie of the coronacio[n], as at thesaid daies of the Iustes & Turney, out of the mouthes of certain beastes, or gargels, did runne red, white, & claret wine.'[19]

For the coronation celebrations of Anne Boleyn, though the celebration tournament was held elsewhere, the Great Conduit was again elaborately embellished and made to run wine, a feat achieved by connecting it by a pipe to a cistern in the Clock Tower. Five more pipes carried the wine from the conduit to five cisterns placed outside the 'pales of the said conduit for people to resort to'.[20]

When tournaments were held at Westminster, the gate at the west end of the yard was transformed into the gate for the answerers. Stow describes it as 'a verie faire gate' known as 'the high Tower at Westminster'[21] and it is shown in the views by both van den Wyngaerde and Hollar. Opening on to King Street, the gate was the principal entrance for anyone coming by land to Westminster. At tournaments it marked the extreme westerly end of the tiltyard, just as the Water Gate marked the extreme east.

It was this 'great and large voide space'— approximately 400 feet from east to west and 210 feet from north to south at its widest points[22]—that provided the site for the most important tournaments of Henry VII's reign and those held in the early years of Henry VIII's reign. In preparation for a tournament at Westminster the tilt barrier, following an east–west line, was 'sett and araysed at the whole length from the watergate vp wel nighe to the entrance of the gate that openeth into Kinges street', and the whole yard, which had been paved in ragstone as early as 1347–8, was 'gravelled sanded and goodly ordered for the ease of the horses'.[23] Around the entire yard in front of the viewing stands a fence was erected, and for any tourneying the tilt would be removed 'and the grounds made smoothe and plaine'.[24] Later, a barrier would be erected for the foot combats if these were to be a feature of the tournament.

Today the eastern side of the Westminster tiltyard is covered by Big Ben and the adjacent Parliament buildings and, although the north front of Westminster Hall still looks out upon New Palace Yard, this is now only a relatively small area well below the pavement level of the much larger Parliament Square and the approach road to the Embankment and Westminster Bridge. King Street is no more and the buildings that once enclosed the yard making it a natural pre-formed arena have long since gone, the victims of fire and of sundry eighteenth- and nineteenth-century improvements. This immensely busy corner of the metropolis, which at times is made even more chaotic by the rush of MPs from their Whitehall offices to the House of Commons when the division bells are rung, is one of London's most visited tourist spots. But few who look down through the railings of New Palace Yard from Bridge Street or take the obligatory photograph of Big Ben are ever aware of the incredible state spectacles that occurred on this spot between 1485 and 1512.

Following the Westminster fire in 1512 and during the succeeding years before the creation of a new royal residence at Whitehall in 1533, all the tournaments held in England were held at the Palace of Placentia at Greenwich. The Court regularly spent the Christmas, New Year, and Shrovetide festivals at this aptly named riverside residence, only a few miles downstream from the City of London. The celebration of these holidays often included tournaments, and Henry VIII engaged in them with tremendous enthusiasm and skill. May was also on occasion a time for light-hearted holiday jousting. When Henry 'with many lusty Batchelers, on greate and well doyng horses'

rode out into the woods to gather may on May Day 1511, for example, he and three others seasonably dressed in green satin were met by another group of courtiers and a pageant in the form of a ship under sail called *Fame,* laden with 'good *Renoune'.* The ship 'shotte a peale of Gonnes' and led the Maytime revellers back to the tiltyard where there followed a jousting match that lasted for three days, the King and his three companions competing against the other group of courtiers. A banquet given by the Queen followed, and Henry was awarded first prize.[25] As can be seen from the list of tournaments in the Appendix, the Palace of Placentia and its tiltyard provided a key site for early Tudor tournaments, including for a time those important state occasions that would undoubtedly have continued to be held in New Palace Yard but for the 1512 fire.

Not surprisingly, once the Whitehall tiltyard became available in 1533, relatively few tournaments were held at Greenwich, though why the holiday tournaments did not continue there during Henry VIII's reign is puzzling. It may perhaps have been because Henry's advancing age and deteriorating physical condition prevented him from personally participating in such activities. During Edward VI's reign the use of Greenwich as a site for Christmas, New Year, Shrovetide and Maytime tournaments seems to have been briefly revived.[26] However, during Queen Mary's reign there were no tournaments at Greenwich, while in Elizabeth's reign there was only one. In the early years of James' reign the tiltyard was used in March and May 1605 and again in August 1606, but after this brief flurry of events, there were no more tournaments there again.

None the less, the Greenwich tiltyard was continually maintained, primarily because it was used for practice by those planning to appear in the lists at Whitehall (see p. 70). Greenwich thus has a very important status among the Tudor and Jacobean tiltyards. Indeed, between 1512 and 1533 it was virtually the only tournament ground in use, and this at a time when Henry's taste for knightly exercises was at its zenith. The length of its tilt barrier (350 feet) has already been mentioned, as has the placing of the main gate at the north end and a much lesser gate at the opposite end. We know too that the tiltyard was laid out with the tilt barrier on a north-west to south-east axis and that it was approximately 700 feet long and 300 feet broad.[27] On the south-west side directly opposite the centre of the tilt was a royal viewing gallery. Since tournaments usually took place in the afternoon with the sun in the southwest, this was virtually an ideal arrangement, placing the sun directly behind the spectators and giving neither challenger nor defender at each end of the tilt any undue advantage with respect to the direction of sunlight.

Just who laid out the tiltyard is unclear. The first real palace had been built by Humphrey, Duke of Gloucester and brother to Henry V, in 1427. On his death in 1447 'The Manor of Pleasance' (as it was now called) reverted to the Crown and quickly became a favourite royal residence. It is probable that the tiltyard was added to the palace

complex some time after this. For an idea of what the buildings and tiltyard looked like in Henry VIII's time we have the evidence of the indefatigable van den Wyngaerde, who made two sketches (see Fig. 52), and one from the north-west (the direction of the river) and one from the south-east (the hill behind the palace). Both show the tiltyard and the wooden barrier down its centre. Van den Wyngaerde's sketches also show the two massive and very romantic-looking towers on the south-west side which provided the permanent royal viewing gallery. These were built between 1516 and 1518 by Henry VIII,

52   Greenwich in 1558. Van den Wyngaerde's drawing of Greenwich from the River Thames (BELOW) shows Henry's grand and fanciful new turreted building at the centre of the picture, which included accommodation for the armour workshops. The tiltyard can be seen to the left of this building and it also appears on the far left in the same artist's view of Greenwich from the hill to the south (BELOW RIGHT). Much of the tiltyard is now buried beneath the Royal Naval College.

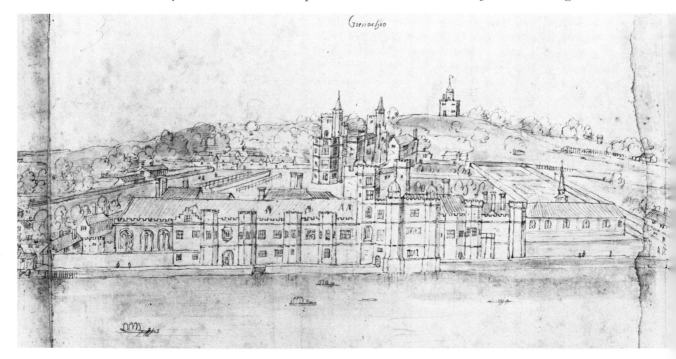

who was anxious to upgrade the royal armouries and to provide suitable accommodation and work space for his imported Almain armourers. The immense sum of £1900 spent on this building provided, as can be seen, a suitably evocative backdrop for the chivalric activities in the tiltyard below its windows.

There was at least one gallery overlooking the tiltyard either within, or connected to, these towers, a fact that can be deduced from the very detailed building accounts for the period 1532–44 provided by John Needham, the Royal Surveyor of Works. These include payments for seventeen feet of new glass 'set in the lower galary in the tylte yard', for 'setting vp of tymberwork for lodginges adioyning to ye sayde armorye', and for the making of lattices on two occasions 'for the galary in the Tylte yerd'.[28] The two towers, the gallery and the various lodgings built by Henry were ideal permanent viewing stands, as he must have intended. Close by, in the tiltyard itself, was a banqueting hall (about 100 feet by 30 feet), and connected to it a temporary amphitheatre for disguisings with a magnificent ceiling by Hans Holbein. Both buildings were constructed in 1527 to entertain the French emissaries at the celebration of the Anglo-French League in May. The buildings were again used for another magnificent entertainment later that year when Henry ratified the Treaty of Amiens in November and was invested by the French with the Order of St Michael. On both occasions jousts, banquets and dramatic presentations followed one upon the other to create a continual flow of festive celebration, all contained within the confines of the tiltyard. In addition to the Banqueting Hall and revelling house, four kennels were built for the King's greyhounds at the end of the banqueting hall in 1532, and in 1533 a cockpit was built, together with a special place in a gallery from which Henry's new Queen (Anne Boleyn) would be able to see the cock fighting.[29] Obviously what Henry had in mind here was the creation of the kind of recreational complex that he had already set up so successively at Whitehall (see p. 116).

Although the use of the Greenwich tiltyard for tournaments declined after 1533, and even

more notably after the death of Edward VI twenty years later, both Elizabeth and James kept the tilt, the lists, and the tiltyard gates in good repair so that those who wished to practise their martial skills could do so. In 1609 or 1610, the Sergeant Painter, John de Critz, was even ordered to paint with 'faire white blewe and vermilion a signe for the Prince to runne at the Tylte',[30] presumably some form of quintain that would allow him to learn how to joust in safety. The eventual fate of the Greenwich tiltyard was anticipated when the long drawn out construction of Inigo Jones' famous and still surviving Queen's House (begun in 1616 but not completed until 1635–6) necessitated moving the southernmost wall of the tiltyard and the small gate in it leading to the park. This very small encroachment was followed, first, by the initial work on a new palace for Charles I (the King's House, completed in 1667), and then by the construction of what is today the great architectural glory of Greenwich, Sir Christopher Wren's Royal Hospital (1696–1705).[31] Now housing the Royal Naval College, the south-eastern block of this immensely imposing building covers the north-western corner of the former Tudor tiltyard (Fig. 53).

Immediately to the south of these buildings there is now a road (Romney Road) and below ground a railway tunnel, both cutting across the centre of the tiltyard. Further to the south, the eastern colonnade of the Queen's House and the National Maritime Museum marks the former south-eastern wall of the tiltyard, and the east wing that juts out north-westwards at right angles to the colonnade extends directly along its centre-line.

Were one to walk a few yards north-westwards from the end of the wing towards the river and towards Romney Road, one would be exactly in the centre of the yard and opposite the spot where once Henry VIII's armoury house and viewing gallery looked down upon so many tournaments. Like Westminster and Whitehall, this is one of the most visited of all England's tourist attractions, yet nothing now remains to conjure up even the faintest reminder of the martial feats and chivalric pageantry so familiar to those who once thronged the spot on tournament days.

Memories of the Tudor love of tournaments are, however, kept alive for today's visitors at the former tiltyard at Hampton Court Palace, although, ironically, this site has far less claim to such memories than any of the tiltyards just discussed. Like Whitehall, Hampton Court was at one time a residence of Cardinal Wolsey, who had begun building work after leasing the site of a small manor house from the Knights Hospitallers in June 1514. The most powerful subject in the kingdom, and on his way to becoming the richest, Wolsey began to create a private palace at his country site beside the Thames to rival, if not excel, any royal palace in the realm. Some time just before his fall from power, Wolsey presented his manor of Hampton Court to Henry VIII, complete with furnishings, tapestries and plate, and Henry assumed full financial control of the building works that were still in progress. In fact, Henry demolished some of Wolsey's work to make way for even further expansions of his own, and the whole history of the buildings is consequently difficult to untangle.

Among Henry's projects was the laying out of a tiltyard and the construction of a group of five highly fanciful towers overlooking it, presumably to serve as viewing stands. Possibly, however, these were in fact 'banqueting' houses, a familiar feature of Tudor and Jacobean country houses. Usually small, romantic-looking towers at some distance from the main house, these houses provided destinations for outings, enjoyable and novel places for banquets, and extra lodgings when guests were numerous.[32] There is quite strong evidence that the towers at Hampton Court were used as lodgings and there is also the inevitable suggestion that they provided convenient accommodation for Henry VIII's mistresses.[33] In view of what will be said in a moment about tournaments at Hampton Court, the common idea that the towers were

53   Aerial view of Greenwich showing the site of the tiltyard. This extended from the Queen's House (the square white building centre right) towards the river, beyond the road, in the centre of the picture.

designed as viewing stands must be treated with caution.

For an idea of what the towers at Hampton Court looked like, we once more have to thank van den Wyngaerde, who included them in his panoramic view of the palace from the north-west produced in 1558 (see Fig. 54). Like the buildings alongside the lists at Greenwich, the Hampton Court towers, with their turrets and crenellations, seem designed to evoke the spirit of chivalry (Fig. 55). Eventually, William III had four of the towers demolished as part of his massive renovation and rebuilding programme at Hampton Court, but one tower still remains. That in the right foreground of van den Wyngaerde's sketch, a rectangular three-storey affair (the sketch shows only two storeys) and the least fanciful of the original

five, has served as a tea-room and restaurant since 1924.

As well as this tower, the site of the tiltyard is also still preserved. Covering an area of seven acres, it was (and still is) enclosed by a high brick wall. William III transformed this large open space into six kitchen gardens (Fig. 56), bounded by further walls, and this arrangement is clearly seen in the painting (see Fig. 57) by Leonard Knyff (1650–1721), best-known for his masterly bird's-eye views of country estates. Today the six sections of William III's kitchen gardens are divided between a car park, a rose garden, tennis courts, flower beds and lawns. Knyff's painting includes the surviving tower (Knyff, like van den Wyngaerde, gives it two storeys) and shows it overlooking the tiltyard but outside the wall, a situation that accords with its present location. However, Knyff's view conflicts with that of van den Wyngaerde, in which the tower is some way from the nearest wall. It is also difficult to reconcile the various references to the towers as being 'in' the tiltyard with the sketch by van den Wyngaerde

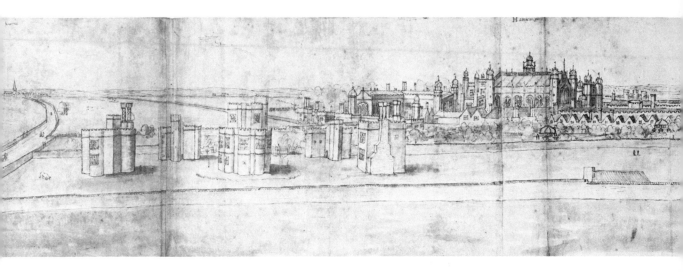

54   Hampton Court Palace from the northwest (1558). Van den Wyngaerde's drawing shows Henry VIII's five romantic and medieval-looking towers that stood close to the tiltyard. The square tower on the right of the group is still there. The tiltyard itself extended to the right from this tower and was later transformed into gardens. The towers were probably designed to serve as viewing galleries, although they were also used as additional accommodation.

55   Hampton Court Palace from the west by an unknown artist. To the right are Henry's five tiltyard towers.

(the perspective of which is distorted because of its horizontal extension), the Knyff painting, and what is to be seen by any modern visitor to Hampton Court.

It would be nice to think that here at last is a site (see Fig. 58) where one could savour the memories of Tudor and Jacobean tournaments, sit on one of the many benches in the gardens and imagine the cheers of the onlookers in the towers, the pounding of horses' hooves, the metallic jingle of harness and armour, and all the colour and pageantry associated with a full-scale Tudor or Jacobean tournament. In spite of attempts by several of those who have written about Hampton Court to do just this, the exercise would be wasted, since there is no clear record that any

A GENERAL PLAN OF
HAMPTON-COURT
PALLACE, GARDENS &
PARKS

House Park.   Bushey Park.
1. The Pallace.   12. My L. Hallifax's
2. The Fountain Garden 13. Mr. Progers's.
3. The Privey Garden   14. New Reserv. & Canal
4. The Wilderness.   15. Old Reserv. & River
5. The Mellon Ground   16. Pheasant house
6. The Kitchen Garden 17. The Round Bason
7. The Canal.   18. Avenue to Twickenh.a
8. The Bowling-green   19. Avenue to Hampton
9. The lower Wilderness 20. The Paddock.
10. Avenue to Kingston 21. The Green
11. Avenue to Ditton   22. The Offices of y Works
FEET

LEFT

56 Bridgeman's plan of Hampton Court Palace shows William III's kitchen gardens (labelled '6'). These were created on the site of the former tiltyard.

tournament was ever held in the Hampton Court tiltyard.

There were only three events which just possibly may have taken place in the tiltyard. The jousting arranged at Hampton Court by Queen Mary and King Philip for Christmas 1557 and attended by Princess Elizabeth may have made use of Henry VIII's tournament ground, with spectators in the five towers, but the surviving account unfortunately does not indicate the exact location: 'On the 29th day of December, she [Princess Elizabeth] sate with their Majesties and the Nobility at a grand spectacle of justing, when two hundred spears were broken. Half of the combatants were accoutred in the Almaine, and half in the Spanish fashion.'[34] There may also have been a tournament at Hampton Court in May 1581, but this seems highly unlikely, and the way in which the tournament ground is described with the Queen sitting 'at one end of the lists' seems to confirm that a Whitehall event is being described, even though the French narrator located it at Hampton Court.[35]

Lastly there is the evidence of James I's first Christmas in England (1603–4), when James and some of his nobles ran at ring while at Hampton Court. However, no mention is made of the tiltyard, and instead we hear of a special viewing stand being set up 'at the Court doore for the Queene to see the running at the Ringe', while the Office of the Chamber accounts, referring to this stand, describe it as being 'in the parke'.[36] Nor is there any indication in surviving records that the Hampton Court tiltyard ever contained a tilt barrier or lists that could have served for practice. As van den Wyngaerde shows, the area, though always referred to as 'The Tiltyard', was a large empty expanse when he saw it, apart from the trees which were permitted to grow around the central tower.

The Hampton Court tiltyard is thus something of a disappointment. Approximately 900 feet by 400 feet (it is not an exact rectangle), it is by far the largest area set aside for Henry's favourite equestrian sport. No doubt palisades around the lists would have reduced the space actually used, but none the less the presence of the five towers (if their function really was related to the tiltyard) and the very large enclosed piece of ground that was involved may indicate that Henry must originally have intended something very grand indeed.

After the disastrous fire at Westminster Palace in 1512, it was the Greenwich tiltyard which was the site of important state tournaments for the next twenty years. Moreover, after 1512 and the beginning of the war with France, the character of Henry's tournaments changed. Though the disguising of knights was still occasionally featured, pageant car entries were abandoned along with the allegorical elements that so often accompanied them. Instead, the emphasis shifted to the use of fanciful horse bards and impresa devices.

It has been suggested that this change was 'a simple change of fashion associated, perhaps, with the development of indoor court festivals which offered more scope for allegorical fantasy, and more variety in its expression'.[37] It is more likely, however, that this change in style was a direct result of the Westminster fire. Important tournaments would still have been accompanied by the full panoply of State magnificence. However, although pageant wagons had been employed at Greenwich in the past and there were several indoor pageants after 1512, and although there is evidence for the occasional use of scenic devices in the lists at Greenwich after 1512, the logistical difficulties of transporting large tiltyard pageants (if they had been built elsewhere), or the lack of suitable facilities for constructing and storing them at Greenwich, may have been a significant contributory cause of this general change in the style of English tournaments.[38]

The use of the Greenwich tiltyard for tournaments marking important state occasions ended on 1 June 1533, when the tournament to celebrate the coronation of Henry's new and controversial bride, Anne Boleyn, was held 'before the King's Gate' at Westminster.[39] The King's Gate was the new gate spanning the public thoroughfare from Charing Cross south to Westminster. The broad upper part of this highway, known as 'The Street', was later renamed Whitehall. Between this road and the River Thames to the east was what had been York Place, an ecclesiastical property belonging to the See of York, which Cardinal Wolsey had turned into a private palace of some considerable magnificence. Here Henry had courted Anne. When Wolsey fell from grace in 1529, Henry appropriated York Place and soon began extensive and hasty building works which were to turn it into the new and magnificent royal palace of Whitehall.

From 1533 Whitehall served as the principal royal residence, just as the older Westminster Palace had done before 1512. At first officially called the 'King's Palace at Westminster', it eventually became known as Whitehall. Though obviously in part to be seen as fulfilling a genuine need for a royal palace to house Henry and his new bride, the creation of Whitehall occurred at the very time when Henry was consolidating his position as Supreme Head of the Church and deliberately enhancing his own imperial status. The massive building works at Whitehall and elsewhere in the early 1530s, made possible by the vast influx of ecclesiastical wealth, were all part of Henry's far-reaching and deliberate policy, vital at a time when the foundations of a radical political and religious revolution were set in place. Significantly, a major feature of Henry's design for the new Westminster palace was a tiltyard overlooked by a sumptuous viewing gallery. Now at last that extremely effective instrument of royal propaganda, the tournament, would have a permanent, purpose-built arena with easy access for the London citizenry.

Henry's building programme not only involved extensive work at York Place. Following the acquisition of land to the west of the road from Charing Cross to Westminster in 1531, he erected a group of buildings designed to accommodate some of his favourite recreations, among them tennis, cock-fighting and bowls. At the same time he obtained the adjacent fields to the west and enclosed them as a game and wildfowl nursery to form what is now St James's Park. Faced with the problem of an important public highway running through what now had become part of the royal residence, Henry had walls constructed on each side of the street and a gateway at either end. Both gateways had passages through them above the roadway so as to provide access from one part of the palace to the other.

The northern gate, initially called the King's Gate or the Cockpit Gate but later generally known as the Holbein Gate,[40] was an impressive neo-Gothic structure with four octagonal four-storey crenellated turrets. Above its arch was a bay window and its walls were decorated with a distinctive chequered design of stone and flint inset with a number of terracotta roundels. The gateway was erected not far from the main Court Gate that stood on the east side of the highway, and the gallery across its centre at the first level above the highway led from the main part of the palace towards the park, the tennis court, the cockpit and other related buildings. At the westerly end where it reached the boundary of the park, two flanking towers were erected and a staircase gave access to the parkland.

Modifications and restructuring of this staircase between 1624 and 1629 resulted eventually in an impressive structure. Looking out over the park was 'a greate Balcony windowe vj foot broad', while the stairway was eight feet wide, with the ballasters and supporting pillars of wood painted and moulded to resemble Corinthian columns. A total of thirty-eight cartouches were carved at the end of the joists.[41]

An excellent illustration of this part of the gallery in its 1629 state exists in Henrick Danckaerts' painting, which also shows the towers of the Holbein Gate and Inigo Jones' Banqueting Hall on the far side of the tiltyard and The Street (see Fig. 59). After coming through the park from St James's Palace, Charles I walked up the staircase to the gallery and across the Holbein Gate to the Banqueting Hall in 1649 on the morning of his execution. The best surviving view of the group as a whole dates from about 1623. It is a drawing by Inigo Jones, designed as stage scenery, and shows Jones' new Banqueting Hall (the one that still exists), the Holbein Gate, the tiltyard gallery, and the towers at the west end of the gallery before the renovations that were shortly to follow (see Fig. 60). Unfortunately, in order to provide a clear view of his Banqueting Hall, Jones totally omits all details of the tiltyard itself from his drawing.

From the windows of the Tiltyard Gallery there was a fine view of the tournament ground which Henry VIII laid out parallel to

59 *Henrick Danckaerts' painting of Whitehall as seen from St James's Park (c. 1680) shows the Banqueting Hall, the Holbein Gate and the adjoining Tiltyard Gallery with its later elaborate staircase. To the left of the staircase is a small guarded doorway. Originally this gave access to the tiltyard. By the time of this painting, however, most of the tiltyard had been encroached upon by the Horse Guards building.*

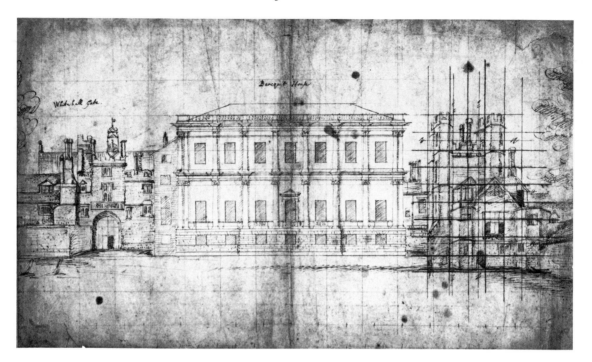

and adjacent with the highway on one side and the park wall on the other. From 1533, the first occasion on which a tournament was held at the new palace, until the death of James I, royalty and nobility watched every major tournament from this lavishly decorated permanent viewing place, the general nature and purpose of which is perhaps best conveyed by Stow. He refers to it as 'a sumptuous Gallery' in which 'the Princes with their Nobility vsed to stand or sit, and at Windowes to behold all triumphant Iustings, and other military exercises'.[42]

The building accounts, for the gallery and the gatehouse through which it passed, show that both were built at great speed. Workers toiled around the clock and were often paid overtime for giving up their rest periods and holidays. For those building the gatehouse, canvas coverings were even erected to permit work to proceed in all weathers.[43] By April 1532 the gallery and gatehouse were virtually complete and, though most of the account book items reveal little of what the structures may have looked like, a few details are clear enough. The roof of the gallery, for example,

60 *This drawing of the Banqueting Hall, Whitehall, was made by Inigo Jones while planning some stage scenery for a Twelfth Night masque performed in 1623. To the right is the Holbein Gate and (though greatly foreshortened) the adjoining Tiltyard Gallery. Unfortunately Jones has omitted all details of the tiltyard.*

was painted and gilded, and garnished with the king's arms and badges, with antique work and with the royal motto. The walls were panelled in drapery wainscot and the floor was tiled and covered with matting. When Lupold von Wedel visited the gallery in 1585, more than fifty years after its completion, he was impressed above all by the collection of pictures on its walls which, as in the case of other galleries in the palace, were arranged to contribute to its decorative impact. Von Wedel was being given the customary tour provided for important visitors, and of the gallery he says: 'On mounting a staircase, we got into a passage right across the tiltyard; the ceiling is gilt, and the floor ornamented with mats. There were fine paintings on the walls, ...'[44]

Whitehall Stairs

The gatehouse was also decorated,[45] and a number of representations of it have survived. One of the earliest is van den Wyngaerde's sketch of *c.* 1558 (see Fig. 61), a drawing that also shows the tiltyard, the cockpit, the tennis court, and the building containing the Tiltyard Gallery, but this last is sketched with tantalizing lack of detail. Hollar's much later drawing of *c.* 1640 (see Fig. 62) provides a clearer and probably more accurate view of the gateway, James I's Banqueting Hall and the Court Gate, but the Tiltyard Gallery is shown in outline only. Later engravings based on Hollar's drawing misleadingly fill in the details of the gallery and are not to be trusted.

Though the gateway did not front directly onto the tiltyard, it was close enough for there to be a view from its windows of any tournament in progress at the time. In 1620, as mentioned earlier, the French ambassador was invited to watch the tournament from the Duke of Lennox' lodgings situated above the gateway.[46] The ambassador was dissatisfied with the arrangement and eventually refused to come, not so much because the view was

61 *Van den Wyngaerde's drawing of Whitehall Palace and the tiltyard (c. 1558) shows the Privy Stairs in the foreground. Behind is the Holbein Gate, with the Tiltyard Gallery beyond it at the second storey level. The tiltyard itself runs from left to right in front of the gallery.*

poor, but because he would have been so distant from the King. Clearly the prized positions for watching tournaments, whatever the view, would always be in the gallery itself to the west of the gateway. For such occasions, as was the custom in specially-erected viewing stands, the gallery was divided by hangings and tapestries into different 'rooms'. The most important of these was for the use of the sovereign, whose window looking out on the yard was distinguished by the 'hanginge of a state without the Tylteyarde in the gallory Wyndowe'.[47]

During Elizabeth's reign and in the early years of James's, the Office of the Works customarily erected a large platform and staircase below this royal window to facilitate the presentation of speeches and impresa shields to the monarch. The tradition of providing

a lavish and comfortable viewing stand for those of highest rank was thus a central part of the design of Henry VIII's Whitehall tiltyard, enabling privileged spectators not only to see the events to advantage but themselves to be seen as part of the general spectacle, admirably set off against the splendours of the special gallery.

As can be clearly discerned in the illustrations of the tiltyard by Braun and Hogenberg and by Agas (see Figs 39 and 45), viewers in the Tiltyard Gallery were ideally situated facing north with their backs to the sun. Not so ideal, however, was the fact that the Tiltyard Gallery was at one end of the tilt barrier rather than facing across it, the tilt being on a north-south axis, not on the more equitable east-west axis used in New Palace Yard, Nor were spectators in the gallery exactly at right angles to the end of the barrier, as John Fisher's plan of 1670 shows (see Fig. 63).[48] This strange feature was caused by the necessity of making the yard parallel to 'The Street', but no one seems to have been concerned. Indeed no comment on the peculiar topography of the tiltyard has survived.

A spectator in the Tiltyard Gallery looking up the length of the yard would have seen

ABOVE

62   This drawing by Wenceslaus Hollar of the Holbein Gate (c. 1640) shows the Court Gate, the Banqueting Hall, and (to the right of the Holbein Gate) the Tiltyard Gallery and tiltyard. There is little detail of the gallery and the yard, but two gates into the tiltyard are indicated and what appear to be a number of tilting lances may be leaning against the storehouse which was within the tiltyard itself.

RIGHT

63   John Fisher's plan of Whitehall (1670) shows how the Horse Guards building has encroached upon the area formerly occupied by the tiltyard. From this plan it is possible to deduce the approximate dimensions of the tiltyard.

small gates in each wall to right and left, providing access to 'The Street' and the park. At the far end of the tiltyard was the main gate for the tournament participants, challengers and defendants alike, who would approach the yard from the north, the direction of the stables. On either side of the yard were a series of viewing stands. By early in Elizabeth's reign, and perhaps before, these seem to have become permanent fixtures. They probably date from 1561 when Elizabeth carried out major renovations to the tiltyard. Unfortunately the Office of the Works accounts contain no record of what was done, but the diarist Henry Machyn stated that the Queen at great cost paved 'from the end of the Tyltt roud abowt the sydes, and closyd in the tylt'.[49]

In 1560 Elizabeth acquired land at the north end of the tiltyard to serve as the palace timber yard. In 1572 Sir Francis Knollys obtained a lease on this area from the crown and built a substantial house. This passed in 1596 to his son William (later Viscount Wallingford) and was later purchased by the Duke of Buckingham in 1622.[50] The history of the buildings at this north end is complex,[51] but in 1606 they consisted of the Knollys property and three tenements held by Lady

Audrey Walsingham. One of the three tenements fronted directly upon the tiltyard, and in 1604 the ambassadors of France, Spain, and Venice were placed at this end 'opposite the King in three several Chambers. The French had the right hand, who thought himself much honoured, the Venetian in the midst, and the Spaniard next coming in, on the left hand, nearest the tilt, where he did not only see best, but was saluted by all the lords as they passed in and out'.[52] In 1620, rooms in this same house were suitably 'apparelled' by the Office of the Chamber to provide the King of Bohemia's ambassador and various other ambassadors with suitable accommodation for viewing the tournament at which Prince Charles made his first appearance as a contestant.[53]

The Whitehall tiltyard was between 480

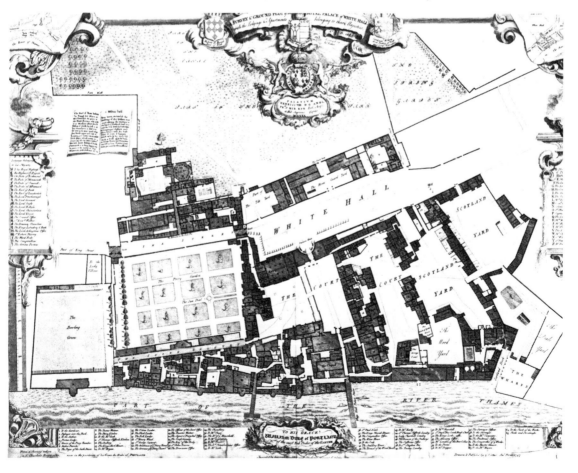

and 490 feet long and approximately 80 feet wide, this width including the space for viewing stands and lists.[54] As already indicated, the tilt barrier was approximately 107 yards long, allowing about 28 yards at each end for mounting blocks, spare weapons, and participants awaiting their turn to joust. When tourneys and foot combats were held, these probably took place in the area immediately below the royal window and the staircase and platform erected in front of it. A description of the marriage tournament for Ambrose Dudley in November 1565 mentions that on the third day 'about ii. of Clocke in the Afternoun, the Queene being com into her Gallery, the iiij. Challengers cam [. . .] armed for the Tourney, and so proceeded to the Tylte Yard; at the upper End whereof was prepared the Place of Tourney'.[55] This same area (the upper end) was occasionally used for bear-baiting in both Elizabeth's and James' reigns.[56] Even after tournaments had long ceased to be held, and even after the building of a Guard House in 1649 and the first Horse Guards Building in the tiltyard itself in 1663–4, sufficient space still remained in front of the gallery for use as a bear-baiting and bull-baiting arena.[57] The original function of the gallery as 'sumptuous' viewing stand was thus not quickly forgotten.

The Whitehall tiltyard was the site of the coronation tournaments of Anne Boleyn, Edward VI and Elizabeth I, and of the Accession Day tournaments of Elizabeth and James I. Here also were held many tournaments in which Sir Henry Lee, Sir Philip Sidney, the Earl of Cumberland, the Earl of Essex and others so dazzled spectators in the 1570s, 80s and 90s, and the later tournaments in which the young Prince Charles participated. The tiltyard is now buried beneath a row of buildings. These extend northwards towards Trafalgar Square on the west side of Whitehall diagonally across from the Banqueting Hall, the one remaining building contemporary (if

only by a few years) with Henry VIII's tournament ground. The Holbein Gate was demolished in 1759 to ease the flow of traffic, and the gallery, though still standing in 1670, was ultimately replaced by Dover House. To the north, where the tiltyard itself once was, were built successive foot-guard and horse-guard buildings in 1649, 1663, and 1751–3. Admiralty House was constructed on the site of Robert Knollys' house. Today the Horse Guards building (1751–3), designed by William Kent and built by John Vardy, is as popular a tourist attraction as Big Ben, but those who come to watch the changing of the guard and the pageantry it offers, like those who peer through the railings at New Palace Yard, are unaware that they stand upon a site which once saw some of the richest displays of pageantry and magnificence ever to be found in English history. Yet one small sign remains: one of the rooms in the Horse Guards building is still known as the Tilt Guard.

*   *   *

These detailed descriptions of the Tudor and Jacobean tiltyards emphasize the manner in which successive English rulers sought to maximize the show of their magnificence by providing appropriately splendid locales for tournaments. The physical grandeur of the tiltyards at Westminster, Whitehall, and Greenwich must have been as significant a factor as the actual spectacle of costume, armour, weapons, horses and pageants in expressing royal power, while national unity was perhaps nowhere better in evidence than in the provision of viewing stands for thousands of spectators, arranged so as to express the accepted social hierarchy. All this was primarily an investment made by the crown. The chapters that follow turn to what individual participants contributed to the events held in the splendid settings supplied by their rulers.

V

Curious Devices

N INDIVIDUAL PARTICIPATING in a Tudor or Jacobean tournament required a suitable horse (preferably several), armour, weapons, colourful, original and sumptuous clothing for himself, his horses, and retainers, and perhaps a pageant wagon complete, if necessary, with actors and musicians. An additional burden during Queen Elizabeth's reign was the newly-established requirement that each knight compose an appropriate impresa. This he would have to have painted upon a small shield which would then be presented to the Queen by his page as part of the ritual preceding the tournament itself. Having to provide an impresa shield was perhaps more likely to strain a knight's wit than his purse, but it was none the less felt to be an extremely important matter.

The impresa generally consisted of a motto and a picture, designed to express the personal intentions, aspirations, or state of mind of its bearer. As William Camden explains in his *Remaines* (1605): 'An Imprese (as the Italians call it) is a devise in picture with his Motte, or Word, borne by noble and learned personages, to notifie some particular conceit of their owne.'[1] The imprese was somewhat similar to what today is a better-known genre—the emblem. During the sixteenth and seventeenth centuries, emblems were ubiquitous in art and literature throughout Europe, and examples of them can be found in so-called 'emblem-books', each containing any number of individual emblems; on illustrated broadsheets; on the title-pages of books; among book illustrations; and in drama, pageants, and masques.

The emblem was composed of three parts that modern theorists have increasingly tended to label with the Latin terms *inscriptio*, *pictura*, and *subscriptio*. The *inscriptio* is usually a brief motto or quotation that introduces the emblem and is generally printed above the *pictura*, a picture (often allegorical). Below the *pictura* is the *subscriptio*, a verse or prose statement by the emblematist, or a quotation from some other author. This third ingredient is frequently in the vernacular tongue of the emblematist and provides an explanation of the meaning of the emblem, although early emblematists disagreed among themselves regarding the degree to which the *subscriptio* should serve this function.[2] For our purposes, Henry Peacham's emblems provide examples of the English emblem during the late sixteenth and early seventeenth centuries (see Fig. 67). However, whereas the emblem had a tri-partite structure of motto, picture, and poem (or prose passage), and expressed some general truth, the impresa (as Camden pointed out in the passage just quoted) omitted the poem and expressed a personal particularity.

In origin, as the many treatises of the mid sixteenth century demonstrated, the impresa was the product of numerous forces, not least of which was the necessity for a man in armour to have some means of identification. In time the coat of arms came to serve this function best, but in many instances the symbolism inherent in heraldry lies at only a small remove from that which is so central a feature in the art of the impresa. The kinship between heraldry and the impresa is evident at the opening of Paolo Giovio's influential *Dialogo Dell' Imprese Militari e Amorose* (Rome, 1555). Following the invasion of the Italian peninsula by the forces of Charles VIII and Louis XII, he explains, whoever followed the military profession in Italy imitated the French by adorning himself with impresas embroidered on his breast and back. These devices were used in battle to distinguish one company from another.[3] In tournaments, where the prime interest had come to be focused on individual combat, the impresa was even more appropriate. In his introduction to his translation of Giovio, Samuel Daniel even suggested that impresas 'are neuer worne but either in true or fained warre, or at Iusts, Turneis, Maskes, or at such like extrauagant shewes'. They were best worn, Daniel explained, on 'the Helmet, the Shielde, the Bardes, the borders of the garment, or the breast'.[4]

In England impresas or impresa-like devices were first introduced into tournaments long before the reigns of Henry VII and Henry VIII, and hence well before the publication in the mid sixteenth century of the influential European collections of impresas by such writers as Paradin, Ruscelli, Giovio and Domenichi. During the reign of Edward III, tournaments and related celebrations often employed some central emblematic motif, such as love-knots, a wreath, honeysuckle, or an olive branch (to name some actual examples). Often these appear to have been accompanied by an appropriate motto and the use of symbolic colours, all designed to comment upon the occasion being celebrated.[5] Over a century later, impresas were employed in the tournament to celebrate the marriage of Prince Richard in January 1477, an innovation apparently inspired by Burgundian tournament practices. On this occasion, for example, Anthony Woodville entered the lists as a hermit. He was dressed in white, and from the top of his helmet to the crupper of his horse he wore brownish orange satin tawny decorated with 'Teres [droplets] of gold'. His motto, we are told, was 'Bane deplesance' [?Do away with discontent].[6]

Then, at Henry VII's tournament in 1494 in honour of the creation of Prince Henry as Duke of York, the challengers on the second day entered New Palace Yard from Westminster Hall beneath portable pavilions, each of which was topped by an impresa-like device. More complex, and more like the type of impresa familiar from the later Tudor period, was Henry Wynslow's deliberately comical picture during the same event of two men playing at dice. This was painted upon his horse's bard and accompanied by 'certain othes writtyn' but, according to the discreet chronicler, 'nott wrothey her to be rehearsed'.[7] There is no similar evidence of the use of impresas during Henry VII's reign, but from Henry VIII's accession onwards there is a succession of allusions to apparel with 'curious deuises, of cuttes and of embrouderies, aswell in their coates, as in trappers for their horses'.[8]

How these devices were used is illustrated by the following two examples. In March 1522, elaborate revels, including a tournament, were held at Greenwich to entertain the ambassadors of Charles V, who were on their way to Spain. At the tournament Henry himself led one group of jousters, and, typical of his personal flamboyance, he entered the lists with cloth of silver bases and a horse bard embroidered with three golden letter 'L's'. Under the letters was an embroidered picture of the 'harte of a manne wounded, and great rolles of golde with blacke letters, in which was written, *mon nauera*'. As Hall explains, the letter 'L', the picture, and the motto were to be understood as a statement that '*ell mon ceur a nauera*' (she hath wounded my heart), an allusion, no doubt, to Henry's Queen who sat in the place of honour. As such it was typical of the tournament impresas of Henry's reign and typical of the way in which various verbal and pictorial devices were used in many of the great European tournaments of the fifteenth and sixteenth centuries. Characteristic, too, was the impresa of Sir Nicholas Carew, also on his bases and horse bard. Carew's impresa consisted of an embroidered picture of a prison with a man looking out through a grating, above which was written, 'in prison I am at libertie, and at libertie I am in prison'.[9] The precise interpretation of this impresa is, as so often, unclear, but perhaps it too was an expression of love and obedient service.

As in the tournament at the Field of Cloth of Gold two years previously, it was these impresas, witty and ingenious in their composition and lavishly presented in complex embroidery work, that seem to have caught the attention of observers, although rarely was there anything quite as elaborate and carefully-contrived as King Francis I's complex and punning impresa (really three impresas in one) that took three days to appear in full.[10] Indeed, it seems that impresas often provided the chief form of pageantry and display at many of Henry VIII's tournaments, becoming increasingly important as a part of tournament ritual just when the use of other forms of scenic display, for whatever reason, began to decline.[11]

In May 1527 there was a tournament held in the presence of the French ambassadors at Greenwich to celebrate the newly-created Anglo-French League. For this occasion the Office of the Revels provided horse bards embroidered with 'knights riding upon mountains, and ladies casting darts at them, and clouds, the spaces between flourished thick with broom'.[12] We have a complete description of this event from Hall, who describes the Marquis of Exeter and his thirteen companions as barded and based alike, the right side 'cloth of golde cut in cloudes engrayled with Damaske golde, the otherside cloth of syluer set with mountaynes full of Oliue braunches, made of gold all mouyng'.[13] The challengers, according to Hall, were all apparelled in bards and bases, the right sides of which were embroidered 'with a compasse or roundell of blacke veluet and in the compas a right hand holding a sworde, and about the sword were pennes and peces of money of diuerse coynes, all enbrawdered, vnder the hand was embraudered *Loialte*, and on that side of the bard was written in embraudery, *Bi pen, pain nor treasure, truth shall not be violated*'.[14] Presumably both impresas on this occasion, as a compliment to the guests of honour, alluded to various facets of the newly-worked out treaty involving a marriage for Princess Mary with either King Francis or his second son, a possible war with Charles V should he not liberate Francis' two sons then being held as hostages, and perpetual amity between France and England.

Surviving descriptions of the tournaments in the remainder of Henry VIII's reign and of those held during the reigns of Edward VI and Queen Mary do not mention the use of impresas. However, the Office of the Revels accounts for the reigns of both Edward and Mary show, as we saw in Chapter 2, that bards and bases from past tournaments were carefully stored and then on occasion had their mottoes reworked for subsequent tournaments. On occasion, too, new bards and bases, complete with impresas, were prepared.[15] Similar evidence of the continued use of tournament impresas during the first twenty years of Queen Elizabeth's reign is somewhat scanty, with one significant exception.

This one exception, however, is of special importance, because it demonstrates that the impresa collections of Giovio and Paradin were not only known in England very soon after their publication in Europe, but that they were used as sources for tournament impresas. In the College of Arms there is a document containing a series of pictures of

pairs of knights jousting, designed to illustrate the different forms of attaint (on the body, on the helm, and man and horse down). The picture of each knight is accompanied by a drawing of a shield on which his impresa is depicted (Fig. 64). We see first a knight with the Dudley family ragged staff on his horse bard. He is jousting against another knight who has a star on his horse bard. Dudley's impresa shield shows an ostrich with a key in its beak and the motto '*Spiritus durissima coquit*' (A noble mind digests even the most painful injuries). His opponent's shield has a picture of waves breaking against a rock and the motto '*Conantia frangere frangunt*' (They break those who are trying to break them).

The next two knights are similarly portrayed. One has a rampant lion on his bard, the other the Dudley ragged staff accompanied by a small crescent, a younger brother's mark of 'difference'. The former has an impresa showing a pot with steam rising from it and the motto '*Sic tua nos virtus*' (Thus are we by your strength), and the second a pyramid encircled with ivy and the motto '*Te stante virebo*' (With you standing, I shall flourish). The next two knights also have

64 *Early Elizabethan impresas. The illustration above shows how knights can score points at a tournament by an attaint on their opponent's head or by striking the coronel of their lance against that of their opponent. The four tournament impresas, belonging (from left to right) to Ambrose Dudley, (?) the Earl of Sussex, William Howard, and Robert Dudley, are of particular interest. The illustration (above right) of scoring by an attaint on the body and by an attaint that throws both man and horse down is from the same source and is equally interesting. The knights may be tentatively identified (from left to right) as Lord Hunsden, Lord Scroop, Lord Windsor, and Lord Darcy. The impresas in both illustrations were all taken from printed sources, but this was not the usual practice in England.*

insignia on their bards. One has a swan, the other a bird of some kind (perhaps a blackbird). Their pictures too are accompanied by impresas. The first consists of three feathers and the motto '*Semper*' (Always) and the second shows the sun breaking from behind clouds and is accompanied by the motto '*Obstantia nubila soluent*' (They dissolve obstructing clouds). The depictions of the last

two knights follow the same pattern. One has a unicorn on his horse bard, the other a bull. The impresa belonging to the former shows a unicorn dipping his horn in water and the motto '*Venena Pello*' (I banish poisons) and that of the latter shows a rock of diamonds with the motto '*Naturae non artis opus*' (A work of nature not of art). Below this second knight, who carries a shattered lance, is a note identifying him as Lord Darcy.[16]

The only tournaments at which the two Dudleys participated alongside Lord Darcy are those of 5 November 1559, and 21 and 28 April 1560. The heralds' score cheques for these events include the names of the Lord Windsor, whose crest was a unicorn; William Howard, whose crest was a lion; Lord Hunsdon, whose crest was a swan; and Lord Scroop, whose crest was a cornish chough or blackbird.[17] It is thus clear that impresas were in use in a tournament at the very beginning of Elizabeth's reign. Far more important, however, is the fact that all of the impresas described, except for two, appear in Paolo Giovio's *Dialogo dell'Imprese Militari et Amorose*. This work was first published in Rome in 1555, its first illustrated edition appearing in Lyons in 1559. In 1556 an edition appeared in Venice with Lodovico Domenichi's *Ragionamente* appended to it, and this was again included in the 1559 edition. It would appear that one of the editions containing the Domenichi appendix was used as the source for the English tournament impresas, since one of the two impresas not in Giovio ('*Sic tua nos virtus*') is none the less to be found in the Domenichi section. The other impresa not in Giovio ('*Te stante virebo*'), the one adopted by Robert Dudley, the future Earl of Leicester, and perhaps suggesting something about his relationship to the Queen, appears in Claude Paradin's *Devises Heroiques*. This was first published with 118 woodcuts in Lyons in 1551 and then expanded in the edition of 1557. Clearly the Dudleys and their companions were quick to obtain copies of both Giovio and Paradin and lost no time in making use of such ready-made sources. However, it is none the less true that this is a somewhat isolated example of such borrowing. The personal nature of the impresa and its importance in displaying a participant's own ingenuity and inventive powers tended, it would seem, to prevent close imitations of the kind just discussed.

Following this early Elizabethan use of

impresas borrowed by Robert and Ambrose Dudley and their companions from contemporary European treatises, there is no record of such devices appearing in the tiltyard until a certain 17 November (probably that of 1577). At this tournament Sir Philip Sidney, the nephew of Robert Dudley, presented himself in the company of a group of ploughmen. He was in the guise of his pseudonym 'Philisides, the Shepherd Knight', his impresa being a harrow with the motto '*Nec habent occulta sepulchra*' (Graves have no secrets). Its presentation to the Queen was accompanied by a song of praise for Elizabeth, the words of which have survived, along with another poem describing how Philisides came to be at the Accession Day tilt.[18] Sidney may also have written a third poem for this same entertainment.[19] It is addressed to the Queen on her 'enitry daye' and seems designed to accompany the presentation of an impresa since it is followed by a note describing the impresa as 'a tree, the one half dying & this word, hoc ordine fata. Such be ye corse of Heavens.'[20]

From the late 1570s evidence of the regular use of impresas at English tournaments is plentiful. Initially, perhaps, it was the enthusiasm for impresas generated by Sidney and others that led to the custom of each knight presenting his impresa to the monarch as part of the ceremonial of the tournament. In Italy the custom of each knight's 'divisa' (a motto or verse alluding to his cause) being presented upon his entry into the tiltyard, when it was recited by a herald at the sound of a trumpet, was apparently well-established in the fourteenth century. At a tournament in Rome in 1332, for example, Galeotto Malatesta da Rimini, dressed in green, presented a device on a pennon which said 'Alone like Horace'. That of Lodovico da Polenta, who was dressed in red, said 'If I die in blood, what a sweet/ soft ("*douce*") death,' and that of Pietro Cappoci, who was dressed in rose, announced 'I am the slave of the Roman Lucrece'.[21]

The Elizabethan ritual involving impresa shields may, on the other hand, have developed from the older custom, already described in Chapter 2, of each knight presenting his coat of arms before a tournament. By the late 1570s and certainly by 1581 shields displaying coats of arms seem to have been replaced by shields with impresas. The Office of the Revels accounts for 1581 record payments totalling £34 10s. for the construction, painting, and gilding of forty-six impresa shields. The construction of a platform below the Queen's window in the Whitehall tiltyard seems to have been in part intended to enable the presentation of these shields to take place, accompanied by suitable speeches delivered by the knights' squires or pages.[22] In January of 1581, the Earl of Arundel's page addressed the Queen in an elaborate speech in which he explained his master's impresa—a pair of compasses[23]—and in May, at the Fortress of Perfect Beauty tournament, there is similar evidence of speeches and impresa shields being presented to the Queen. Henry Goldwell's description of the May event makes clear that every knight entered with 'his sundrie inuention', and when Goldwell goes on to quote several of the speeches, he explicitly notes that Ratcliff's page presented his shield to the Queen during one of them.[24] Once the presentation of impresas became a well-established ritual, that ritual was regularly maintained until the end of James I's reign.

Usually, as already indicated, it was the knight's page who presented his impresa, often with an explanatory speech, though in 1602 Sir Thomas Gerard provoked considerable comment because, having entered the tiltyard on a tiny horse 'no bigger than a goode bandogge' (bloodhound), 'he delivered his scutchion with his *impresa* himself, and had goode audience of her Majestie, and made her very merry'.[25] Five years later when Sir James Hay selected someone '(according to custom) to present his *Shield*, and *Device* to the King', he sent Robert Carr to do the office. The historical implications of this choice were considerable, since Carr's injury when he fell from his horse in front of James was what sparked the King's initial

*65 Designs for impresa shields by Inigo Jones
(c. 1610). In that above a space has been left blank
for the painting of the impresa. On either side are
female warriors, perhaps Minerva and Chivalry.
Jones' other design (right) shows a knight or
squire, dressed à l'antique. His impresa shield
includes a scroll for the impresa's motto.*

interest in the young man.[26]

The necessity to produce an impresa for each tournament, though it may have fired the creative imagination of a Sidney, seems to have caused difficulties for others, and those who did not feel equal to the task responded by employing the services of third parties to invent impresas for them. In 1600, when Lord Herbert (the future Earl of Pembroke) was preparing to make his first appearance at a tournament, Rowland White wrote to Sir Robert Sidney asking for advice concerning an impresa (see p. 72).[27] In 1613 Shakespeare was paid forty-four shillings to compose an impresa for the Earl of Rutland, and Richard Burbage £4 8s. for constructing and painting it.[28] For the same tournament Ben Jonson composed a speech for Robert and Henry Rich to accompany the presentation of their impresas. Possibly he composed the impresas too.[29] Jonson, however, seems to have had very mixed feelings about such commissions, and one of his epigrams, entitled 'To Sir Annual Tilter',[30] is a hard-hitting satire on a knight who lacks the necessary wit to compose his own impresa:

Tilter, the most may admire thee, though not I:
And thou, right guiltlesse, may'st plead to it, why?
For thy late sharpe deuice, I say 'tis fit
All braines, at times of triumph, should runne wit.
For then, our water-conduits doe runne wine;
But that's put in, thou'lt say. Why, so is thine.

There is not much information on what the typical impresa shield looked like, although Inigo Jones' two designs for impresa shields are very suggestive (see Fig. 65). One of these is shown held by a knight or squire. The shield is small, approximately eighteen inches by ten inches when seen in relation to its bearer. Both this and the other design are characterized by their highly elaborate borders. These shields are entirely decorative and would have been quite impractical in real combat, since the purpose of a shield was in part to force an antagonist's blow to glance away. A knight would not want an opponent's weapon to find lodging in some decorative crevice. Hilliard's full-length portrait of the Early of Cumberland is also helpful. It was probably painted in 1590 to commemorate Cumberland's appointment as Queen's Champion (Fig. 70) and it shows the Earl's impresa shield hanging on a tree. The border of the shield is not quite so elaborate as those in Jones' drawings, but it is just as small relative to the size of the man.

Unfortunately no Tudor or Jacobean impresa shield specifically designed for a tournament has survived, but in the British Museum there are two wooden impresa shields, one of them English, that perhaps come close to what each knight was expected to produce (Fig. 66). The English example dates from the late fifteenth century and once belonged to Sir William Belknap. Originally in Burton Dassett Parish Church (Warwickshire), the shield is decorated with another shield suspended from a burning beacon, below which is a salamander with a crown around its neck. The original significance of Belknap's impresa is not known, but it is certainly in character with many Tudor tournament shields. A late fifteenth-century Flemish shield hangs

66 *The knight's motto on this late fifteenth-century Flemish impresa shield is* Vous ou la Mort. *Death, it appears, will take him if the lady does not.*

alongside it in the museum. This shows a kneeling knight with poleaxe, helmet and gauntlets in front of him. Before him stands a lady and behind him Death. His motto '*Vous ou la Mort*' seems to express his plea to the lady : she must choose him or he will die.

Although no Tudor or Jacobean tournament impresa shield has survived, we none the less know about an extraordinary number of them. Early in the 1580s, and perhaps before, it became customary to hang impresa shields up in a special gallery at Whitehall Palace after each tournament. This collection eventually grew to a considerable size. Bearing in mind the number of tournaments and the numbers of participants, it is clear that hundreds of shields must have been hanging in the gallery by the time the last tournaments took place in the early 1620s. From quite early on, the collection became a major attraction for visitors taking the guided tours of Whitehall that seem to have been available. Fortunately, a number of those visitors described the gallery and even wrote down descriptions of some of the impresas they saw there, so that William Segar's statement in his *Booke of Honor and Armes* (1590) that the 'Emblemes, Devices, Poesies, and other Complements', used in tournaments 'cannot be recovered' is far from accurate.[31]

Von Wedel gave us the first description of the gallery itself, which eventually became known as the Shield Gallery. 'We were taken into a long passage across the water,' he says, 'which on both sides is beautifully decorated with shields and mottoes. These shields originate from tournaments [. . .] Everybody who wishes to take part must ask permission; this being granted, he offers the shield to the queen, who orders it to be hung up there. In this passage the queen has secret doors to the river if she wishes to take a trip on the water.'[32] The term 'secret doors' is an allusion to the Privy Stairs which Henry VIII had constructed at the same time as his workmen were building the tiltyard gallery.[33] The stairs are shown in both van den Wyngaerde's sketch

of Whitehall and in the Agas map (see Figs 61 and 45) and they provided the monarch with private access to the river. The gallery connected with the second storey of the Palace, and actually projected out over the Thames. Below it was the river and the Queen's landing stage.

Fourteen years after von Wedel's account, Paul Hentzner, another visitor from abroad, described seeing a variety of emblems on pasteboard ('*papyracea*') shields, 'with mottoes, used by the nobility at tilts and tournaments, hung up here for a memorial'.[34] Shortly after, in 1599, Thomas Platter recorded his visit to 'a chamber built over the water, hung all round with emblems and mottoes'.[35] Like a number of other visitors, Platter was so impressed that he copied down descriptions of some of the devices he saw. Other visitors followed, among them the nineteen-year-old Moravian Baron Waldstein, the young Philip Julius, Duke of Stettin-Pomerania, the London lawyer John Manningham, and the English emblem writer Henry Peacham. These, together with William Camden, recorded descriptions of a number of the impresas in the gallery. Peacham, who made use of some of them in his *Minerva Britanna* (Fig. 67), even appears to have made a collection of the majority of them. Unfortunately for us, he was dissuaded from publishing it because of the prohibitive cost.[36] Many years later Samuel Pepys mentions going to the Shield Gallery in Whitehall on two occasions in his diary. Clearly the name survived, even if the shields themselves were perhaps no longer on display, as one suspects they were not, given the ravages that beset the palace during the Commonwealth.[37]

These accounts describe only a small fraction of the great wealth of emblematic material that was originally hung up for all to see. A much more important source is the long list of impresas appended to the diary of one of those who accompanied the Landgraf Otto of Hessen-Kassel on his visit to England in the summer of 1611. The son of Landgraf Moritz of Hesse, the seventeen-

27
Sine refluxu.

T O the honourable Lord, the L : Harrington .

D : Philippi Syd-
næi.

THE CASPIAN Sea, as Histories do show,
(Whome Rocky Shores, on every side surround,)
Was never seene by man, to ebbe and flow:
But still abides the same, within his bound;
    That drought no whit, diminisheth his store,
    Nor neighbour streames, augment his greatnes more.

Thus should we beare, one and the selfe-same saile,
In what ere fortune, pleaseth God to send,
In mid'st of trouble, not of courage faile,
Nor be to proude, when fortune is our frend:
    And in all honest actes, we take in hand,
    Thus constant, in our resolutions stand.

Statius 5 silvar: 1.

Nec tamen hic mutata quies, probitasve secundis
Intumuit, tenor idem animo, moresq́, modesti
Fortuna crescente manent .----

His

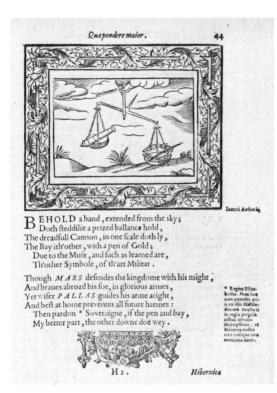

Que pondere maior.   44

Inerti Authoris

B EHOLD a hand, extended from the sky;
    Doth steddilie a peized ballance hold,
The dreadfull Cannon, in one scale doth ly,
The Bay ith'other, with a pen of Gold;
    Due to the Muse, and such as learned are,
    Th'other Symbole, of th'art Militar.

Though *MARS* defendes the kingdome with his might,
And braues abroad his foe, in glorious armes,
Yet wiser *PALLAS* guides his arme aright,
And best at home preventes all future harmes:
    Then pardon * Soveraigne, if the pen and bay,
    My better part, the other downe doe wey.

* Regina Eliza-
betha. Nam hoc
cum paucissi ali-
is ex illis Hasti-
diorum trophæis
in regia pergula
adhuc servatis
descriptsimus, vt
Minerva nostra
non vndique non
concinna luceæ.

H 2.   Hibernica

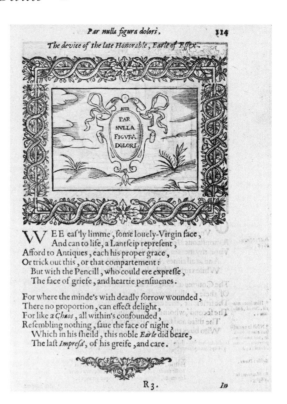

```
Par nulla figura dolori.   114
The device of the late Honorable, Earle of Essex.

PAR
NVLLA
FIGVRA
DOLORI

W EE eas'ly limme, some louely-Virgin face,
    And can to life, a Lantscip represent,
Afford to Antiques, each his proper grace,
Or trick out this, or that compartement:
    But with the Pencill, who could ere expresse,
    The face of griefe, and heartie pensiuenes.

For where the minde's with deadly sorrow wounded,
There no proportion, can effect delight,
For like a Chaos, all within's confounded,
Resembling nothing, saue the face of night,
    Which in his sheild, this noble Earle did beare,
    The last Impresa, of his greife, and care.

R 3.                    In
```

67   *Tournament impresas recorded by Henry Peacham. In his emblem book* Minerva Britanna *(1612), Peacham acknowledged that he used tournament impresas as one source for his emblems. The picture of the tideless Caspian Sea* (LEFT) *and the accompanying motto ('Without flowing back') on Sir Philip Sidney's tournament impresa are presumably intended to represent his own constancy in the face of the ebb and flow of fortune. Another* (ABOVE LEFT) *expresses the familiar idea that the pen is mightier than the sword (or in this instance a gun). The third impresa* (ABOVE RIGHT) *was used by the Earl of Essex, and was included in* Minerva Britanna *with a suitable poem. The motto (it means 'Nothing can represent his sorrow') and an otherwise blank shield may be related to the Accession Day tournament in 1586 and hence be an expression of grief for the death of Sidney. Alternatively, the impresa may have been used in 1590 when Essex appeared dressed in black, perhaps as a sign to Queen Elizabeth of his abject sorrow at having married Sidney's widow without her permission. The poem on the fourth example* (RIGHT) *is Peacham's addition.*

```
Hei mihi quod vidi.   143

Incerti. Ex per-
gula Regia :

L OOKE how the Limbeck gentlie downe distil's,
    In pearlie drops; his heartes deare quintescence:
So I, poore Eie, while coldest sorrow fills,
My brest by flames, enforce this moisture thence
    In Christall floods, that thus their limits breake,
    Drowning the heart, before the tongue can speake.

Great Ladie, Teares haue moou'd the savage feirce,
And wrested Pittie, from a Tyrants ire:
And drops in time, do hardest Marble peirce,
But ah I feare me, I too high aspire,
    Then wish those beames, so bright had never shin'd,
    Or that thou hadst, beene from thy cradle blind.

XI.                    Sic
```

year-old Otto, came to seek the hand of James I's daughter, Elizabeth.[38] Much of his time was spent in the company of her brother, Prince Henry, and Otto's followers were often left to find their own amusements.

The description of the London theatres that resulted is well known, but what has never been published is the thirty-four page list of impresas that the compiler made after taking a boat to Whitehall and visiting the Shield Gallery with some of his companions one July afternoon. Part of a lengthy travel diary known as Quarto MS. Hass. 68, the document in question is now in the Kassel Landesbibliothek und Murhardsche Bibliothek. It is one of four such manuscripts recording the details of the young Landgraf Otto's visit.[39] According to its compiler, the small group of sightseers that spent the afternoon in Whitehall that day wrote down descriptions of about half the devices in the gallery.[40] Since the number of impresas listed in the manuscript is just over 400 (one marvels at the diligence of these tourists), the total number in the gallery in 1611 may well have been about 800. After that time, of course, the collection would have grown still larger with each additional tournament. When the Kassel list is combined with all the previous known sources—and these, it should be noted, are often duplicated by it— the total number of known English tournament impresas turns out to be approximately 520. The Kassel text is thus the single largest surviving source of information about the English impresa. Though it tells us about only one limited aspect of the tournament, it is, nonetheless, the largest existing text concerning English tournaments, and a major addition to the corpus of English Renaissance emblem literature in general.

Yet, despite the abundance of impresas, and despite what Jonson may have thought, composing an impresa cannot have been easy. It had to express succinctly the entire meaning of any accompanying pageant; it had to display the personal intentions or aspirations of its bearer, which often involved some matter related to his political status at court and in particular his relationship to the monarch; and it also had to provide an entertaining exercise in wit, its deliberate obscurity challenging the skill of the would-be decipherer. Sometimes such obscurity defeated all efforts at interpretation. Sir Henry Wotton, for example, when describing the tournament of March 1613, noted the 'bare Impresa: whereof some were so dark, that their meaning is not yet understood; unless perchance that were their meaning, not to be understood'.[41] Often also a motto would in reality be a quotation and one which the interpreter would have to place in context in order to be able to unravel the impresa or enjoy the full 'wit' of its invention. The Ditchley manuscript, which contains a great deal of material connected with Sir Henry Lee's appearances in tournaments, includes a note (perhaps by Lee) of Latin phrases suitable for impresas. One is a quotation from Seneca's *Phaedra* ('*Curae leves loquuntur, ingentes stupent*': Light cares speak, but heavy ones are dumb), but it is suggested that only '*ingentes stupent*' be used for the impresa itself.[42] Camden gives several examples of the technique in his *Remaines*, among them the following based on a line in Ovid's *Epistulae* (V, 149): 'Hee played with the Name, and hoped remedy to his Love, which devised a Rose, with that of *Ovid*, (leaving out the negative) AMOR EST MEDICABILIS HERBIS.'[43] The original lines in Ovid, as Camden and other educated contemporaries would have recognized, state, not that 'Love is curable with plants', but that there are no plants that can cure love.

Such demands upon the composers of impresas also, as Wotton's complaint makes clear, placed a parallel burden upon interpreters. However, the problem of interpretation was often lessened by the explanatory speeches offered by each knight's squire or page when the impresa shield was presented in the tiltyard. Typical examples would be the song ('Singe neighbours sing') that probably accompanied the presentation of Sidney's impresa shield in 1577 (see, pp. 155/6), the 'sweet speech or Oration' delivered to the Queen by the Earl of Oxford's page at the tournament on 22 January 1581, the poem by Ben Jonson for the brothers Rich at the tournament on 24 March 1613, and the much later poem by John Beaumont to accompany the presentation of the Marquis of Buckingham's impresa in the early 1620s, the impresa in question being a bird of paradise.[44]

Unlike the emblem, the impresa depends for its interpretation upon some knowledge of the personal situation of its bearer at a particular date. Sidney's famous '*Speravi*' impresa provides an excellent illustration of this. In 1579 (the exact month is unclear), Sidney participated in a tournament with the Earl of Oxford, Lord Windsor and others, and when he entered the tiltyard, according to William Camden,[45] he bore an impresa consisting of the word '*Speravi*' (I hoped) crossed through. In Camden's view this impresa made a pointed allusion to the child recently born to Sidney's uncle, Robert Dudley, the Earl of Leicester. Sidney had been the Earl's heir apparent, but in September 1578 Leicester, abandoning all hope of marriage to the Queen, married his old love, Lettice Knollys, who had recently been widowed and was already in an advanced state of pregnancy, if some of the not altogether reliable accounts of the time are to be believed. The consequent birth of a son completely dashed Sidney's hopes.

Camden's explanation is colourful, but probably inaccurate. Sidney would surely never have been so tactless as to reproach his uncle in this way and at the same time remind Elizabeth of an event that had evidently deeply upset and angered her. Camden, who probably knew the impresa from observing it in the collection at Whitehall, no doubt considered that the birth of Leicester's son would have been an apt moment for Sidney to have used this unusual device. Unfortunately, it is not now possible to authenticate a precise date for it. One scholar has suggested that the '*Speravi*' impresa was used just after the marriage of Lord Rich to Penelope Devereux, the

'Stella' of Sidney's sonnet sequence *Astrophel and Stella*, on 1 November 1581.[46] The impresa would then be an expression of Sidney's disappointed love. There is a further possibility, and one more in character with the way in which most of the Elizabethan and Jacobean tournament impresas were concerned with the relationship between the bearer of the impresa and the monarch.

According to George Whetstone's commemorative poem, Sidney at one time used the impresa '*Spero*' (I hope) in token of his desire for the honour to be gained from learning and from martial skills.[47] After Sidney had written a letter to Elizabeth some time early in 1580 urging her against marriage with the Duc d'Alençon, he was forced to withdraw from court for a time, but in January 1581 he appeared in a tournament at Whitehall in answer to the open challenge of the Earl of Arundel, who called himself Callophisus. Arundel's challenge was answered in the name of the White Knight, the Knight of the Tree of the Sun, and the Blue Knight. The Earl of Oxford was the Knight of the Tree of the Sun, and Lord Windsor and Sidney used the other fictitious names, though which was which is now impossible to tell.[48] As a sign of his humility and contrition, and also as a sign of the blow received to his ambitions, did Sidney enter the tiltyard on this occasion, not with his '*Spero*' impresa—one that he had presumably used on some earlier occasion—but with the '*Speravi*' impresa described by Camden. For a New Year's gift, Sidney had just given the Queen a bejewelled whip as a symbol of his subjection to her will, and this had helped bring about a reconciliation. '*Speravi*' dashed through would not have been out of harmony in this context.

Although we have mottoes and descriptions for several hundred English tournament impresas, in only about a hundred or so instances do we know both the names of their original bearers and their precise or even approximate dates. As a result it is often difficult, as in the case just cited, to attempt detailed interpretations. Indeed, it is often quite futile. Although at one level impresas often express some broad general truth that is obvious enough, as in Ambrose Dudley's '*Spiritus durissima coquit*' (A noble mind digests even the most painful injuries) or in the Earl of Montgomery's impresa for 6 June 1610, '*Fides sine pulsu*' (Faith resounds without influence),[49] it is our inability to interpret the personal particularities that is frustrating.

This may matter very little in the case of some of the early Tudor impresas which were largely concerned with compliments to the Queen, by Henry VIII and others. The presence of the Queen at this period offered the traditional feminine object for the knights' devotions and chivalric exploits. In Elizabeth's reign, however, this familiar pattern took on added political significance when the Queen became the object of an elaborate cult which defined her (among other things) as Virgin Queen of the Reformed Church. Her Accession Day of 17 November, as already noted, developed as a great national holiday in which her virtues, England's delivery from Popish bondage, and the people's subsequent peace and prosperity were celebrated throughout the land. The tournament at Whitehall was indeed an occasion for the right kind of personal/political compliments, as in Sir Henry Lee's '*Caelumque solumque beavit*' (She makes blessed both heaven and earth). But it is also clear that Elizabeth's courtiers learned to exploit the opportunity it offered in another way, like the annual giving of gifts to her each New Year's Day.

Sidney's '*Speravi*' impresa, for example, probably contains an appropriate implicit compliment to Elizabeth. Whatever hopes Sidney may have had, only she can now assist him. Elizabeth is thus complimented as the source of authority and power, but at the same time, of course, Sidney is making a personal plea. He himself is seeking some advantage at her hands. Similarly, whoever presented either Elizabeth or James with the impresa of a fruit tree with the motto '*Speramus regalem pluviam*' (We hope for royal rain) was doing more than merely complimenting his ruler as the source of all bounty.[50] Robert Dudley's use of the '*Te stante virebo*' impresa from Paradin works in a similar way. Elizabeth is complimented by being represented as a golden pyramid-like column without whom her subjects (the ivy) cannot flourish.[51] But Dudley's impresa is probably also a plea that Elizabeth should offer him assistance, though in fact she had just made him a Garter Knight and Master of the Horse. On a more subtle level, the impresa may hint at something more personal, a tempting idea given the rumours at the time about the possibility of marriage between Dudley and Elizabeth. A host of further examples in which compliments are mixed with personal pleas could be cited, among them such impresas as '*De lumine petimus lumen*' (We seek for light in the light), depicting a burning light; '*Dum splendes floreo*' (While you shine, I flourish), depicting a rose just below the sun; '*Fatum subscribat Eliza*' (Elizabeth writes below my fate), depicting a blank space below the motto; and '*Si non sustenatus pereo*' (I perish if not held up), depicting vines held up with supports.[52]

As Elizabeth's courtiers quickly learned, an appearance at a tournament, when they had been out of favour, together with a suitable impresa, might well turn the tables again. When Sir Robert Cary appeared at the Windsor tournament in 1593 disguised as a forsaken knight who had vowed solitude, he presented Elizabeth with an extremely expensive gift, but presumably his impresa also conveyed in some fashion his contrition for having earlier displeased the Queen (he had

68 *This portrait of Robert Devereux, 2nd Earl of Essex, by William Segar (1590), shows Essex as he probably appeared at the Accession Day tournament in November 1590. On this occasion he arrived in the tiltyard 'all in Sable sad' in a chariot 'Drawn on with cole-blacke Steeds of duskie hue' (George Peele).*

ABOVE

69 *Impresa portrait of George Clifford, Earl of Cumberland, by Nicholas Hilliard (1585–89). This miniature shows Cumberland in his Greenwich tournament armour, that still exists in the Metropolitan Museum, New York. Above his head is the motto* Fulmen aquasque fero *('I bear lightning and rain'). The portrait was probably to commemorate one of the several tournaments Cumberland participated in during the late 1580s before he came Queen's Champion in 1590. He wears a blue favour on his right arm.*

FAR RIGHT

70 *Impresa portrait of the Earl of Cumberland by Nicholas Hilliard (c. 1590). In this famous full-length miniature, Cumberland is dressed for a tournament, probably that in 1590 when he became Queen's Champion.*

married without her permission). Such a situation would have been well served by the impresa '*Dolor meus apertus*' (My sorrow is open), although there is now no way of knowing to whom this particular device originally belonged.[53] In 1590 the Earl of Essex (particularly renowned, like Sidney, for his impresas)[54] faced a similar situation to that of Cary. He had enraged Elizabeth by secretly marrying Sidney's widow. At the tournament in November, he and his train entered as a funeral cortège. George Peele vividly described the dramatic scene in *Polyhymnia* (1590). Essex, we are told,[55] was

> . . . all in Sable sad,
> Drawn on with cole-blacke Steeds of duskie hue,
> In stately Chariot full of deepe device.

Though Peele interpreted the pageant as an expression of grief for the death of Sidney some four years earlier, those in the know would have understood Essex' need at this particular moment in his career to reconcile himself with Elizabeth. For his impresa on this occasion he may have carried a black shield with the motto '*Par nulla figura dolori*' (Nothing can represent [his] sorrow). This was attributed to Essex by Manningham, Frederic Gershow (tutor to Philip Julius), and Camden, all of whom recorded descriptions of it. Unfortunately none of them provided a date, so its use in 1590 remains conjectural. Alternatively, Essex may have used this impresa for his first entry into a tournament in 1586, just after the death of Sidney, whose body had only just arrived in London and was still lying in state. Some fragments of text survive for this tournament. Entitled 'A rem[em]brance of Sir Ph: Sidnie Knight', they are probably by Sir Henry Lee, and they show among other details that a riderless horse in mourning accoutrements was led into the tiltyard as a tribute to the dead knight.[56] Clearly Essex' black shield, devoid of anything except its motto, would have been equally suited to either this occasion or that in 1590.

Essex decided to commemorate his appearance at the 1590 tournament by having his portrait painted by William Segar (see Fig. 68). The painting, now in the National Gallery of Ireland, shows Essex dressed completely in black, presumably as he appeared in the tiltyard at Whitehall when he made his entrance in a chariot drawn by coal black horses and driven by the personified figure of Time. Several of those who participated in tournaments decided to have such portraits made of themselves, and sometimes these portraits include the tournament impresas. Essex himself had Nicholas Hilliard do a miniature of him in armour, standing before a tent. On either side of Essex' bases a series of diamonds with the motto (somewhat damaged) 'Dum formas minuis' (While you shape, you diminish) are embroidered within a circle. On his right sleeve is tied what must be the Queen's glove and in the background a page wearing the Queen's colours of black and white is holding Essex' horse. This miniature was probably commissioned to commemorate the Accession Day tournament of 1595 at which Elizabeth gave Essex her glove.[57]

An impresa shield belonging to Essex and probably created for this occasion appears to have hung in the Shield Gallery. It showed a large diamond with the motto 'Dum formas minuis'. John Manningham says he saw it in the gallery in 1602, the year after Essex' execution. Its presence there and its attribution to Essex is further confirmed in Camden's *Remaines*, in Jonson's *Conversations with Drummond*, and in the Kassel manuscript.[58] Without a proven date, it is impossible to be sure about an interpretation, but there appears to be some intended allusion to the bearer's relationship to the Queen. The image of the diamond and the accompanying motto are a reminder, so Camden suggests, that diamonds are always impaired when they are cut. Essex perhaps felt that Elizabeth should recognize his great virtues and accept with them any flaws in his behaviour. The sentiment has more in it of

personal pleading than compliment, but this would have been not entirely uncharacteristic of the egocentric Essex.

Several other portraits show their respective subjects in tilting armour and display their impresas in some way (Fig. 69). Among them, for example, is Hilliard's portrait miniature of the Earl of Cumberland (Fig. 70). As was mentioned earlier (see p. 130), this probably commemorates the Accession Day tournament of 1590 at which Cumberland succeeded Sir Henry Lee as Queen's Champion. In his cap Cumberland wears the Queen's glove, and his gauntlet lies as a challenge on the ground before him. In his right hand he grasps his tilting lance, and his helmet and second gauntlet lie to his left. Behind him hanging in the tree is his impresa shield on which is depicted the sun, the moon and the earth, and his motto 'Hasta Quando'. The meaning of the device seems to be that Cumberland, the new Champion, will serve his sovereign with his lance (hasta) until the sun, the moon and the earth are in eclipse.[59] Cumberland is dressed as the Knight of Pendragon Castle, a role in which he appeared in 1590 at Whitehall and in 1593 at Windsor. In the background is a panoramic view of London, an allusion to his role in the Whitehall tiltyard.

Another such portrait is that of Robert Ratcliffe, by an unknown artist, painted when he became Earl of Sussex on 14 December 1593 (Fig. 71). A month earlier he appeared at Windsor in his first tournament, and the portrait, now at the Tower of London, appears to commemorate a foot combat related to this event. Ratcliffe, the top part of whose body is in white armour (leg armour was not required for foot combat), is shown

71 *Portrait of Robert Ratcliffe, Earl of Sussex, by an unknown artist (1593). Ratcliffe is dressed for foot combat at barriers and so wears no leg armour. His foot combat helmet has a typically elaborate crest. Above his left shoulder is his impresa motto.*

Sir James Scudamore Knt: ob:1619
Ær 61.

holding a lance in one hand and a sword in the other. His white helmet has an elaborate jewelled and feathered crest.[60] To one side is the motto '*Amando et fidando troppo son rovinato*' (Being too much loving and faithful was his ruin), presumably his impresa motto for the occasion, though no accompanying picture is given. Was Sussex' impresa a reproach of some kind to Elizabeth, either on his own behalf or that of someone else?

Sussex appeared again at a further eight tournaments, including that in March 1595 at Whitehall at which James Scudamore made his first tournament appearance. Scudamore appeared in six further tournaments, and at some time during this period or shortly thereafter he too commissioned a portrait of himself, dressed in his Greenwich tournament armour, lance in hand, his bases of velvet laced with silver (Fig. 72). An orange scarf, perhaps a lady's favour, is worn diagonally across his chest. As in the Cumberland portrait, Scudamore is placed in a romantic outdoor setting, in this instance a sylvan Arcadian scene reminiscent of the pastoral imagery evolved by Lee, Sidney and others for their own appearances in tournaments (see Chapters 6 and 7).[61] The unknown painter of Scudamore's portrait did not include his tournament impresa, but perhaps none was needed. In the Accession

Day tournament in November 1595, Scudamore used his own name as motto, and, according to the Kassel manuscript, he carried a shield shaped like a heart with a turtle painted on it. Peele described his entry on this occasion, but without the Kassel text one could easily miss the fact that he is actually describing Scudamore's impresa:

> Le Scu d'Amour: The armes of Loialtie
> lodgd Skydmore in his harte . . .[62]

These examples are obviously only a tiny representative sample of the tournament impresas that have survived. When Sir John Harington translated *Orlando Furioso* and came to discuss the devices of Orlando and Olivero, he mentioned the many Elizabethan Accession Day tournament impresas that he had seen, and he went on to remark: 'In this kind we haue had many [. . .] of which if I should speake at large, it would aske a volume by it selfe.'[63] Confronted by such richness of material, one senses that Harington was probably right, and that a full exploration of this complex and neglected art form must be taken up elsewhere. In the context of this book, the English tournament impresa is chiefly important for the evidence it frequently offers of the political motivations of those that participated. In their investment of wit and sometimes money in the creation of a suitable impresa, participants were anxious to glorify their monarch and thereby add to the general magnificence of the occasion, but they were also invariably anxious to use the impresa as a means of enhancing their own relationship with the monarch. These joint aims were frequently further pursued by means of participants' speeches, as the next two chapters will show.

72 *Portrait of Sir James Scudamore by an unknown artist (c. 1595–1600). Scudamore is dressed for jousting but placed within an Arcadian setting. The scene behind him with the horse and the seated man may have some symbolic significance.*

Winged Words

HE COMPOSITION OF impresas was not the only demand made upon the creative wit of tournament participants. Three other types of literary endeavour commonly led knights, or the authors they had hired, to exercise their pens and imaginations. The resulting texts have a special place in the history of the English Renaissance since they do more to reveal the true nature of Tudor and Jacobean tournaments and the inspiration that lay behind them than any other surviving information, including the heraldic and financial records so frequently referred to in earlier chapters. They also, in their own right, have a special place in the history of English literature alongside the (to date) better known texts of pageants, masques, and plays. What is more, anyone familiar with the English tournament texts cannot but gain a very special insight into the characters, settings, events, and ideology of many literary works, including those two seminal masterpieces of this period, the *Arcadia* and *The Faerie Queene*.

The three most common texts were petitions, challenges and the articles setting out rules of combat. Because the holding of tournaments was strictly controlled, anyone wishing to issue a challenge on his own initiative had first to petition the monarch for licence to do so. The only surviving petitions date from the early Tudor period, the earliest of these originating from four knights in 1492 who wanted to join Henry VII's military campaign in France. The knights asked the King for permission to serve in the army that was to cross the Channel, but they first wanted to prove their martial skills against all-comers in two days of tilting.[1] Two years later, another group of knights petitioned Henry VII when it was known that the young Prince Henry was to be created Duke of York, it being 'accustomed of auncientie within this your noble Realme for the laude and honor of the ffeast to haue Justs and Tourney for the exercise of feats and deeds of Armes'.[2] A third extant petition, probably dating from 1510, was addressed to Henry VIII and sought permission to hold a combat at barriers at Greenwich.[3] It referred to the open-air pastimes customary at court in May and June and was no doubt inspired by the colourful and light-hearted May/June tournaments at Greenwich three and four years before.

Neither these petitions nor their accompanying articles venture into the fictitious romantic world that characterizes many Tudor and Jacobean tournaments. Instead, and in character with the majority of the early tournaments of Henry VII's reign, they rather mundanely stress the opportunities provided by such events to 'learn the exercise of the deeds of arms', to assay and prove a knight's 'habilities', and to eschew 'Idlenes the ground of all vice'.[4] Quite different in character, however, is the petition from the Lady May addressed to Henry VII's daughter, Princess Mary, in 1506. The fictional personification of May, who is a subject of 'my Ladye and sou[er]aigne Dame Somer', has just returned from a voyage in the company of 'divers gentlemen and yeomen apt and active to any exercise that shall of them be demaunded'. On behalf of her 'poore servants' and possibly speaking from the deck of a flower-decked pageant representing her ship (she refers to '*this* ship apparelled and tackled after my judgement' [my italics]), the Lady May beseeches Princess Mary to offer her 'gratious licence' so that Lady May's knights can 'exercise against all comers in waye of pleasure and pastime'.[5]

This petition is clearly literary in character, establishing fictitious characters for the petitioner and the challengers (the servants of Lady May), and implying the kind of fictitious roles suitable for those who might choose to respond as answerers. As such the Lady May's petition has much in common with a number of challenges of the age. Although these can be mere down-to-earth calls to arms, as prosaic and straightforward as the early petitions, they often take on a very different character. Challenges of this latter kind show just how the Tudor court, following in the footsteps of the court of Burgundy,[6] transformed tournaments from straightforward martial exercises into displays of chivalric romance and allegorical pageantry that had more to do with literature, masque and theatre than the preparation of knights for battle. But it was not all a matter of the immediate and direct influence of Burgundy. Of considerable significance also was the earlier English tradition of pageantry, disguisings, and allegory. This appears sporadically throughout the thirteenth century and becomes a hallmark of the tournaments of Edward III in the fourteenth century.[7]

One of the earliest examples of such a challenge appeared in 1507 when a copy of a joint proclamation, delivered by the Herald April and supposedly from the Queen of May and Lady Summer, was sent to Sir Rowland de Vieilleville with a covering letter from Sir Rowland's friends. In effect it is a challenge to 'all noble men desyrous of honour or exersyse in armes' to come to Kennington, 'nygh to the noble citie of London', where a tilt is 'redy for iustus, by whiche tylt standing an hawthorne, and on that tree hangyng a shyld of whyt and grene'. There two of the servants of the Queen of May and Lady Summer will challenge all-comers on successive Sundays and Thursdays.[8] The challenge thus not only sets out an allegorical identity for the tournament participants, but also establishes in advance an elaborate *mise-en-scène*. This was exploited to the full when the challengers were answered, as is clear from two anonymous poems of 1507, *Here begynneth the Iustes of the moneth of Maye* and *Here begynneth the Iustes and tourney of the moneth of Iune*.

During each day of the May tournament a beautiful lady, 'yonge of age' and dressed in green, appeared beneath a hawthorn tree on a high platform. In her hand was an hour glass that was designed to mark each half hour.[9] It is just possible that this figure of May was played by Princess Mary herself, who is known to have presided at the continuation of the jousts in June.[10] The May Queen's knights (Charles Brandon, Thomas Knyvet, Giles Capell and William Hussey) were also dressed in green and each entered with a cockleshell badge attached to his neck. As a sign of fidelity to the lady, the badge was not removed until the month of May was past.

The use of the Tudor colours of green and white, the hawthorn tree (an heraldic badge used by both Henry VII and Henry VIII), and the possible fusion of May Queen and royal princess transformed this event into a celebration of Tudor chivalric and political aspirations. This point was made clear in the letter to Sir Rowland which referred to the manner in which 'thys noble realme of Englonde hath long flowryd in honour by conqueste of warre and hygh actes of armes (whiche be regestyrde in the noble howse of fame, to the great honour therof and perpetuall memory to the worldes ende)'. At the same time, the elements of fictional narrative in the challenge have become of primary significance, and with this the English tournament has become a dramatic and literary form in its own right. For the first time, as far as the evidence permits us to judge, the challenge, the setting, and the costumes are all subordinated to a single dramatic fable.[11] In this process the challenge has played a key role because it has defined in advance the fictional world that is to be created by challengers and answerers alike. However, as will be clear in a moment, a close relationship between challenge and tournament and the subsequent potential for unity of effect are comparatively rare.

Just before Christmas, on St Thomas's Day, 1524, for example, sixteen challengers sent Windsor Herald to the Queen's Great Chamber at Greenwich where the king and court were gathered. The herald bore a coat of arms consisting of a castle with four silver turrets, in each of which was a beautiful lady.[12] After a trumpet fanfare, the herald, who identified himself as the 'Herault called *Chasteau Blanche*', then issued a challenge to 'all comers gentlemen of name and of Armes' to tilt, tourney and barriers, and to an assault upon the Castle of Loyalty, which the King 'hath most aboundantly given vnto fower maidens' of the court 'to dispose of according to their pleasures'. He explained that the defence of the castle had been placed in the hands of the challengers.[13] Near the castle was to be erected a mount on which would stand a unicorn and four shields representing the four forms of combat that answerers could choose. In their challenge the sixteen defenders of the castle refer to themselves as 'straungers' who have 'departed their farre Countries'. They are thus given a fictional identity, but they also retain an allegorical status as defenders of loyalty and of loyalty to fair womanhood in particular.

It is clear from Hall's *Chronicle* and from the Office of the Revels accounts that a mount, a castle, and a unicorn were duly erec-

ted and that a lengthy assault upon the castle took place (see Fig. 73),[14] but it seems unlikely that the fictional context established when Chasteau Blanche appeared on St Thomas's Day was sustained as the tournament progressed. Henry VIII and Charles Brandon, for example, made a sudden appearance as 'ancient knightes, with beardes of siluer'. They were dressed in robes of blue damask and led by 'twoo ladies on twoo palfries'.[15] In their petition to the Queen, the two men asked permission to fight even though 'youth had left them, and age was come'. From the chronicler's report it would seem that this petition was in no way an extension of the initial allegorical and fictitious context. Instead, the surprise appearance of the two ancient knights and the drama involved when they removed their outer garments and revealed themselves as the King and the Duke of Suffolk created a quite separate fiction. Variety and novelty, one assumes, were valued on this occasion over any desire for artistic unity.

There was a more integrated relationship between challenge and ensuing combat at the Greenwich Christmas celebrations during Edward VI's reign in January 1552. After a tourney on 6 January, a play was put on in the evening and there followed 'talk between one that was called Riches, and the other Youth, whether [one] of them was better'. After some 'pretty reasoning' twelve combatants entered, six for Youth and six for Riches, and a fight at barriers followed.[16] None of the speeches used on this occasion has survived, but presumably either Youth or Riches offered a challenge to the other, the subsequent combat then retaining an allegorical dimension. The use of the debate formula here was very reminiscent of Henry VIII's coronation tournament in 1509.[17] At this event 'a Castle, or a Turret, wrought with fine clothe of Gold: the toppe wherof was spred with Roses and Pomegranates' was carried in. Inside the structure was a woman playing the role of the goddess Pallas Athene, patron of arts and learning. Her armed followers were

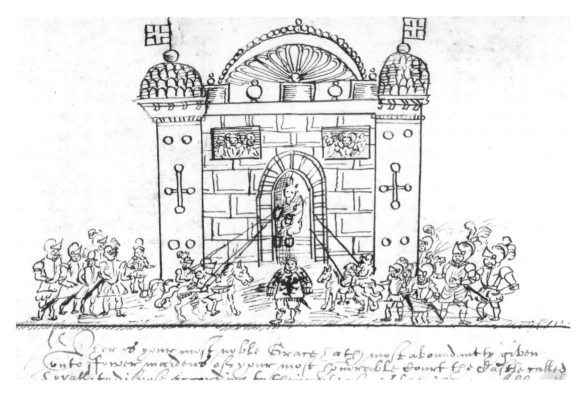

73 *A drawing of the device for the tournament at Christmas 1524–5. The mock castle was built in the lists at Greenwich and surrounded by fences and deep ditches. It was defended by sixteen knights. On its gate was the picture of a unicorn and four shields. Those who wished to respond to the challenge could approach the gate and touch one or more of the shields. The white shield represented a challenge to joust, the red a challenge at tourney, the yellow a challenge at barriers, and the blue a challenge to assault the castle.*

introduced to Henry as the Scholars of Pallas and their challenge to all-comers was accepted by another group of knights representing Arms. The audience was thus presented with an allegorical portrayal of the familiar Renaissance debate between the pen and the sword. On the following day the knights defending Arms declared themselves to be servants of Diana, the virgin goddess of the hunt. They further explained that they had broken off from hunting to fight with Pallas' scholars. This kind of allegorical combat between two

groups, with its pattern of *discordia* moving towards *concordia*, was most highly developed in the Jacobean masque and in certain later related works by Ben Jonson for combats at barriers and tiltings.

Other attempts to preserve the initial fiction of a challenge took various forms. On Sunday, 16 April 1581, four challengers (the Earl of Arundel, Lord Windsor, Philip Sidney and Fulke Greville), calling themselves the Four Foster Children of Desire, sent a boy dressed in the symbolic colours of Desire, red and white, to deliver their challenge to the Queen as she came from chapel. It was an unusual challenge in that it offered to the Queen herself 'the sounde of a defie', whereas challenges were usually issued on her behalf. It announced that nearby were encamped 'foure long haples, now hopeful fostered children of Desire', who maintain that the Fortress of Beauty belongs to them. If the Queen does not yield to them, they will 'besiege that fatal FORTRESSE, vowing not to spare (if this obstinacie continue) the swoorde of faithfulnesse, and the fire of affection'.[18] The challenge then went on to offer combat at tilt and tourney to all the knights of Elizabeth's court.

At the tournament which followed in May, the royal gallery (the Fortress of Beauty) and its occupant, Queen Elizabeth (Beauty), were besieged. As Henry Goldwell explained: 'The Gallary or place at the end of the Tiltyard adioining to her Maiesties house at *Whitehall,* wheras her person should be placed, was called and not without cause, the Castle or *Fortresse of perfect beautie,* for as much as her highnes should be there included, whereto the said Foster children layde Tytle and claime as their due by discent to belong vnto them.'[19] The event had considerable political overtones because Elizabeth was at the time under a very different kind of siege. Vigorous attempts were being made to arrange a marriage between her and the Duc d'Alençon, and the contrived failure of the tiltyard siege was no doubt meant to suggest that Elizabeth was unassailable. She was not about to yield (nor should she) to any French love-siege. If this was the point addressed to the French, the message for Elizabeth was that her Foster Children (her English subjects) wanted her to maintain the status quo i.e. not get married. In many respects this tournament was making the same point as Sidney had made in his famous ill-advised letter, when he urged Elizabeth not to consider marriage with a foreigner; however, the 1581 tiltyard extravaganza was more tactful and it was deliberately ambiguous in what it said. Whatever the Queen may have thought in private, on this occasion she chose not to show any offence.

At this tournament the fictional and thematic framework of the challenge was maintained by the challengers, and the defendants also seem to have followed suit, a key point for those who have argued that the characters and speeches were created by a single author, Philip Sidney being the most likely person.[20] The speeches of the defendants, while developing a separate fiction relating to the disguise and situation of each defender, were none the less direct responses to the central fiction of the initial challenge and the concept of Beauty besieged, with all its political implications.

A similar unity marks the challenge and surviving answers of those who took part in a tournament a few months earlier on 22 January. The challenger was the Earl of Arundel, and, as already mentioned (see p. 93), he took to himself the name Callophisus (Lover of Beauty). For his tiltyard appearance he certainly maintained the role established in his challenge, as can be seen from his surviving entry speech.[21] Arundel's initial challenge exists in the form of a printed broadside, the only surviving copy of which is in the Folger Shakespeare Library. So far as I know, no other challenge was issued in this way. In it Callophisus declared that he was imprisoned 'by the greatest perfection in another' and with his assistant would be 'at the Tilts ende vpon the two and twentie day of Ianuarie next ensewing, at one of the Clocke' to run six courses against all-comers in defence of a series of propositions that he then lists. The propositions all have to do with the beauty and virtues of his mistress, by whom one assumes he means the Queen, especially since he suggests that those who concur with his opinions of his mistress need not be embarrassed by having to fight him 'to defend the contrary against him' but can instead join in combat with him in mutual honour and affection for the lady.

Arundel's challenge was answered by seventeen knights led by the Earl of Oxford, Lord Windsor, and Philip Sidney. These three responded as the White Knight, the Blue Knight, and the Knight of the Tree of the Sun, this last being the Earl of Oxford. The texts of their answers still exist, together with a further speech by Sir William Drury, Arundel's assistant, who styled himself the Red Knight,[22] and they show us how a challenge could spark a verbal combat between participants in their adopted fictional roles even before they entered the tiltyard. In his response the White Knight obviously sought to upstage Callophisus by ignoring the obvious identity of the latter's mistress: 'Vnto vs is Callophisus a mere straunger and his mistress likewise whose name he hath Concealed.' Rather than 'worship an vnknowne sainct', the White Knight will combat Callophisus at the tilt, tourney and barriers in defense of his own 'soueraigne mistres that royall virgine that peereles Prince that Phenix and Paragon of the world whome with all deuoc[i]on I doe serue loue honor and obey in all perfecc[i]ons as farre surpasseth the Concealed ladie as the Clerest daie doeth the darkest night or the fairest flower the fowlest weede'.[23] The White Knight was answered by the Red Knight 'because Callophisus must be better occupied in dischardging of that w[hi]ch he hath most honorable vndertaken'. Rather than be drawn in by the White Knight's deliberate failure to recognize the identity of Callophisus' mistress, the Red Knight merely affirms that Callophisus' loyalty to his mistress is greater than that of anyone else.[24] The remaining two responses by the Blue Knight, who included a drawing of his impresa, and by the Knight of the Tree of the Sun similarly question whether Callophisus' loyalty and devotion can match their own and offer combat on those grounds.

At the tournament itself, we know that at least one of the defendants developed his fictional role yet further. The Earl of Oxford (the Knight of the Tree of the Sun) appeared, as already described in Chapter 3 (see p. 93), in 'rich gilt Armour', and this golden motif was matched by his 'statelie Tent of Orenge tawny Taffata, curiously imbroydered with Siluer, & pendents on the Pinacles'. In addition his staves were 'gilded cleane ouer,' but these props were far surpassed by his 'Sun Tree', a 'great high Bay-tree, the whole stocke, branches and Leaues whereof, were all gilded ouer, that nothing but Gold could be discerned'. Only when his page delivered his speech to the Queen, however, did the full meaning of Oxford's fictional title and scenic attributes emerge. In his wanderings the

knight (Oxford) had met an aged 'Pilgrime or Hermit' who showed him 'a Tree so beautiful, that his eyes were daseled'.

As the speech unfolds, it becomes clear that this 'Tree of the Sunne' represents Elizabeth. It is unique like the Phoenix, and it eclipses all other trees. In an allusion to Elizabeth's virginity, we are told that '*Vestas* bird sitteth in the midst, whereat *Cupid* is euer drawing, but dares not shoote, beeing amazed at that princely and perfect Maiestie'. In the shade of the tree, the knight has found 'such content, as nothing coulde bee more comfortable', and has 'made a sollemne vowe, to incorporate hys harte into that Tree, and ingraft hys thoughts vppon those vertues. Swearing, that as there is but one Sunne to shine ouer it, one roote to giue life vnto it, one toppe to maintaine Maiestie: so there should be but one Knight, eyther to lyue or die for the defence thereof. Where-vppon, hee swore himselfe onely to be the Knight of the Tree of the Sunne, whose life should end before his loyaltie'. The speech then concludes with his assertion that, hearing the measure of his loyalty questioned, he now stands ready 'to die vppon the poynts of a tousande Launces, then to yeeld a iote in constant loyaltie'.[25] Lack of any detailed account of the other defendants' tiltyard speeches and pageants unfortunately makes it impossible for us to know whether the fictions of the responses by Windsor and Sidney and their fellow answerers were also developed with such imaginative fervour, but we can probably assume that they were.

Another type of literary composition that a knight or someone on his behalf might be required to write would be delivered as part of his processional entry into the tiltyard. The example of Callophisus' speech to Elizabeth on 22 January 1581 has just been cited. Speeches, poems or songs of this kind often appear to have accompanied the presentation of a knight's impresa, as was mentioned in the previous chapter. Such an opportunity to address the monarch was one that was responded to in a number of ways. A knight might, for example, simply explain his impresa, as we have seen, or he might confine himself to extravagant praise of the occupant of the royal viewing stand. The ode 'Of Cynthia' is typical of the latter. Published by Francis Davidson in 1602 and probably written by either John Lyly or John Davies, it was sung, according to an accompanying note, 'before her sacred Maiestie' as part of a device presented by the Earl of Cumberland on May Day, not long before its appearance in print.[26]

Th'Ancient Readers of Heauens Booke,
Which with curious eye did looke
Into Natures story;
All things vnder *Cynthia* tooke
To bee transitory.

This the learned only knew,
But now all men finde it true,
Cynthia is descended;
with bright beames, and heauenly hew,
And lesser starres attended.

Landes and Seas shee rules below,
Where things change, and ebbe, and flowe,
Spring, waxe olde, and perish;
Only Time which all doth mowe,
Her alone doth cherish.

Times yong howres attend her still,
And her Eyes and Cheekes do fill,
With fresh youth and beautie:
All her louers olde do grow,
But their hartes, they do not so
In their Loue and duty.

Very similar is the 'song to ye Queene' which may have been part of the Accession Day tournament in November 1602 (the last in Elizabeth's reign), although John Manningham, who recorded the text in his diary, dated the song 2 November and referred to it as deriving from 'the Maske at Court'.[27]

The conventional praise of such poetic tributes, however sincerely meant, cannot have engendered the same degree of interest and curiosity as those speeches accompanying the entry of a knight who had adopted a pseudonym and had put on a disguise in keeping with his assumed role. Where no previous challenge had established the fictional context for such an entry, the speech of the knight or his page was essential to explain the identity that had been assumed and the circumstances that had supposedly brought the knight to the tiltyard. When Charles Brandon entered the Westminster tiltyard on 13 February 1511, for example, he was enclosed in a pageant representing a jail. When the door was unlocked by a jailer, Brandon rode out dressed 'In a long & course prisoners wede wyth a pylgrymms long staff In his hand, and a pylgrymmys hat upon his heed wyth a long & fforgrowyn berd Rechyng to his Sadyll bowe'.[28] Brandon's request for the Queen's licence to participate in the jousting was made in the form of a letter passed to her on the end of his staff. Presumably it explained his fictional circumstances, but unfortunately its precise contents are not known. Other knights then entered in other assumed roles and also presented petitions, but the texts of these have not survived and it is not clear whether these were read out aloud. We do not have the text of an entry speech explaining a knight's fictional identity from the earlier Tudor period, but the frequent earlier use of disguises makes it more than probable that accompanying interpretations (either written or oral) were familiar.

The earliest surviving speeches interpreting a knight's disguise date from the period in the 1570s when the influence of Sir Henry

74 *Portrait of Sir Henry Lee by Antonio Mor (1568). This portrait shows Lee at about the time when, according to his contemporaries, he revived English tournaments and established the tradition of annual Accession Day tournaments. One report claims that he made a vow to appear annually in the tiltyard at Accession Day until 'infirmity, age, or other accident did impeach him'. His ability to participate appears to have lasted until 1590 when he resigned as Queen's Champion.*

Lee (Fig. 74) began to make itself felt. On 11 September 1575, when Queen Elizabeth arrived at Woodstock in the course of her summer progress, she suddenly encountered the spectacle of a fierce combat between two knights on horseback (Loricus and Contarenus). A hermit appeared, and 'at his comming hee caused them to dismount themselues'. This quotation comes from the unique quarto text in the British Library of *The Queenes Majesties Entertainment at Woodstocke* (1585). Unfortunately the first signature of this copy is missing, the text beginning with signature B and a fragmentary sentence containing the words just quoted. What follows is the tale told by the hermit, who explains who the knights are and why they are fighting.

Later George Gascoigne, who was present on this occasion and noted the Queen's interest in the tale, presented the text to her with appended translations in Latin, French and Italian, but the actual author of the tale was almost certainly Sir Henry Lee, the Lieutenant of the Manor of Woodstock, who later developed his entire story yet further in a subsequent entertainment some seventeen years later when Elizabeth visited him at his home at Ditchley in 1592. Significantly, texts of the 'Hermit's Tale' and the later 1592 entertainment are both contained in the so-called Ditchley manuscript in the British Library which contains a great deal of other material probably by Lee.[29] A further link with Lee derives from the use in both texts of the name 'Loricus'. This was Lee's fictional identity at Woodstock and again in the 1592 entertainment when he appeared as an old man now in retirement, one who, he explained, 'sometymes [. . .] consorted with couragious Gentlemen, manifesting inward ioyes by open justes, the yearlie tribute of his dearest Loue'.[30]

Although the circumstances of the recital of the Hermit's Tale do not precisely match those of a tournament presentation speech, it serves a very similar function. It is also related to Lee's other efforts to create an entire romance mythology, not only for court tournaments but for other court entertainments too. This attempt to achieve an ongoing unity can be seen in the text of the 1592 Ditchley event, a work which refers back both to the 1590 tournament at which Lee retired and to the much earlier occasion at Woodstock when Loricus, still very much an active knight at arms, had fought before his mistress.

The 'Hermit's Tale' of 1575 is long and involved. It employs a number of the stock devices of Greek and chivalric romance, including the separate quests of its three protagonists (the two knights, Loricus and Contarenus, and a lady, Gaudina), a tyrannical father's opposition to his daughter's love, the interaction of gods and goddesses, and the suspense and mystery deriving from the riddles posed by oracles and prophecies. Its plot concerns the noble but thwarted love of Contarenus and Gaudina, the hopeless love of Loricus for a matchless lady, and the situation of the hermit, once a 'knight knowne and accounted of' but now blinded by Venus and forced to live in a hermitage on a hill for venturing to enter her temple.

Apollo has told the hermit that he will only recover his sight when 'at one time, and in one place, in a countrie of most peace, two of the most valiant knights shal fight, two of the most constant louers shal meet, and the most vertuous Lady of the world shall be there to looke on. And when thy eyes shal beholde what thy heart delighteth in, euen a Lady in whom inhabiteth the most vertue, Learning, and beauty, that euer yet was in creature, then shal they be opened'.[31] For his part Contarenus has been told by an enchantress that he will not recover Gaudina until he has first fought 'with the hardiest knight' and seen 'the worthiest Lady of the world'. Gaudina and Loricus have been told by a mythical prophetess, the Sibyl, that their situations will not be eased until they have 'found out a place, where men were most stro[n]g, wome[n] most fayre, the countrey most fertile, the people most wealthy, the gouernment most iust, and the Princes most worthy'.[32] With the coming of Queen Elizabeth to Woodstock, as the hermit explains, his sight has been restored, Contarenus and Gaudina have found each other, and Loricus has been freed to pursue his honourable purpose and earn his reputation in the service of his unattainable mistress.

Lee's knight-turned-Hermit is one of the stock figures of chivalric romance and of the English tournament pageants (Fig. 77). As we shall see, Lee introduced the character on a number of occasions in tournaments at Whitehall, and eventually he himself symbolically removed his armour and put on hermit's weeds at his retirement tournament in 1590. However, Lee's use of the figure at Woodstock was by no means new. A century or so before, at a tournament in 1477, Anthony Earl Rivers had entered the tiltyard fully mounted but dressed with a white hermit's cassock over his armour. He and his horse were concealed inside a pageant on the subject of his namesake, Anthony, consisting of a richly-adorned hermitage with black velvet walls and windows made of the finest linen.[33]

In 1501 the Marquis of Dorset also employed a hermitage-like pageant and entered the Westminster tiltyard accompanied by thirty beadsmen and led by a hermit. Ten years later, as has already been mentioned, Charles Brandon entered the same tiltyard in hermit's garb, a motif that he repeated in May 1514, when he and Henry VIII were challengers and presented themselves to the Queen as hermits.[34] Traditionally, as Caxton's translation of Ramon Lull's *Ordre of Chivalry* (printed between 1483 and 1485) makes clear, the elderly knight who has retired to a life of contemplation as a hermit was responsible for advising and instructing novice knights. During his active career in the tiltyard, Lee could and did present himself as the knight advised by a hermit. At his retirement, the roles appropriately became reversed when he became the hermit.

The Hermit in the Woodstock entertainment, once his sight had been restored and Contarenus and Gaudina reunited, acted as wise adviser to Loricus: 'Knight, prosecute thy purpose, it is noble, learning by me not to feare of thy self to take paine: remembring, nothing notable is woon without difficulty, *Hercules* had by his laboures his renowne, and his end by Loue: *Loricus*, thy end wilbe reward, at least most reputation, with noblest women most esteemed.' His tale completed, the elderly hermit then escorted Elizabeth to a kind of latticed bower below an oak tree. Inside this piece of pastoral fantasy was a crescent-shaped table as a compliment to Elizabeth/Diana, and on the walls were various pictures and allegorical verses referring to various members of the court. The hermit left the Queen at the door, and she was then banqueted and entertained by music emanating from an underground room.

Later, the Fairy Queen arrived in a chariot. This was surely one of the most amazing moments in Elizabethan pageantry as, mirror-like, one Fairy Queen confronted the other. It was an event, too, of some consequence to literary history, for the Fairy Queen was here making her first appearance in English literature. Later, during Elizabeth's stay at Woodstock, a play was staged which continued the plot begun in the 'Hermit's Tale'. Gaudina's father, Duke Occanon, comes in search of her. She is his only child and hence is heir to his dukedom. Now she has to choose between her love for the humbly-born Contarenus and her duty to her father and her country. After what is clearly intended as an agonizing debate between the conflicting claims of love and duty, Gaudina and Contarenus both yield, with some prompting from the Fairy Queen, to the call of duty, and Gaudina parts from Contarenus.

At Kenilworth earlier in Elizabeth's progress, the Queen had been entertained by the Earl of Leicester in a show that depicted her as King Arthur returned and Leicester as the guardian of Arthur's castle. The whole gist of the entertainment was that, through marriage, Leicester and Elizabeth could bring about a renewal of the Arthurian golden age.

A second show, probably by George Gascoigne, had been planned but it was never performed. This was ostensibly because of bad weather, but probably because the show urged the virtues of marriage over virginity and would have added to Elizabeth's displeasure over the first entertainment.[36]

Lee's Woodstock entertainment, however, urged a quite contrary course. His implying that personal desires should be subjected to the interests of the State, we are told, pleased Elizabeth, who asked for a copy of the text. She and her ladies also seem to have found the show extremely moving: 'it was as well thought of, as anye thing euer done before her Maiestie, not onely of her, but of the rest.'[37] But if there was a message in all this for the Queen, there was also one for her courtiers. Inherent in the fates of Loricus, Hermetes and Contarenus is the suggestion that the lovers of Elizabeth should serve their mistress to their utmost. However, they must recognize that their service is its own reward; they will be recompensed by their ensuing honour and reputation, but with nothing more. The fiction of the jousting knights, Loricus and Contarenus, was thus more than playful fantasy. Lee and others fully understood the potential of such devices and explanatory speeches as a means of conveying their concerns and point of view to the most important member of the audience at a tournament, as is clear from some of the following examples.

The Arcadian mixture of Greek and chivalric romance established by Lee at Woodstock in 1575 was echoed repeatedly in subsequent tournaments. Nowhere is this more apparent than in the imagery and fictions of the entry speeches and songs that introduced a whole panoply of characters, many of whom seem to have stepped straight from the pages of some chivalric romance. There are Hermits, Wandering Knights, Stranger Knights and Unknown Knights, a Frozen Knight, a Blind Knight, a Restless Knight, a Clownishly Clad Knight, a Black Knight, an Enchanted Knight, a Disenchan-

ted Knight, and an Indian Prince. There are also knights with such names as Loricus (Lee), Philisides (Sidney), Callophisus (Arundel), the Knight of Pendragon Castle (Cumberland), the Red Knight (Drury), and Meliades (Prince Henry).

In November 1577, two years after Lee's Woodstock entertainment, Sidney, who had probably been present at Woodstock,[38] appeared in the Whitehall tiltyard on Accession Day as 'Philisides, the Shepherd good and true' (see p. 128 and Fig. 75). The name was obviously a barely-disguised version of his own, but it may also have alluded to his love for Penelope Devereux (assuming that he had met her by this date), since it could be taken to mean 'lover of a star',[39] an anticipation of his later use of the name Astrophel in his great sonnet sequence on his love for Penelope.[40] When Sidney entered the tiltyard in 1577, he was attended by a group of ploughmen, and his progress along the length of the tilt barrier was accompanied by the sound of 'rusticall musick'. When he arrived in front of the gallery, one of the ploughmen recited the poem 'Philisides, the Shepherd good and true'. It tells how Philisides, the shepherd, called upon Menalcha, the husbandman, to persuade him to set aside his plough in order to celebrate the forthcoming Accession Day ('the chief of Cupides Saboathe daies').[41] The ploughman's recital was followed by a song ('Singe neighbours singe') in praise of Elizabeth that probably accompanied the presentation of Sidney's impresa, a picture of a harrow with the motto '*Nec habent occulta sepulchra*' ('Graves have no secrets' or 'Secrets cannot be hidden').[42]

This may have been Sidney's first appearance at an English tournament.[43] Aged twenty-three, popular, ambitious, and with a certain amount of experience following his recent service with his father in Ireland and on an important European mission for Elizabeth, his dramatic entry into the tiltyard would have provided him with the perfect 'coming out' before the thousands of onlookers who thronged the Whitehall viewing stands. For the first time, also, he could demonstrate his martial prowess in the very best of company, his fellow challengers being the Earl of Arundel, Lord Windsor, and Sidney's close friend, Fulke Greville. Among the defendants was Sir Henry Lee, a seasoned veteran in the tiltyard, against whom Sidney fought his second set of courses. Unfortunately, the poems (the two just mentioned and a third to be discussed below), the impresa descriptions that accompany them in the Ottley manuscripts, the brief note on Philisides' entry in the same source, and the heralds' score cheque are all that survive of the occasion, but it is sufficient, I feel, to show that from the very beginning Sidney understood the full political potential of the tournament and accompanying speeches. On this occasion he used the opportunity to offer himself to Elizabeth as her good shepherd. Later, as already mentioned, he was to use a tournament in an attempt to influence Elizabeth in her deliberations concerning the vital question of a French marriage.

A few years after his appearance at Whitehall as Philisides, Sidney incorporated a self-portrait under this same fictional name in the revised *Arcadia* (Fig. 76). In his description of the Iberian jousts, he had an Iberian knight called Philisides enter the tiltyard to the sound of bagpipes rather than the more customary trumpets, thereby creating an equivalent for the 'rusticall musicke' he had used at Whitehall. The knight's page was a shepherd boy. His retainers were dressed as shepherds, who then sang an eclogue, and his lances, carried as was customary by his retainers, were made to look like shepherds' crooks. Philisides himself was 'drest over with wooll' and 'enriched with Jewels'. Like Sidney at Whitehall, he carried a suitably pastoral impresa, a picture of 'a sheepe marked with pitch, with this word *Spotted to be knowne*'.[44] Philisides' opponent was Lelius, an older and more experienced jouster ('knowne to be second to none in the perfection of that Art'),[45] an obvious allusion to Sir Henry Lee, one of Sidney's opponents at Whitehall.[46]

For Sidney, the fictional fantasies of the romance world of the Iberian tournament were clearly very close to the actual practices of his own day. Indeed, when placed against

75 Portrait of Sir Philip Sidney by an unknown artist (c. 1576). Shortly after this portrait was painted, Sidney made his first appearance at a tournament. Subsequent appearances were colourful and dramatic and did much to encourage the use of tiltyard pageants and impresas as a means of glorifying Elizabeth while at the same time enhancing a participant's public image.

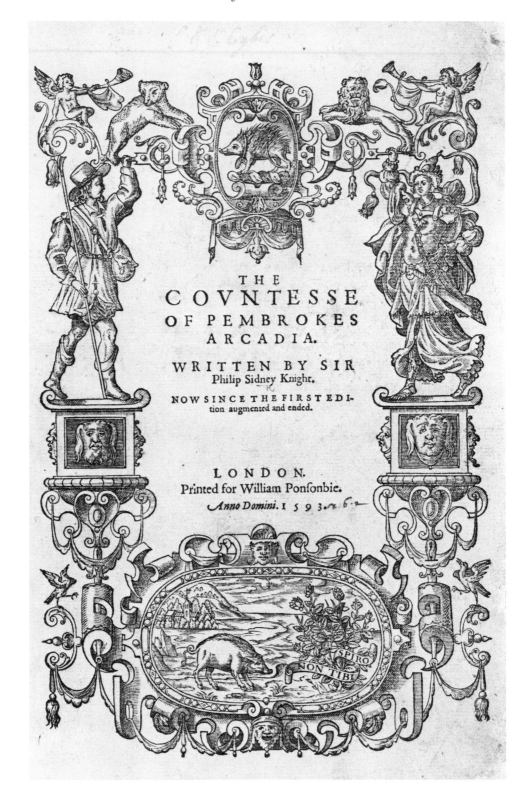

THE
COVNTESSE
OF PEMBROKES
ARCADIA.

WRITTEN BY SIR
Philip Sidney Knight.

NOW SINCE THE FIRST EDI-
tion augmented and ended.

LONDON.
Printed for William Ponsonbie.
Anno Domini. 1 5 9 3.

SPIRO
NON TIBI

the list of fictional characters who actually appeared at the Elizabethan tournaments, those in the *Arcadia* offer few surprises—a wild man covered in leaves; a knight with a completely blank shield; a knight who rose from within a burning phoenix; and a frozen knight. Sidney's use of the name Philisides for his pastoral persona appears to have caught on with his contemporaries, for it was by this name that Sidney was memorialized by many of them after his death.

The full significance of Sidney's fictional name makes it clear that his assumed role in the 1577 tournament and his accompanying poem were no mere playful exercises. By 1577 Sidney had already begun to see himself as the self-appointed saviour knight of Protestantism. This image was cultivated by Sidney, his friends and his relatives, and it was strengthened by his successive appearances in the tiltyard, by his daring (perhaps rash) opposition to Elizabeth's possible marriage to a foreigner, and by his ultimate sacrifice at Zutphen in the service of the Protestant cause. The image of the shepherd in this connection linked both nationalist and religious ideals, for Sidney saw himself as the protector of his mistress's business, that mistress being head of both State and Church. The shepherd in this context faithfully preserved 'his charges against any dangerous and popish wolf, risking his life for any helpless ones who strayed. And, too, he represented the poten-

tial purity of the country against the possible corruption of the court'.[47] The seemingly playful evocation of the pastoral world that occurred when Philisides first entered the Whitehall tiltyard thus had a serious underlying intent. Something of significance was being said, and I think we may assume that Sidney's contemporaries were aware of it.

It was probably at the same tournament at which he first used the name Philisides that Sidney also appeared as a 'desert knighte', or one who had come from a deserted and uncultivated land, his armour covered in 'barke & mosse of faded tree', his impresa a tree with the motto '*Hoc ordine fata*' (Such is the course of Heaven). The poem explaining his situation was 'inclosd in a tre sealed w[i]th a grene leaf' and it was addressed to the 'Sainte of the saboath', an epithet that provided a link with the 'Philisides' poem and the song which followed it, in which Elizabeth is described as a saint and her Accession Day as being on the sabbath. One half of the tree on Sidney's impresa was verdant, the other half dying, suggesting that his fortunes were in the balance. All now depended upon what his motto refers to as 'ye co[u]rse of Heavens' (*Hoc ordine fata*), an obvious allusion to Elizabeth herself.

Sidney's choice of imagery for this second entry was apt. In the past two years, as already noted, he had been in Ireland to visit his father, who was Lord Deputy there, and more recently he had visited various European states as Elizabeth's emissary, ostensibly to convey her condolences following the death of the Emperor Maximilian, but also to report on the possibilities for the formation of a Protestant League. Somewhat to his annoyance, Elizabeth felt that he had exceeded the bounds of his mandate, and he had been summoned home earlier than he would have chosen.[48] What is more, official recognition failed to follow. Indeed, it was not until the autumn of 1585 that Elizabeth was to give Sidney any significant position at court or any crown business of consequence. We have benefited from Sidney's enforced

76 *Title-page of Sidney's* Arcadia. *Sidney's revised version of* Arcadia, *which includes some elaborate descriptions of tournaments and knightly combat, was published posthumously and was one of the most popular books of its day. In it he included a fictionalized account of a tournament (probably that in November 1577) in which he jousted against Sir Henry Lee. Sidney was famous for his impresas. A number are in the* Arcadia, *and the title-page includes one that is the invention of the editor. It humorously implies that those of coarse tastes will not enjoy the book (as in the proverb: 'It is folly to strew roses among swine').*

semi-retirement, since it provided the necessary leisure for his excursions into literary composition.

The 'desert knighte', according to his accompanying entry poem, had been 'Waynd [i.e. 'weaned' or 'alienated'] from the hope w[hi]ch made affection glad,' and he had been 'in deserts'. This last phrase was a pun referring both to Sidney's absence in foreign parts and to his being in past receipt of favour:[49]

Waynd from the hope w[hi]ch made affection
   glad
to show it self in himnes of delight
yet highly pleasd w[i]th those conceipts I had
made me in deserts grow a desert knighte . . .

The poem goes on to say how, having heard of the approaching Accession Day celebrations, he has come joyfully to participate. As befitting 'a desert knighte', his armour is of 'barke & mosse of faded tree', and his lances are 'wild poles'. As with the shepherd-knight motif, Sidney's use of the fiction of 'the desert knighte' and the accompanying impresa comparing himself to a tree only half in leaf is no mere playful romance fiction. It has an underlying serious purport directly alluding to his own situation at a particular moment in his career. Thus, as with many of the impresas discussed in the preceding chapter, there is a surprisingly close relationship here between fancy and the reality involved.

It is generally believed that Sidney was probably the author of the texts for the tournament in May 1581, at which the Four Foster Children of Desire besieged the Fortress of Beauty. For this topical moral discourse on the inviolate nature of Elizabeth's situation as monarch, woman, and symbol of virtue and beauty, Sidney (assuming that he was the author) composed not only the challenge and the teasingly ambiguous impresa *Sic Nos Non Nobis* (Ours But Not For Us), but also the various speeches and songs presented in the tiltyard. After the four challengers had entered the lists in great splendour, the same boy who had

some time before delivered the challenge to the Queen as she came from church offered her the opportunity to yield. She of course refused, at which point a 'Rowlling trench or Mounte of earth was mooued as nere the Queen's Maiestie as might be'.[50] A song was then sung to the Queen by a boy accompanied by cornets ('Yeelde yeelde O yeelde, you that this FORTE do holde'), and when that was ended another boy sang to the challengers ('Allarme allarme, here will no yeelding be').[51] The challengers' attack then followed, involving the shooting of sweet powder and water, 'very odoriferous and pleasant', the throwing of flowers against the gallery walls, and a 'verie excellent consert of mellodie within the Mounte'.[52]

The defendants then entered the tiltyard and six of the speeches they made have been preserved. These show clearly how the central theme of Beauty besieged with all its topical ambiguities was sustained through a series of highly elaborate variations over the two days during which the event lasted. Thus, Sir Thomas Parrott and Anthony Cook entered the tiltyard in armour 'beset, with apples and fruite'. Parrott represented Adam, and Cook, who 'had haire hung all down his Helmet', was Eve. Their page was dressed as an Angel, who explained that a certain Frozen Knight, observing that the Sun (Elizabeth) was besieged, had died. Once in the Elysian Fields, the Frozen Knight had complained bitterly about the arrogance of humankind and the folly of such an attack on the Sun. Hearing his cries, the gods have sent down Adam and Eve, the parents of the human race, to correct their foolish offspring. The Angel then addressed the challengers: 'Will you subdue the sunne, who shal rest in the shadow where the weary take breath, the disquiet rest, and all comforte?' The Angel urges the knights to desist from an impossible task, comparing their pride to that of the giants Otus and Ephialtes, who attempted to usurp the gods by scaling Olympus, and to the doomed 'soaring' of Icarus and Phaethon, and he then throws down a gauntlet as Adam and Eve's challenge in defence of Beauty (Sun/Elizabeth), 'the lighte of the worlde, the maruell of men, the mirour of nature'.

The eloquence, imagery, and one might even say grandeur of this speech strike a new note in English tournament literature, making it especially tempting to think of it as the work of Sidney. Apart from its intrinsic literary merit, however, the speech is striking for its appeal to and concept of divine order. Were Elizabeth to marry, and especially were she to marry a foreigner, it is implied, that order would be shattered as surely as it was when Adam and Eve fell to temptation. As Sidney was aware, Elizabeth had indeed been tempted by the prospect of marriage. Little wonder that Sidney's sonnet in *Astrophel and Stella* describing the first day of the tournament refers to the presence among the onlookers of those sent by 'that sweet enemy France'.[53]

Other speeches then followed. When Thomas Ratcliffe arrived before the Queen his page explained that the knight, 'always crossed by fortune', had sought refuge in solitude and had spent a long time by the seashore in a mossy cave where his chief sustenance had been moss and where in time he lost his memory. One morning he had come upon some men 'either cast away by shipwrake, or cast ouer-borde by Pyrattes'. Their leader was dead but had been carrying 'a scrowle containing a claime, a challenge, nay a conquest of BEAWTIE'. At this his memory gradually returned:

O Beawtie where thy Fortresse is founded I know, but what these brethren should mean I maruaile, for as I am assured that to winne thee none could be so fortunate, so did I thinke that to claime thee none coulde be so fond, when as thou O divine BEAWTIE art of euery one to be desired, but neuer to be conquered of DESIRE.

Roused from his melancholy, the knight has come to Whitehall to take up the challenge, his shield hewn 'out of the hard cliffe enriched onely with soft mosse'. One must assume that Ratcliffe's costume, in keeping with the page's narrative, was suitably 'mossie'. He represented the knight maddened by love who become a wildman, like his fellows in Malory and Spenser.

Ratcliffe was followed by Sir Francis Knollys' four sons, all cousins of Elizabeth, and all dressed in matching armour. The covert theme of the tournament was barely disguised when the page who spoke to the Queen on their behalf stated: 'O rare & most renowmed BEAWTIE, O goddes to be honored of all, not to be equalled of any, become not nowe a prisoner, your FORTRESSE in inuincible' (sig. B vib). The French visitors at Whitehall, who included the Prince Dauphin of Auvergne and others, could hardly have missed the almost blatant topicality of such sentiments. That Elizabeth herself chose to ignore them says much for her political acumen. To protest too much would have strengthened the hand of her French wooer, whereas her strategy at this stage of the negotiations appears to have been to keep everyone in a state of uncertainty. Some form of alliance with France was necessary, given the threat from Spain, though secretly she no longer wished for an alliance through marriage.

Other speeches are recorded by Goldwell. The boy who had first delivered the challenge spoke at the end of the first day, and a Herald spoke at the opening of the second when the challengers entered in a magnificent chariot accompanied by 'a beautiful Lady, representing Desire'. The Herald explained that the Foster Children were now virtually without hope, but wished Elizabeth to watch their combat. Finally, when tourney and barriers were over, a boy dressed in ash-coloured clothes came to the Queen carrying an olive branch. He reported the submission of the challengers, who now acknowledged that Desire had been defeated by the defenders of the Fortress of Beauty. The central fiction with all its accompanying political overtones first established in the challenge was thus maintained throughout the entire two-day event, and throughout all the succeeding speeches. Although this was not the last occasion at which Sidney appeared in the tiltyard, it was the last tournament for which texts survive that can be associated with his name. Had he lived longer, his literary skills and political ambitions combined with an imagination ideally suited to the extravagant excesses of tiltyard entertainments would no doubt have left a greater imprint.

If the career of Sidney as a deviser of tiltyard entertainments was short-lived, that of Sir Henry Lee appears to have spanned more than two decades. It was probably Lee who wrote the speech given by Arundel's page when he presented Elizabeth with the Earl's impresa in January 1581. Also probably by Lee is a sonnet on behalf of a Blind Knight which is dated 17 November 1584. Both speeches appear in that rich collection of materials associated with Lee, the so-called Ditchley Manuscript (see footnote 29). The Blind Knight's sonnet uses the same fiction as that attached to the Hermit at Woodstock. In this case, not only is the knight blind in the Queen's presence but his page has been struck dumb, and it is not clear whether the sonnet was read aloud by another or merely handed to Elizabeth to read. As with the Woodstock Hermit, the Queen's presence has of course the power to cure:[54]

This Knight made blynd, & I made dombe you
    see
proue thus thy power, of sweet receauinge smarts
but sith to vertue grace doth more agree,
now helpe our happs, thou m[istr]es of o[u]r harts.

Whether the Blind Knight was Lee's role for the occasion is not clear, but certainly the rather simple design, which lacks the kind of political complexity of Sidney's work, seems much more in keeping with the general tenor of Lee's inventions, quite apart from the anti-Leicester undertones of the Woodstock entertainment.

Immediately following this sonnet in the Ditchley manuscript, and for this reason perhaps related to the same tournament, is a speech on behalf of some Wandering Knights and the Black Knight (now in 'new habite'). What is particularly striking about this speech is the author's clear attempt to create continuity between successive tournaments. The Black Knight, we learn, was present at the previous year's tilting, but the Wandering Knights were not. Since that time, the Black Knight has been in solitude and has consulted with an old hermit (this figure again!) who has directed him to bring the Wandering Knights to the current tournament.[55] Without being certain of the date of the speech, we cannot know the identity of the Wandering Knights, but it may be significant that Lee was present in both 1583 and 1584, whereas Sidney, having incurred Elizabeth's displeasure for his marriage to Frances Walsingham, was absent at the earlier event. Was he, one wonders, one of the Wandering Knights?

Equally difficult to date, but very much in character, it seems to me, with the other examples that appear to be by Lee are several other extant speeches in the Ditchley manuscript. First is a speech to Queen Elizabeth by a Hermit on behalf of a 'clowneshly clad' knight and his rustic companions (it is tempting to think of Philisides and his ploughmen). The countrymen cannot participate in the jousting because they are not of gentle birth; however, they would like to demonstrate their prowess, perhaps at the quintain (see p. 102). The knight, reminiscent of the Loricus of the Woodstock entertainment, has fallen in love with a precious but unobtainable jewel at court, but he has been forced to retire to the country. There he has since remembered the 'vowe he had made, w[hi]che was whilest he cold sett on a horse, & carye a staff in his hand, to sacrefice yearly the strength of his arme, in honor of her that was m[is]tress of his hart' on the occasion of the 'holidaye wich passed all the popes holidayes, & that shold be kepte the Seavente[en]th daye of Nouember'.[56] The vow identifies the knight

as Lee, but it is impossible to assign any particular year to the speech, though clearly it was used when the Accession Day tournaments had already become established as a regular annual event.

More fanciful as a fiction is the group of speeches for a tilt and tourney spoken by a Priestess of the Temple of Peace. The Priestess introduces two knights, one who follows desire and innocence, and the other truth and constancy.[57] The knights have fallen out on their way to the Temple of Peace

77 Hermit instructing a squire. It was traditional in the chivalric romances for knights to be instructed by old hermits, themselves often former knights. Ramon Lull's widely-read treatise on chivalry, published in England by Caxton as The Book of the Ordre of Chivalry or Knyghthode *(c. 1484), was set out as a treatise presented by an old knight turned hermit to a young squire about to be knighted. The scene depicted here comes from a fifteenth-century manuscript version of Lull's work.*

and have been denied entry as a consequence until they have done a suitable penance. This penance is to visit the island of Terra Benedicta (Britain), which is ruled by a princess, the greatest friend to peace in the world. In Terra Benedicta, so the knights are told, they will find an altar consecrated to peace (probably there was some structure in the tiltyard to represent this), and there they will be permitted 'to ronne six courses with the launce, and to have tenne blowes with the sword'.[58] The knights then presented their impresa shields.

The jousting followed and then another short speech, and the next day, after the tourney, there was a further speech promising the knights entry into the temple. Since each knight had originally entered the tiltyard with an equal number of armed followers, it may be that the two groups made up the entire number of tournament participants. If this was so, a single fiction would have governed the entire event, as happened in May 1581. There does not seem to be any means of dating the Temple of Peace tournament, but it may have been part of the Armada victory celebrations in November 1588, when a two-day tournament was held. The subject of peace would have been appropriate, but the dispute between the two knights does not seem particularly relevant.

The final undated tournament speech in the Ditchley manuscript is the 'message of the damsell of the Q[ueen] of fayres' on behalf of an enchanted knight, who, because of his enchantment, has been unable to participate adequately in Elizabeth's Accession Day tournament when it was held 'not far hence'.[59] The speech is thus not a tournament speech proper but appears to create a fiction after the event to explain a particular knight's situation. Apparently he did appear in the lists but 'was nyther able to charge staffe nor stricke blowe'. None the less he 'was content to byde the brunt of the strongest knight, & the blowes of the sturdiest staues'. To show his love, the knight presents Elizabeth with a golden cupid which he hopes she will choose to wear, leading one to think that the speech was perhaps made when Elizabeth received her New Year's gifts at Greenwich ('not far hence' from Whitehall).

The use of the Fairy Queen's 'damsell' to speak on behalf of the knight harks back to the first appearance of the Fairy Queen at Woodstock; however, it is possible that this speech was written by Lee very much later on behalf of the Earl of Cumberland for the last tournament in Elizabeth's reign in November 1602. Although we can only speculate about this, it is a striking coincidence that Cumberland wrote on three occasions to Sir Robert Cecil in October 1602 asking to be excused from the coming tournament and explaining that he had injured his arm in a fall from his horse and would be unable to carry a tilting stave. He did say, however, that if necessary he would be 'ready to ride alongst the tilt, though I can do no more'.[60] The surviving score cheques for the event show that Cumberland's attempts to excuse himself were unavailing, and he ran on both 17 and 20 November, though whether he actually ran without a stave is not recorded.

Unfortunately this rich material is largely undatable, but there are some compositions for tournaments in the Ditchley manuscript that can be assigned a specific date. The 'rem[em]brance of Sir Ph: Sidnie Knight the 17th Nou[em]ber 1586' has already been noted in the previous chapter. In addition there is material, probably by Sir Henry Lee, for his retirement tilt in 1590 and a speech for the introduction of his relative in 1597.

The best description of the 1590 tournament, at which Lee surrendered his office as Queen's Champion and put forward the Earl of Cumberland as his successor, is contained in George Peele's *Polyhymnia*. Apart from describing Lee's entrance, his dress and his caparison decorated with crowns and a withered vine ('As who would say, My spring of youth is past'), Peele has some thirty-four lines describing the resignation ceremony. To these he added some verses that are now generally ascribed to Lee and appear to have been part of the ceremony, although Peele does not explain their role. For this we must turn to another description of the event, that of William Segar in *Honour, Militarie and Ciuil* (1602). Segar's description of Lee's device of the Temple of the Vestals has already been described (see p. 100). Before this temple stood a crowned pillar 'embraced by an Eglantine tree', and hanging upon the pillar was a Latin poem, which is included by Segar. The poem is a hymn in praise of Elizabeth, the crowned Vestal Virgin, and of her Empire, which extends beyond the Columns of Hercules to the New World. The temple, the eglantine, and the column were all three part of the elaborate symbolism relating to Elizabeth. The temple is part of her representation as Vestal Virgin, and the eglantine, a single white rose, is emblematic of her chastity. The pillar is a version of Emperor Charles V's impresa of the two pillars of Hercules with the motto *Plus Ultra*, an expression of his imperialist ventures in the New World. As applied to Elizabeth, the crowned pillar is representative of her power and military might and after the defeat of the Spanish Armada it appears in a number of engravings of the Queen.[61] The column also represented Elizabeth's constancy and fortitude, in keeping with her favourite motto '*Semper Eadem*' (Always the same), but in Lee's version it seems intended to refer also to his own constancy in serving her.

The sudden appearance of the temple and the crowned column encircled by eglantine was, so Segar tells us, accompanied by music and by a song sung by the royal lutenist Robert Hales, the verses of which Peele appended to his *Polyhymnia*. In the version in Segar the song is in the first person, giving it an immediacy and intimate appeal unusual for tiltyard presentations. Because they were given by third parties (usually the knight's page), such verses were nearly always in the third person. Other surviving versions of the poem, which was set to music by John

Dowland and has as a result achieved a fame quite separate from its original context, are in the third person.[62]

My golden locks time hath to siluer turnd,
(Oh time too swift, and swiftnes neuer ceasing)
My youth gainst age, and age at youth hath spurnd.
But spurnd in vaine, youth waineth by encreasing.
Beauty, strength, and youth, flowers fading beene,
Duety, faith and loue, are rootes and euer greene.
My Helmet now shall make an hiue for Bees,
And louers songs shall turne to holy Psalmes:
A man at Armes must now sit on his knees,
And feed on pray'rs, that are old ages almes.
And so from Court to Cottage I depart,
My Saint is sure of mine vnspotted hart.

And when I sadly sit in homely Cell,
I'le teach my Swaines this Carrol for a song,
Blest be the hearts that thinke my Souereigne well,
Curs'd be the soules that thinke to doe her wrong.
Goddesse, vouchsafe this aged man his right,
To be your Beadsman now, that was your Knight!

Those who had followed Lee's career, Elizabeth among them, would have perceived from Lee's presentation that Loricus (Lee), once advised some fifteen years earlier by a hermit at Woodstock, had now himself (at the age of 47) become a venerable and aged hermit. Yet this was by no means the end of Lee's use of the conceit of the knight turned beadsman. As already described, when Elizabeth visited him at Ditchley two years later, Lee presented an entertainment which returned to the story of Loricus that had so pleased Elizabeth in 1575.[63] Having retired to the country, Loricus has erected a 'Crowne Oratory', at the entrance of which he has placed his device on a pillar. Though he is near to death, the Queen's presence miraculously restores him—yet one more reiteration of the symbolic royal power to heal the sick.[64]

The elaborate entertainment of the Ditchley show ended with Loricus signing his will 'Loricus, Columnae coronatae Custos fidelissimus' (Loricus, the most faithful guardian of the crowned pillar). Everything, of course, harks back to the crowns on his caparison in the 1590 tilt and the crowned pillar before the Temple of the Vestals. The Ditchley entertainment makes many other references to the Woodstock entertainment, most notably in its allusion to the Fairy Queen, in the pictures containing riddles in the banqueting house, and in the 'Justes and feates of Armed Knightes'. In this way Lee managed to create a remarkable display of sustained imagery spread over seventeen years and divided among three major entertainments.

In addition to Lee's verses in Segar, there exist some verses which may have been used, not in the resignation ceremony which followed the tilting in 1590, but when Lee first entered the tiltyard on that occasion. They are to be found in John Dowland's *Second Booke of Songs or Ayres* (1600) and also inscribed in a copy of a book owned by the Oxford musician John Lilliat.[65] The latter version attributes the verses to Lee 'In yeelding vp his Tilt staff'. The central theme of the verses concerns the elderly knight turned hermit who continues to serve Elizabeth by substituting thanks and prayers for his previous shows, masks, and jousts. Much of the poem is directed towards praising Elizabeth, who is accorded a status identical or surpassing that of the Virgin Mary in the third stanza. In Lilliat's original, the three stanzas of Dowland's song ('Tymes eldest sonne') are followed by the last six lines of 'My Golden lockes', although here transposed to the second person. It is not clear how the two poems became conflated. One can only assume that Lilliat took his copy from Dowland and, having either Peele's or Segar's version of the other poem, added the extra stanza.

Lee made one further contribution to English tournament literature some time after his retirement as Queen's Champion, when he addressed those planning to participate in an Accession Day tournament on behalf of his 'only sonne'.[66] Describing himself as 'a pore faythfull, feble knight, yet once (thoe

vnworthie) yo[ur] fellowe in arme[s] & first celibrator in this kynd of this sacred memorie of tha[t] blessed rayne', and as one who has been disabled by age and has turned 'from a staffe to rune with, to a staffe to rest one', Lee asked the assembly to accept into their fellowship his young 'sonne.' Whether he is using the word 'sonne' literally is not completely clear; however, it is known that a John Lee (died 1609), probably the illegitimate son of Cromwell Lee (Henry's brother), appeared at the Accession Day tournament on 17 November 1597.[67]

Apart from the speech given by the 'damsell' of the Fairy Queen, which I have suggested may have been written in 1602 for the Earl of Cumberland, the 1597 speech in effect concludes Lee's long career as a deviser of tiltyard speeches. Except for the Woodstock entertainment, Lee's work seems to have avoided the kind of direct and potentially controversial topical subject-matter so characteristic of Sidney. Instead, Lee developed a sustained glorification of his Queen, using many of the images central in the cult of Elizabeth: Cynthia, Fairy Queen, Vestal Virgin, Virgin Mary, the 'Best flower of flowers, that growes both red and white',[68] and the miraculous healer of the blind and dumb. Drawing upon the ideal of service familiar from chivalric romance, he developed an elaborate fantasy around himself. He was first the faithful knight and then the devout hermit, willing to sacrifice all in service and worship of his mistress, whom he addresses as beautiful and chaste woman, queen, and goddess. No one did more than Lee by way of example and organizing influence to establish the essential character of the Elizabethan tournament. Incongruous as it may seem in purely literary terms, he is only matched by Ben Jonson, who dominates the final phase of the English tournament. Between the work of these two figures, however, stand the contributions of two of Elizabeth's greatest devotees to chivalry and the cult of Elizabeth—the Earl of Cumberland and the Earl of Essex.

━━◄ *VII* ►━━

Apt Words Have Power

HE SAME ROMANTIC imagery that characterizes Lee's work appears in the surviving speeches of the Earl of Cumberland, his successor as Queen's Champion (Fig. 78). When Cumberland entered the tiltyard in 1590, he already knew of his forthcoming appointment, and for this important occasion he appeared as the Knight of Pendragon Castle riding upon a pageant car representing the castle. He was attended by the magician Merlin and possibly by Uther Pendragon, the legendary father of King Arthur. The name 'Pendragon' derived from one of Cumberland's ancient family strongholds in Westmoreland.

When Merlin delivered Cumberland's speech to Elizabeth, he spoke of the founding of Pendragon, his account apparently modelled on the legendary story of the building of the fortress of King Vortigern, the ancient British king who ruled from Wales to the southeast of Britain in AD 425. According to Geoffrey of Monmouth's *Historia Regum Britanniae*, when this building was under construction it kept sinking from sight and supposedly could only be completed if sprinkled with the blood of a fatherless boy. When the boy was found, he turned out to be the prophet Merlin, who revealed that the real reason for the problem was the presence below ground of two fighting dragons, one white and one red (see Fig. 79).

Cumberland's speech retells this familiar legend and explains that the castle was completed once the two dragons had ended their combat.[1] The corresponding section in Geoffrey of Monmouth's history leads into a long list of the weeping Merlin's prophecies, a text familiar to the Tudors, who, so their supporters liked to claim, were descended lineally from Cadwallader, the last British king. Henry VII's accession, according to the more enthusiastic of his contemporaries (particularly his Welsh supporters), marked the beginning of a new period of British triumphs, a kind of second Arthurian golden age in fulfilment of the prophecies made to King Vortigern.

Henry must have had this in mind when he christened his first son Arthur, having chosen Winchester (noted for its Arthurian connections and the Round Table in the Great Hall) as his birthplace in 1486. The year before, he had marched to Bosworth with a banner displaying a fiery red dragon upon a background field of white and green. At his entry into London (see pp. 24/5), the banner was also conspicuously present, and when his Queen was crowned a year later the river procession included a Bachelors' Barge made to appear like a red dragon spouting fire into the River Thames. The dragon features conspicuously on the parapet of St George's Chapel, Windsor, in keeping with the fact that Henry

LEFT

78 *The Earl of Cumberland's Greenwich armour, now in the Metropolitan Museum (New York), is the most complete of all surviving Elizabethan armours and includes a second helmet and plates for an armoured saddle.*

ABOVE

79 *Combat between the Red and White Dragons. When the legendary Vortigern attempted to build a castle, it kept falling down. A clairvoyant boy with prophetic powers (Merlin) told him to drain the pool beneath its foundations; when this was done, a red and a white dragon were discovered. They fought each other, the white conquering the red. The boy explained that this foretold the Saxon victory over the British. The revival of the Red Dragon, a heraldic badge of Henry VII, was part of the Tudor mythology linking the new dynasty with King Arthur.*

used the red dragon as the dexter supporter for his coat of arms. Significantly, it was Henry who created a new pursuivant named Rouge Dragon. What had been a symbol of both Uther Pendragon and Arthur had become an important heraldic emblem, representative of both the Tudors' Arthurian and Welsh connections.[2]

Henry VIII, whose martial prowess frequently led to comparisons with Arthur, had the dragon emblem prominently displayed in his contributions to King's College Chapel, Cambridge. Similarly, combining Tudor and Arthurian motifs, he had the great Round Table at Winchester repainted with a Tudor rose in the centre surrounded by the dominant Tudor colours of green and white. When he entertained Francis I at the Field of Cloth of Gold and the young Emperor Charles V in Calais shortly after, Henry carefully included symbolic reminders of his Arthurian connection.³ Two years later, when Charles V came to London, one of the pageants for his processional entry with Henry into the city showed King Arthur sitting at the Round Table inside a palace, attended by the Kings of Wales, Scotland and Ireland, Norway, Denmark and Iceland.⁴

At first sight it would thus appear that Cumberland's fictional role and use of a familiar pattern of motifs was not only meant to evoke patriotic echoes, but was also intended to present him as a kind of second Arthur in service of Elizabeth. This was perhaps a rather dignified way of alluding to his own series of privateering expeditions against the Spanish since 1586, his major role in the battle against the Spanish Armada, and his future office as Queen's Champion. Since Elizabeth herself was more properly to be perceived as the 'Arthur' figure according to Tudor mythology, Cumberland's portrayal of himself as a second Arthur may seem odd, but in fact he is actually making an adaptation somewhat similar to that worked out by Spenser. In his *The Faerie Queene* (1590), the future King Arthur appears as Gloriana's (Elizabeth's) champion, though elsewhere as an ancestor (II, x, 4, lines 1–6):

> Thy name, O soveraine Queene! thy realme, and race
> From this renowmed Prince derived arre,
> Who mightily upheld that royall mace
> Which now thou bear'st, to thee descended farre
> From mighty kings and conquerours in warre,
> Thy fathers and great Grandfathers of old . . .

Cumberland certainly seems to have his past service in mind when he refers in his speech to Merlin's prophecy that 'till a Red Draggon did fly into ye Sea, to encounter ye black Eagle, the castle should not be fortunate'. The speech then goes on to tell of how 'oftentimes with great courage, but with noe lookd for successe, hath this Draggon pulled some feathers, but not seized on ye Bodie of this displayed Eagle'. Here the allusion to the Red

Dragon not only refers to the Arthurian myth but also to Cumberland's own family crest,⁵ a fiery dragon. The speech is thus an apt comment on Cumberland's military service against the black eagle, the heraldic device of Spain. Having neither received reward for his loyalty on land, nor profit for his service at sea, the Red Dragon has none the less recently received encouragement by finding a new prophecy hidden 'between two stones' in the castle:

> When a Virgin hath reigned thirty three yeares,
> When a Vine on ye Walles in one night shall grow,
> When Castor, and Pollux, on the Land appeares,
> and the Red Draggon shall seeme like Snowe;
> Then shall ye Cormorant, that now the Eagle hight [is called],
> have his feathers moulten by a Virgins might.

The vine that Cumberland refers to is Lee, who, as we have seen, entered just before Cumberland, his caparison 'charg'd with Crownes', but 'Oreshadowed with a withered Vine,/As who would say, My spring of youth is past'.⁶ The allusion to Castor and Pollux, the twin sons of Zeus, is not clear to me, unless Cumberland was referring to the presence of the Knowles brothers among the participants (but as there were three of them this may not be so). Peele's account tells us that Cumberland was 'yclad in coate of steele,/ And plumes and pendants al as white as Swanne',⁷ something which explains the fourth line. Cumberland used white feathers on his helmet and was wearing a surcoat of white (a tribute to his Virgin Queen), a point clearly illustrated in Hilliard's miniature commemorating the occasion. The final lines of Cumberland's verses are apparently a further allusion to Spain and the Roman church. The rest of Cumberland's speech continues to emphasize the Arthurian associations, but in humorous vein. Merlin mentions, tongue in cheek, that Cumberland once thought of inviting Elizabeth to Pendragon Castle, but decided there was nothing there of much interest except for such things as 'this world hath worne out of fashion. Excalibers Sworde, ye Sleeve that S[i]r Lancelott bare for his Ladie, Balyns Speare, S[i]r Braumins Smyter, Dinidans Dittie, S[i]r Gawins Spurres' and so on.

This humorous touch at the end of the speech raises the entire question of tone. It is often impossible to be sure whether tiltyard speeches contain a degree of self-conscious comic affectation. The (to us) exaggerated rhetoric of so many of the speeches can easily mislead us into thinking that this was so when perhaps none was intended, as the speeches of courtiers addressing the monarch on other occasions make only too clear. Then, too, as already mentioned, the fusion of romance and reality can easily be missed by the modern reader not fully conversant with the seriousness of what is being said by means of some chivalric fantasy. Nevertheless, the humour that characterized some of the impresas and the conclusion of Cumberland's 1590 speech suggest that a certain amount of playful jesting with the themes, legends and characters of medieval romance was not uncommon.

Cumberland's next appearance at an Accession Day tilt was in November 1593, when, as we have seen, the annual tournament was held at Windsor. Here he once more appeared as the Knight of Pendragon Castle, and his Squire explained that he had been absent from the tiltyard while on service at sea. Accompanied by some of his mariners, he now entered the tiltyard upon 'the old Castle, which was founded in Westmorland and once removed to Westminster' and now 'strangely erected in Windelysore'. Once more the Arthurian theme is repeated as more Merlin-like prophecies are pronounced:[8]

When Windesore and Pendragon Castle doe kiss
The Loyon shall bring the Red Dragon to blisse.

and:

When Nature shall spend all perfections in one,
When all for that one of themselves shall thinke worse,
When duety shall move very castles of stone,
When Albion prospers by outlandish curse,
And when the Red Dragon led shipmen on dry land,
Then blest be the earth for a maide in an iland.

Cumberland's Arthur-like role as the Knight of Pendragon Castle, so flattering both to himself and Elizabeth, was sustained at least for a while. At the Accession Day tournament in 1595 he entered, as Peele tells us, with a device which represented his castle, its treasure guarded by a dragon. When Elizabeth arrived, Cumberland in gilded armour and 'enflamed with honors fire' rode out from his 'castle' to do her service.[9]

However, five years later, at the Accession Day tournament in November 1600, Cumberland completely abandoned the Arthurian theme. Instead, his squire took up a subject in no uncertain terms that had been lightly touched on ten years before when Cumberland had expressed his disappointment at receiving little reward on land and little profit at sea. Before 1590 and in the years that followed, Cumberland had used up a great deal of his personal estate in outfitting ships for his various privateering ventures, some of which had greatly benefited Elizabeth without bringing much actual profit to Cumberland. Most of his efforts to receive what he considered a just reward had then fallen upon deaf ears, as was so often the case at Elizabeth's court. In April 1597, he had, for example, written to Lord Burghley asking him to petition the Queen on his behalf concerning his desire to be made Governor of the Isle of Wight, but in the end Cumberland was passed over.

It is consequently not surprising that Cumberland chose to present himself at the 1600 tournament as a melancholy wandering knight who, 'removyng from castell to castell, now rowleth up, and downe in open feild, a field of shadow, having no other m[istres]s but night-shade, nor gathering anie mosse but about his own harte'.[10] The squire, recalling his master's past services, says 'that he hath made ladders for others to clymbe, and his feet nayled to the ground not to stirr. That he is lyke him that built ye ancker to save others, and themselves to be drowned. That when he hath outstript manie in desert, he is tript upp by Envy, until, thos, overtake him, that undertooke nothing'. To apologize for such importunity, Cumberland then has his squire go on to observe that the knight he represents is obviously mistaken. None the less, the central point is made yet again in another telling image referring to Cumberland's sales of his land to pay his debts: 'Is it not, as I have often tould ye, that, after he had throwne his land into ye sea, ye sea would cast him on the lande for a wanderer?'

Cumberland, an inveterate gambler and spendthrift, whose ambitious attempts to thrive by privateering had led to his desperate state of debt, probably dressed as the personification of melancholy, like the moss-covered Thomas Ratcliffe did in 1581. If his self-assumed role as the Knight of Pendragon Castle had been sustained in all his previous tournaments, his new guise would have provided a dramatic shock, one which he no doubt hoped would stir some positive response in the heart of his mistress. Such contrived dramatic effects, combined with personal pleading are, however, more typical of the tournament devices of Cumberland's contemporary, the Earl of Essex, that brightest of Elizabethan stars, that 'Faire branch of Honor, flower of Chevalrie', as Spenser called him, who fell so tragically and predictably at the close of the Tudor period.[11]

Essex first made his appearance at an English tournament in November 1586, just after he had returned from Zutphen in the black-draped ship bearing Sidney's body. Thereafter, when not serving overseas and when not in dire disgrace at court, he appeared at virtually every English tournament until his misguided rebellion and subsequent execution in 1601. His renown as an impresa writer has already been mentioned, but it is clear from other sources that he possessed an imaginative, albeit egocentric flair for other kinds of tiltyard drama. In 1590, for example, Essex arrived before the Queen in the lists dressed completely in black in a chariot drawn by black horses (see p. 138), and this at a celebration, the central event of which was to be Lee's retirement.

Essex' penchant for self-dramatization shows clearly in his various portraits (e.g. Figs 68 and 80), as well as in many events of his career. On the English expedition to Portugal in 1589, Essex demonstrated his knightly valour by being the first Englishman to wade ashore; at Lisbon he later offered to fight all-comers in honour of his mistress; and at the siege of Rouen in 1591 he challenged the enemy commander to single combat. It was to Essex that Sidney bequeathed his best sword as he lay dying, pleading with him to marry his pregnant wife, Frances Walsingham, and it was Essex, more than anyone else, who assumed Sidney's role as self-proclaimed Protestant activist hero, the knightly champion of English Church and State against the threat of Rome and Spain. Like Sidney, he seems to have modelled his behaviour on the ideals of chivalric romance,

80 *Portrait miniature of the Earl of Essex in tournament attire by Nicholas Hilliard (c. 1593–95). This shows Essex before his tent, and the military background suggests that some allusion to his involvement in the campaign in Normandy in 1591 is intended. However, in other respects the portrait may well commemorate his participation in a tournament, perhaps that in 1595 at which Elizabeth gave him her glove. On his right arm Essex wears a lady's glove and round his bases is embroidered the emblematic device of a diamond with the motto 'Dum formas minuis', an impresa that Essex is known to have used in a tournament. The fancifully-dressed page wears the Queen's colours of black and white.*

and it is no surprise to find that Peele, when he wrote *An Eclogue Gratulatorie* to welcome Essex home from Portugal, linked the two military heroes:[12]

> Fellow in Armes he was, in their flowing deies,
> With that great Shepherd good Philisides:
> And in sad sable did I see him dight.
> Moning the misse of Pallas peereles Knight.
> Io Io Paean.
>
> With him he serv'd, and watcht and waited fate,
> To keepe the grim Wolfe from Elizaes gate:
> And for their Mistresse thoughten these two swains,
> They moughten never take too mickle paines.
> Io Io Paean.
>
> But, ah for griefe, that jolly groome is dead,
> For whome the Muses silver teares have shed:
> Yet in this lovelie swaine, source of our glee,
> Mun all his Vertues sweet reviven bee.
> Io Io Paean.

Elizabeth, however, saw things differently. Though she was frequently affected by the young Earl's magic and was willing to be flattered by knightly shows in the tiltyard, she saw the folly that so-called chivalric attitudes could induce in the real world and in particular on the battlefield. More than once she was led to chastise Essex for what she considered irresponsible recklessness, while in Sidney's death (had he worn leg armour he could have protected himself) she saw nothing but pointless waste.

Unfortunately, in spite of all the attention focused on Essex in his lifetime, few records remain to tell us about his tiltyard appearances and the speeches he presented there. In fact, only fragments of the text of his elaborate 'Love and Self-Love' device for November 1595 survive. The year before he had hired 'certeine schollers' from Oxford to present some kind of show to the Queen[13] and experienced scholar-actors, suitable for the very special kind of rather learned disputation that Essex had in mind, were again hired for the 1595 tournament. The names of the actors and an account of the event are given in a letter from Rowland White to Sir Robert Sidney,[14] and various versions of the fragmentary text have survived in a variety of manuscript sources, chief among which are some papers in the hand of Francis Bacon, who was closely associated with Essex at the time.[15]

The authorship of the text has never been completely determined, although Sir Henry Wotton, who was a secretary for Essex at one time, later praised Essex' 'inventions of entertainment', and in an apparent reference to the 1595 entertainment spoke of Essex' 'darling piece of love, and self-love'.[16] The exact sequence of the text is also not certain and there is the problem of which surviving fragments were only drafts, and which were actually used. In what follows I shall use Rowland White's letter as my guide where possible and, using the internal evidence of the texts, I shall suggest what seems to me to have been the most likely sequence.[17]

The essence of Essex' entertainment consists of an allegorical dispute among various conflicting loves, loyalties, and choices of occupation. Essex, who is represented under the name Erophilus (Lover of Amorousness), loves the Queen, and, in a speech that may be missing, he has apparently had his squire express that love. In two draft speeches in French,[18] Philautia (Self-Love), representative of a principle opposed to Love and hence opposed to Essex or committed to converting him, first addresses Elizabeth and speaks against the love expressed by Essex. In the much shorter second speech, having listened to the Squire's defence of Erophilus' love (the Squire's speech has not survived), Philautia withdraws her opposition. Next comes a further speech by Philautia. It is a draft in Bacon's hand and, like the first two Philautia speeches, perhaps never used.[19] In it Philautia addresses Elizabeth. Since her last audience, she says, she has reported the opposition she has encountered 'to Pallas, vpon whom *Philautia* depends'. Pallas has urged her to assail Erophilus once more. The nature of the planned assault is not revealed, but we may assume that Philautia is referring to the device involving 'one dressed like a Heremite or Philosopher' (representing Contemplation), a Soldier (representing Fame and the life of action), and a Secretary/Statesman (representing Experience).

It was probably at this point that the Squire entered the tiltyard with the Hermit, Soldier, and Secretary/Statesman. The Squire explains to Elizabeth that 'coming hither to your Majesty's most happie day he [Essex] is tormented with the importunity of a melancholy dreaming Hermitt, a mutinous, brainsicke Souldier and a busie, tedious Secretary. His peticion is that he may be as free as the rest, and at least while he is heere troubled with nothing but with care how to please and honor you'.[20] To this the Secretary/Statesman responds, explaining to the Squire that the three men have been sent by Philautia 'to treat with him [Essex] for his own goode'.[21]

At about this stage, though it is not explicitly referred to in any of the texts, Essex' page arrived in the tiltyard with a message for the Queen. Having spoken to her, he was given her glove to take to his master as a sign of special favour. Then Essex himself entered, presumably wearing the favour, and was 'mett with an old Hermitt, a Secretary of State, a braue Soldier, and an Esquier'. This last 'was but his own Follower, to whom thother three imparted much of their Purpose, before his Coming in'.[22] Texts and description now match for a moment. The Hermit, speaking to Essex' Squire (though Essex is, of course, present) hands him a 'Booke of Meditations', and urges that Essex not 'borowe other mens opyniones to direct himself' nor 'tie himself to the courses he is already entred into'. The Hermit then goes on to say of Essex: 'Will he never discern manacles from bracelets, nor burdens from robes? Will he neuer ceasse to professe that is not beleeued, to offer that is not accepted, and to tax himself at that which is not remytted?'[23]

According to White, other speeches then

followed. The Secretary/Statesman offered a book of political discourses, the Soldier a book of 'Oracions of braue fought Battles', and another (White does not identify this character, but perhaps it was Philautia) 'devised with him, persuading him to this and that Course of Liffe', but none of the texts for this part of the entertainment in the tiltyard has survived. To conclude this section of the entertainment, the Hermit then addressed the Queen, asking her to assign 'a tyme when we may before you [speak] for our selues'.[24]

The spectators gathered in the Whitehall tiltyard were by now doubtless anxious for the day's events to move ahead. They no doubt felt that more speeches by the three agents of Philautia could well be left to another occasion. Essex, after all, was only the second person to have entered. According to Peele, Cumberland, having entered first and presented his device, stood 'impacient of Delaie/awaytinge there his freindly foes approche', but Essex, true to form, had no compunction about upstaging the Queen's Champion. Already he had added the Queen's glove to his costume of red and white (the colours of love), and now he had one more surprise in store.

Just as everyone must have expected the arrival of the Earl of Sussex, there rode into the tiltyard 'thordinary Post Boy of *London*, a ragged Villain all bemired, vpon a poore leane Jade, gallaping and blowing for Liff, and deliuered the Secretary a Packet of Lettres, which he presently offered my Lord of *Essex*'. This comical moment involved no speeches. As White says, 'with this dumb Shew our Eyes were fed for that Time'. Presumably the entries of the other participants then followed, the remainder of Essex' show having been reserved for after supper that evening.

What, if anything, would Essex' contemporaries have made of his entertainment thus far? It was well known, for example, that Essex had recently gone through a period of considerable discord with Elizabeth. For two years he had sought by every means in his power, and often in the most strident terms, to have Francis Bacon appointed, first as Attorney-General and then as Solicitor-General. In both matters he had failed. There was also the business of the office of Secretary of State. In 1591, while Essex was absent in France, the Queen had appointed the newly-knighted Sir Robert Cecil, Lord Burghley's younger son, to the Privy Council. Since Walsingham's death, Elizabeth had deliberately left the Secretaryship open, despite Essex' attempts to have William Davison appointed.

In retrospect we can now perceive that both she and the elderly and infirm Burghley, to whom unofficially she handed over the responsibilities of the post, must have seen Burghley's son, Robert Cecil, as a good choice, and it was indeed he she eventually appointed in 1596 when Essex was conveniently abroad, this time in Spain. From the first Essex caused trouble over this long drawn out issue, but the Queen remained adamant, to the great frustration of the young Earl. When she knighted Cecil at Theobalds and appointed him to the Privy Council while Essex was out of the way in France, it was generally assumed that Cecil would soon be appointed Secretary. Not surprisingly the expectation alone was sufficient to set off that bitter and intense power struggle between the gifted, highly intelligent politician and the flamboyant, ambitious, high-born courtier, which only ended when Essex was executed.[25]

We have it from White's letter that there were some among those present at Whitehall in 1595 who believed that the Hermit and the Secretary represented 'two of the Lords' at court. This is not surprising. When Elizabeth visited Burghley at his home at Theobalds in May 1591, she had been welcomed by Robert Cecil dressed as a hermit. In a long verse speech excusing the absence of Lord Burghley, the hermit explained that he had led a solitary and retired life nearby for ten years until his founder (i.e. Burghley) removed him, and, 'oretaken w[ith] excessyue greefe', took over the hermit's cell for just over two

years.[26] Burghley had been grief-stricken by the deaths of his wife and daughter. The hermit, who has been carrying out some of his 'founder's' responsibilities, is anxious to return to his cell and asks Elizabeth to help him out of his predicament. In this way Cecil reminded Elizabeth of his own administrative talent while making show of not being ambitious.

That same day Elizabeth appears to have drawn up a teasing and cajolling mock charter. Written on vellum, attached to which was the Queen's Great Seal, and signed by the Lord Chancellor, the impressive-looking document, dated 10 May, was addressed 'to the disconsolate and retired spryte, the Heremite of Tybole'. In it Elizabeth commanded the hermit to return 'to yoor old cave, too good for the forsaken, too bad for oour worthily belooved Coouncillour'.[27] Three years later on another visit to Theobalds, the playful joke about the so-called hermit (now increasingly recognized as an able figure in court affairs) was continued. Elizabeth was again met by the aged hermit, now restored to his hermitage, who thanked her for her previous assistance and presented her with gifts.[28] Thus Essex could hardly have expected anything but speculation regarding his Hermit and Secretary. Indeed, given Burghley's frequent retreats to Theobalds, and given the fact that Robert was increasingly carrying out the duties of Secretary, Essex' two characters could have been read almost interchangeably.

We may also wonder, as Essex' audience certainly did, what he meant by having the postboy deliver letters to the Secretary who then passed them on to Essex? Was this Essex' way of reminding Robert Cecil that he outranked him? Or was this a way of commenting on the fact that Burghley's control of state affairs was by now, due to his ill-health, often largely through letters that were sent to Robert, who then forwarded them to their intended recipients? We cannot know, but we can be sure that between the first introduction of the characters in the tiltyard and their reappearance after supper there must have been a great deal of conjecture as to what Essex was up to, especially as he may also have been parodying another Cecil entertainment in which a postboy with letters from the Emperor of China asks for Secretary Cecil, even though the Queen is present.[29]

When Essex moved away from his position below the royal window, the other tilters were then able to make their entries. For one of them, Essex (or Bacon) composed some elaborate presentation speeches. There is, however, no indication as to which participant used them.[30] None of the descriptions of the participants in Peele's *Anglorum Feriae* seems to match the text, and the manuscript itself contains no clues, although it does contain several references to Philautia and to the main theme of the rest of the entertainment. Furthermore, the squire who introduces the entrant to the Queen is clearly not the entrant's squire but the same character as the squire who figures so prominently elsewhere. Such links (and there are more) suggest that the speeches were intended as part of the 1595 entertainment.

Two characters are involved—a tilter disguised as a young Indian prince from the New World and his attendant, this latter 'white of complexion' and conveniently 'expert in language'. After their initial introduction by the squire, the attendant explains that the young prince was born blind. However, an ancient prophecy has foretold that the young man will 'expell the Castillians, a nation of strangers, which as a scourge hath wounde it self about the bodie of that continent', and a recent oracle has told of a wonderful and wise queen 'Seated betweene the olde world and the newe' to whom the young prince 'must make his sacrifice If he will haue the morning of his eyes'. At this point we seem to be seeing yet another repetition of one of Lee's favourite plot-motifs with some anti-Spanish sentiments thrown in for good measure, but when the prince, as we expect, gains his sight, he is transformed into something more than an Indian prince. He becomes a figure of 'Seeing Loue, a prince indeed, but of greater territories then all the Indies, armed after the Indian manner with bowe and arrowes and, when he is in his ordinary habitt, an Indian naked or attired with fethers, though nowe for semelynes clad'.

Blind Cupid, symbol of erotic and irrational love, has thus been transformed into Seeing Cupid, a very different being, who goes on to present Elizabeth with 'his gifte and propertie to be euer yong; his winge of libertie to fly from one to another; his bowe and arrowes to wound where it pleaseth you'. Though denied access to Elizabeth before, he hopes that in his new form he will be vouchsafed entertainment. The Queen, it is suggested, will now see clearly who merely flatter and who truly love her, and Philautia will take second place to this new insight. The message then given to the squire (Essex' squire, that is) to take to his master concludes the attendant's speech: 'And so, Squier, for guyding vs our right way, we haue taught your Master parte of his.'

Following the tournament, there was the usual banquet, after which Essex' entertainment resumed. Four speeches make up this section of the text. As Rowland White's letter explains, the Hermit, the Soldier, and the Secretary/Statesman each delivered a speech. That of the Hermit urged Erophilus 'to leaue his vaine following of Loue, and to betake him to hevenly Meditacion; the Secretaries all tending to haue him follow Matters of State, the Soldiers persuading him to the Warr'. The lengthy statements by the agents of Philautia and the squire's response to them are the most important part of Essex' entertainment. The three agents allegorically represent three choices available to Essex at this moment in his career. One course is to retire from an active role in public affairs, 'offer his seruice to the Muses' (as Sidney did for a time), and pursue truth and knowledge.

Such a choice would naturally have played into Burghley's and Cecil's hands, and presumably it was one that Essex never really contemplated. The choice offered by the

Soldier, on the other hand,[31] may clearly have had its attractions for Essex, but he had already discovered that military service, however successful in bringing him honour and popular fame, was no guarantee of royal recognition and favour. In the early 1590s, but especially after he joined the Privy Council in 1593, he had made a token effort to show himself capable of dealing with what the Secretary/Statesman defines as 'the instruccions to emploied men, the relacions of embassadours, the treaties betweene princes, and accions of the presente tyme'. But Essex' presence in the Privy Council only brought him into direct confrontation with Cecil, and with Burghley when he was well enough to attend, and there was little sign that his hot, tempestuous pride allowed for much skill in the conduct of state affairs.

In the Secretary/Statesman's speech it is recommended that Essex follow 'pollicy and matter of state', and the speaker then goes on to urge Essex to adopt a particular mode of behaviour. This turns the speech into a biting satire that many must have assumed was directed at Burghley and Cecil, however unjust in what it suggested. The Secretary/Statesman's advice is that, if Essex take up statecraft, he should not sound into any matter too deeply, but 'know onlie so much as may make him able to make vse of other men's witts, and to make againe a smooth and pleasing reporte'. Let him not sound too confident, 'for that will rather make him obnoxious to the successe, but let him follow the wisdome of oracles, which vttered that which might euer be applied to the event. And euer rather let him take the side which is likeliest to be followed, then that which is soundest and best'. Fortunately the care-worn Burghley, who in fact frequently expressed differences of opinion with Elizabeth in his pursuit of the 'soundest and best', was not present at Essex' entertainment because he was unwell but his son Robert was presumably there, and one cannot help wondering what he made of this rather tasteless attack on his chosen career.

The three speeches just described were then followed by a very long final speech, 'The replie of the Squier'. In this Essex invested all his hopes for a positive response from Elizabeth. The Squire rejects all three choices offered by 'the inchaunting orators of *Philautia*', whom he accuses of attempting to turn 'resolued *Erophelus* into a statua depriued of action, or into a vulture attending about dead bodies, or into a monster with a double harte'. Instead, he stresses his master's love and devotion to Elizabeth: '*Erophilus*' resolution is fixed: he renounceth *Philautia*, and all her inchantments. Ffor her [i.e. Elizabeth's] recreation he will conferre with his muse, for her defence and honor, he will sacrifice his life in the warres, hoping to be embalmed in the sweete odours of her remembrance. To her seruice will he consecrate all his watchful endeuors.'

Essex' show, whatever satirical jibes it may have contained concerning his political rivals, thus concluded with a grand renunciation of personal ambition (the self-love of Philautia) and an expression of his intention to devote his entire energies to the service of his true love (Elizabeth) by whatever means he could (as poet, as soldier, as careful statesman). Given the effort and expense Essex had put into the production of his device and given the manner in which it had monopolized the tournament during the afternoon and the suppertime recreation period during the evening, Essex doubtless hoped for much, but Elizabeth, rather than comment and thereby commit herself to any definite response, stalked off to bed, saying 'that if she had thought their had bene so moch said of her, she wold not haue bene their that Night'.[32] Perhaps she had enjoyed herself, perhaps not. From Essex' point of view, however, I think we must deduce that his show was something of an expensive flop, at which Cecil doubtless had the last laugh.

Where the Earl of Essex was the major creative force in tiltyard entertainments in the 1590s, Ben Jonson, the celebrated writer of plays and masques, was the dominant figure during the Jacobean era. In his three major contributions to the literature of the tournament, Jonson employed his considerable talents and professional experience to produce spectacles that seem almost indistinguishable from the elaborate court masques that became so fashionable in the early years of King James' reign. Indeed, Jonson's innovative use of perspective scenery and the subtle visual and auditory effects achieved through the use of indoor lighting and bands of musicians probably helped to speed the progress of court interest away from the open-air pageantry of the tiltyard towards the very different forms that he and his scenic collaborator, Inigo Jones, were learning to exploit in night-time entertainments indoors.

Gone is the gentlemanly amateurism of those tiltyard extravaganzas created by the tiltyard participants themselves. Jonson's (and Jones') works are the polished products of professionals. Their collaborations are also representative of the Stuart tendency towards exclusiveness. The tiltyard was losing its attraction as a place where all ranks of society from the monarch down could celebrate their common bonds. Significantly, King James, who in any case tended to shun crowds, preferred the very different glorification of his status accorded by the masque which required an indoor setting.

Jonson's first major work of concern to us here was *Hymenaei, or the Solemnities of Masque and Barriers at a Marriage.* This was written to celebrate the nuptials of the new holder of the title Earl of Essex and Frances Howard, the daughter of the Earl of Suffolk. As befitting an occasion calculated to unite two powerful families, both the masque, which took place on the wedding night, and the masque-like entertainment for the barriers, which occurred the night after, were held, as far as is known, in the Whitehall Banqueting House. On the first evening the court witnessed a lavish and intricate affair (decor and scenic effects by Inigo Jones) involving the figures of Hymen, Reason, Juno, and Order,

the whole dazzling display concluding in an Epithalamion or song in praise of the bridal pair. On the second evening (6 January) two women dressed exactly alike and representing Truth and Opinion emerged from a mist at one end of the hall to the accompaniment of music imitating the sounds of battle. The two engaged in a quarrel, Truth offering a challenge in defence of the proposition that marriage is a more honourable state than the single life.

As in the speeches of Hymen and Reason on the previous evening, the allusion was to the topical political concern (one dear to James' heart and about to be discussed in Parliament) of possible union between England and Scotland.[33] The challenge was followed by further debate and the entry of sixteen challengers (the champions of Truth and the Bride) and sixteen defendants (champions for Opinion and Virginity). A combat at barriers followed and was brought to a halt by an Angel who heralded the reappearance of Truth, Opinion having ignominiously vanished. All was then resolved in favour of unity and concord, and the discordia/concordia pattern so typical of the masque was thus merged with the quintessential adversary pattern of the tournament. Indeed, there were precedents for what Jonson did in the long tradition of the *débat* culminating in a banquet hall combat at arms, the 1552 Epiphany dialogue *Youth and Riches* (discussed in the previous chapter) and the ensuing combat at barriers in the hall at Greenwich during Edward VI's reign being a typical example. In Jonson's skilled hands everything is subsumed to the debate-like allegorical fiction, and the accompanying challenge and combat are completely at one in sustaining that fiction. Furthermore, although there was some fighting for spectators to enjoy, this was probably subservient to the larger spectacle and the subtle underlying political commentary that it offered James and his Court.

If Jonson believed in 1606 that the display of martial skills should be a secondary ele-

ment in the production of a combat at barriers, he tactfully showed no sign of it when he and Jones were given the responsibility of staging the combat at barriers for Prince Henry in 1610 (Figs 81 and 82). The background and a brief description of this event have already been given in Chapter 1. The entire event was designed as a spectacular piece of ceremonial with the Prince as centrepiece. Furthermore, in keeping with the chivalric cult that had developed around Henry during the preceding few years, Jonson not only had to stress the Prince's chivalric virtues, which he did by exploiting the mythology of Arthur, but he had also to

81 *One of Inigo Jones' designs for Prince Henry's barriers (6 Jan. 1610) was for the Fallen House of Chivalry* (ABOVE). *At the beginning of the spectacle the Lady of the Lake bemoans the fall of the House of Chivalry, which she says is in ruins. Shortly after King Arthur appears with a shield to be handed to Prince Henry. The entire allegory*

stress Henry's potential as successor to England's earlier warlike kings (Figs 83 and 84). This he did, but with some qualifications that emphasized the importance of leadership and government at a time of peace. Britain had undergone an immense transition since ancient times and Arthur's age was no more:

made clear that in Henry chivalry and the glories of Arthur would be revived. A second design by Inigo Jones (ABOVE RIGHT) was for the same event and shows St George's Portico. In the course of the spectacle Prince Henry (Meliadus) and his knights are discovered in St George's Portico 'yet undemolished'. Prince Henry's presence revives Chivalry, and the barriers follow.

> But here are other acts; another stage
> And scene appears; it is not since as then:
> No giants, dwarfs or monsters here, but men.
> His arts must be to govern and give laws
> To peace no less than arms.[34]

Not only are the days of knights rescuing ladies from giants long past, but successive British kings have nurtured the development of a judicial system, of trade and agriculture, of domestic industry, and of a strong network of national defence that keeps foreign enemies at bay. As Jonson has Merlin explain to the young Prince (Meliadus), 'civil arts the martial must precede'.[35] The supreme model of kingship, according to Merlin, is Henry's father, and we must imagine at this point how all eyes in the Whitehall Banqueting Hall momentarily shifted from the glittering armed figure of Prince Henry to the enthroned person of King James:

82 *Costume design for a lance-bearer by Inigo Jones. At any tournament, a knight required a page or attendant to carry his lance. This was then ceremoniously handed to him after he had mounted his horse. This costume design may have been created for one of the lance-bearers at the special tournament in June 1610 to celebrate the creation of Prince Henry as Prince of Wales.*

83 *Portrait miniature of Prince Henry by Isaac Oliver (c. 1612). Henry is shown surrounded by all the trappings appropriate to his image as soldier-hero and national leader. Henry himself, in his blue garter sash, wears armour. In the background, in keeping with the chivalric antique dream world that was so much a part of the cult of Prince Henry, are warriors à l'antique holding lances, shields and spears.*

SOIT QUI MAL Y PENSE

ICH DIEN

Si: Paß: sculp: A°: 1612.

Are to be soulde by Compton Holland, ouer against the Exchange at the signe of the Globe.

ILLUSTRISSIMI GENEROSISSIMIQUE PRI. HENRICI
MAGNÆ BRITANNIÆ ET HYBERNIÆ PRINCIPIS,
Vera Effigies.

Royal and mighty James, whose name shall set
A goal for all posterity to sweat
In running at, by actions hard and high;
This is the height at which your thoughts must
    fly.[36]

All this followed the initial appearance of the
Lady of the Lake, who set off the whole chain
of Arthurian allusions that dominate the
speeches that follow. Generally Jonson was
contemptuous of the literature of Arthur, but
clearly he recognized its suitability on this
occasion for providing Prince Henry's first
appearance in armed combat with an
appropriate chivalric context in keeping with
the warmth of popular adoration. Arthur
himself appears, presents a shield to Henry,
and argues that 'Defensive arms th'offensive
should forego',[37] and just before the start of
the combat, Meliadus (Prince Henry) hangs
his shield upon his tent—the traditional sign
of a challenge to all-comers in chivalric
romance—and Merlin awakens Chivalry
from her cave where symbolically she has
been sleeping. Her one short but telling
speech then introduces the barriers:

Were it from death, that name [Meliadus]
    would wake me. Say
Which is the knight? O, I could gaze a day
Upon his armour that hath so revived
My spirits, and tells me that I am long-lived
In his appearance. Break, you rusty doors
That have so long been shut, and from the
    shores

84 *Engraving of Prince Henry by Simon van de
Passe (1612). Although Prince Henry was not old
enough to participate in jousting, he did
demonstrate his skill at running at ring and at foot
combats. Most notable was the carefully-staged
combat at barriers in 1610 when Henry, with six
companions, fought at barriers against fifty-six
answerers. In this engraving he is seen dressed (but
without his helmet on), as for a combat at barriers.
His long stave is of the kind used in this event. In
the background can be seen other men practising
their tournament skills, perhaps at Greenwich.*

Of all the world come knighthood like a flood
Upon these lists to make the field here good,
And your own honours that are now called
    forth
Against the wish of men to prove your worth![38]

The combat then followed, during which the
fifteen-year-old Henry with six assistants
fought on foot against fifty-six defendants
across a barrier erected down the centre of
the Banqueting Hall. This colourful Twelfth
Night event began, we are told, at ten in the
evening and lasted until the next morning.
According to his biographer, the young
prince did admirably, 'giving and receiving
that night, 32. pushes of Pikes, and about 360.
stroakes of Swords, which is scarse credible
in so young yeares, enough to assure the
World, that *Great Britaines* brave Henry
aspired to immortality'.[39]

When the excitement of the barriers was
over, one last speech by Merlin served to
conclude the event by reiterating the idea that
military glory and the pursuit of arms cannot
be ends in themselves ('He that in deeds of
arms obeys his blood/Doth often tempt his
destiny beyond good' lines 398–9). Once
more, too, he turns to James, whom he
praises in elaborate terms, prophesying that
Prince Henry will also achieve wonderful
things, that his brother Prince Charles will
follow him in the practice of arms, and that
the Princess Elizabeth will be the mother of
nations and have sons to rival her brother
Henry. As we now know, fate decided things
very differently—Henry was shortly to die,
Prince Charles would eventually lose his
crown and his head, and the Princess would
suffer with her future husband the loss of the
Palatinate of the Rhine and the Kingdom of
Bohemia.

Jonson's third text for use at a tournament
was *A Challenge at Tilt at a Marriage*. It was
first published in the Folio edition of his
works in 1616, although the actual
tournament occurred on 1 January 1614. As
in the case of the Folio text of *Hymenaei*,
Jonson deliberately avoided mentioning the
actual occasion for which the work had been

written. This was because it had originally been composed in honour of the wedding of the Earl of Somerset and Lady Frances Howard. Lady Howard's earlier marriage had been celebrated by Jonson's *Hymenaei*, but had then been declared null and void after a notorious divorce case and she had subsequently married her lover Robert Carr, the Earl of Somerset. What Jonson thought of all this, we shall never know, but he was no doubt as shocked as anyone else when further scandal erupted in 1615 and Lady Frances and her new husband were both convicted of the murder of Sir Thomas Overbury, a crime for which they were condemned to death, though the sentence was never carried out. No wonder, then, that Jonson suppressed the names of the guilty pair when he proudly (some thought arrogantly) gathered together his works and published them in a grand single-volume edition a year later.

The first part of *A Challenge at Tilt at a Marriage* was presented on 27 December 1613, the day after the marriage. Following a celebratory running at ring by the King, Prince Charles and the bridegroom, the initial challenge for a tilt, to be held on the ensuing New Year's Day, was presented. In place of a formal call to arms, Jonson created a dramatic fiction by having two cupids (Eros and Anteros) appear before the court, posing as the husband's page and wife's page respectively. Each claimed to be the true son of Mars and Venus and each said that the other was an imposter. After comic and somewhat salacious descriptions of their roles on the wedding night, one cupid challenged the other: 'But, that this royall and honor'd assembly be no longer troubled with our contention: behold, I challenge thee of falsehood; and will bring vpon the first day of the new yeere, into the lists, before this palace, ten knights arm'd; who shall vndertake against all assertion, that only I am the child of MARS and VENVS: and, in honor of that ladie (whom it is my ambition to serue) that, that loue is the most true and perfect,

that still waiteth on the woman, and is the seruant of that sexe.'[40]

On New Year's Day, the court assembled in the tiltyard at Whitehall and the two cupids arrived, each in a handsome chariot, and each accompanied by ten knights. The knights of the challenger (the bride's cupid) entered first, dressed in murrey (a reddish purple colour) and white. Dismounting from his chariot, the bride's cupid comically regaled all the women present by reminding them of his power over them. With the entry of the defendant (the husband's cupid) and his ten knights, all dressed in the bridegroom's colours of green and yellow, further lighthearted contention between the two cupids ensued, and this was quickly followed by the tilting match. At the conclusion of this, neither side having clearly won the prize, Hymen suddenly appeared to resolve the dispute. First he urged them to engage in a quite different kind of tilting—'to meete lips for lances; and crack kisses in stead of staues'.[41] Then, in more serious vein, the god explained that one cupid was Eros and the other Anteros, each being necessary to the other: 'This is the loue that *Hymen* requires, without which no Marriage is happie.'[42] Did Jonson have in the back of his mind the fact that the Lady Frances' first marriage had ended because of the supposed impotence of her husband? With the submission of both cupids to Hymen's call for concord, the entertainment came to a close.

Reading the text, it would almost seem that the tournament itself was merely secondary, and so it may have been in Jonson's opinion. Perhaps the colourful costumes of the knights and the excitement of the encounters between them still had the power to hold the interest of the assembled crowds, but it is significant none the less that this was the last tiltyard event to involve the use of actors, speeches, and fiction. Henceforth, Stuart delight in such entertainments would be transferred to the theatre and the masking hall, despite the fact that tournaments were to continue at Whitehall for at least a further ten years.

Epilogue

THERE IS NO DOUBT that tournaments throughout the Tudor and Jacobean periods were largely anachronistic exercises, though convenient politically and, we may assume, as enjoyable socially as a modern foxhunt or polo match. The Tudor and Jacobean tournaments were also the most recognizable outward manifestation of the last vestiges of medieval chivalry, that courtly code of behaviour involving service to king, country and mistress and the performance of noble and valorous deeds. Of value to the first Tudors principally as propaganda spectacles (though we should not forget Henry VIII's sheer delight in the tournament as recreative sport), tournaments underwent something of a revival during Queen Elizabeth's reign. They were a concomitant of the cult of Elizabeth as Virgin Queen and saviour of the reformed Church. They permitted her knights to demonstrate their service in symbolic fashion by acting out elaborate fantasies and allegories, often complete with speeches, pageants and fictional characters, that are at one with such contemporary romances as *Amadis de Gaul*, *Orlando Furioso*, the *Arcadia,* and *The Faerie Queene.*

During the reign of James I, the tiltyard ceremonies of Accession Day continued their ritualistic role in demonstrating royal ascendancy while implicitly making clear the continued fascination with both the trappings and values of chivalry. It is no mere arbitrary quirk of taste, for example, that caused so many designers of Tudor and Jacobean houses to include ornamental defensive towers, domed turrets, and roofline crenellations. Such features were an integral part of the survival of chivalry, though they may well strike us as increasingly fantastic as they became more and more detached from the realities of Renaissance warfare and military engineering. We have only to compare the delightful mock fortifications of Bolsover Castle in Derbyshire, for example, with the functionalism of contemporary defensive structures along the English south coast to see the difference.

In the same way, Sidney's bravado at Zutphen when he went into battle without leg-armour, or Essex' thrusting of his pike into the gates of Lisbon to offer single combat on behalf of his mistress, are acts that cannot be explained in terms of either Renaissance *realpolitik* or military science. Yet they are quite in harmony with the fantasies of the tiltyard and contemporary literary romances. No wonder some of the early humanist educators, among them Erasmus, Thomas More, and Juan Luis Vives, had so long before mistrusted the romance as a form of literature likely to mislead young men into acts of pointless violence, not to mention bawdry.

None the less, though the external trappings of chivalry more or less disappeared in England along with the tournament, its code of values survived, in spite of the alternative neoclassical culture that prevailed during the eighteenth century.[1] For much of this period the Middle Ages and the associated cult of chivalry were dismissed as of no account, and as representative of human barbarity and folly at their worst; none the less, during the last decades of the eighteenth century, an age that so glorified the rational in man, the beginnings of a revival occurred. During these years and the century that followed, this rediscovery manifested itself in painting, in the architecture of public buildings, churches, country houses and castles, in wealthy Englishmen's insatiable interest in collecting armour, and in the decoration of homes with mementoes of the age of chivalry.

This is the context for the publication of Sir Walter Scott's historical fictions, among them *Ivanhoe* (1820), *Quentin Durward* (1823), and *The Talisman*, all set in the Middle Ages. More than any other single factor, Scott's novels must be considered responsible for popularizing the great nineteenth-century revival of interest in the Middle Ages and with it the cult of the English gentleman and the accompanying code of chivalric values. Especially notable, also, was the connection between this revival and a kind of nostalgic conservatism that was increasingly an influential force in British politics as the English looked across the Channel at the violence and turmoil of post-revolutionary France. Indeed, even as the eighteenth century had come to its close, George III, the upper and middle classes (Tories and conservative Whigs) and the established Church had all been united in their mistrust of change and their repressive and often persecuting resistance to reform.

The Middle Ages, with its feudal social structure, its powerful Church, and its unquestioning acceptance of monarchy, offered an attractive image to those who felt threatened by the proponents of change.

Reverence for the Middle Ages continued through the nineteenth century and is exemplified by such appropriately unrelated phenomena as George IV's coronation in 1821, at which participants wore specially-made 'Elizabethan' outfits, his remodelling of Windsor Castle, the widespread decorative use of chivalric motifs, the publication of numerous medieval romances, ballads and chronicles, the publication of Meyrick's *A Critical Inquiry into Ancient Armour* (1824), the widespread building of neo-Gothic castles and mansions, the setting up of a new gallery to display the collection of armour at the Tower of London, Queen Victoria's fancy dress ball on the theme of Edward III and Queen Philippa in 1842, and a countless stream of other examples.

Inevitably, within such a context, tournaments offered a special kind of attraction. Scott provided the perfect imaginative revival in *Ivanhoe*, and in 1827 some Sussex gentlemen held a country house tilting party, but nothing anticipated the scale of the Eglinton Tournament in 1839, perhaps the most renowned manifestation of the nineteenth-century English revival of chivalry. Organized by a young Tory, Archibald William Montgomerie, the 13th Earl of Eglinton, the tournament may originally have been inspired by the rumour published in a newspaper in 1837 that the Queen was planning a tournament, that heralds were going to all parts of Europe to announce it, that a hundred English knights would defend her name, and that on the final day the last six combatants would fight to the finish, the victor to become Victoria's prince.[2] A year later, just after Queen Victoria's coronation, the same newspaper, the *Court Journal*, put out the story that the Earl of Eglinton was going to hold a tournament, and a few weeks later Eglinton confirmed this.

As a lover of chivalry, Eglinton was to some extent protesting against the Whig penny-pinching that had accompanied the coronation. Particularly disappointing had been the cancellation of the traditional banquet in Westminster Hall (George IV's had cost £25,000) and the traditional ceremony of the entry on horseback of the Queen's Champion. The publication of the news that Eglinton was to hold a tournament was received with enormous enthusiasm by some, and furious opposition by others. The event became, as Mark Girouard has pointed out, 'a symbol of Tory defiance, of aristocratic virility, of hatred of the Reform Bill . . .'.[3] Thus, in a quite new way in English history, the mere holding of a tournament became a decidedly political act, an expression in the face of indignant verbal protest of belief in the status quo of the English class structure and of faith in the superiority of the gentlemanly virtues.

As had been the case some centuries before, would-be participants found themselves spending large sums on armour, weapons, crests, pavilions, tents, shields, banners, and costumes for themselves and their retainers. The Earl himself not only furnished the tournament ground but also, in order to mock the to him unseemly tight-fistedness of the Whig government, he laid on a magnificent banquet and ball. His subsequent expenses were so vast that he then had to pledge a large part of his ancestral estate.[4] But money alone could not buy the necessary training of horse and knight. In a large garden behind a London tavern, knightly aspirants first had to practise their jousting skills by riding along a tilt barrier against the 'Railway Knight', a mechanical opponent on wheels who sped towards them down a pair of grooves. The training of horses proved more difficult, however, and of the 150 original knights, only thirteen ultimately took part in the tournament itself.

At the tournament, which was held at Eglinton Castle, about twenty miles from Glasgow, the participants assumed various fictional names (the Knight of the Red Lion, the Knight of the Burning Tower, the Knight of the White Rose, etc.), and Lady Seymour was given the role of the Queen of Beauty. A large tournament ground was prepared, complete with suitably Gothic viewing stands (see Fig. 85), and it is estimated that some 100,000 spectators assembled, among them fifty-five peers and peeresses and various foreign aristocrats. The great event was to begin with a procession from Eglinton Castle of all the knights and their retainers, together with the Queen of Beauty. As is well known, disaster struck in the form of that old enemy of British tournaments—heavy rain. All was turned to mud, the Queen of Beauty was taken from her white palfrey and placed in a closed carriage, the roofs of the stands leaked to the great discomfort of their occupants, and everywhere (including, it was said, among the knights in the procession) umbrellas were anachronistically unfurled. Attempts at tilting were disastrous, everyone got cold, wet and muddy, and the banquet and ball had to be postponed. As far as the delighted Whig press was concerned, the occasion was a flop, and there is no doubt that in popular memory this image has survived in spite of the fact that a few days later the tournament, banquet and ball all took place very successfully in perfect weather.

The Eglinton experience probably prevented any further attempts at an extended revival of the tournament in England. In other European countries tournaments had been held sporadically throughout the eighteenth century, and after 1800 they were held in Sweden (1800), Austria (1800, 1814), Malta (1828), Spain (1833) and Italy (1839, 1842, 1853, 1863, 1868, 1883, 1893).[5] Across the Atlantic, the fashion for Sir Walter Scott's novels gave added impetus to a particular kind of romanticism that flourished in the southern United States. In this area, it has been argued, the extravagant worship of women, the leisured life of an agrarian aristocracy served by slaves, and the fanatical love of horses combined to make life on a plantation analogous to life in a medieval manor, the master-slave relationship being a kind of parallel to the stratifications of the feudal system.[6] Tournaments provided an ideal expression of the cult of woman, loyalty

to caste, chivalric manners, and superior horsemanship with all that this last implied for a ruling class. Before the Civil War, tournaments were particularly common during the 1840s and 1850s in Virginia, Louisiana and South Carolina. Indeed, Mark Twain believed, not perhaps without considerable insight, that Sir Walter Scott and the southern cult of chivalry were in great measure responsible for the war.

In Britain, the rains of Ayrshire prevented the tournament from playing any sustained role in the propagation of nineteenth-century chivalric ideals, and before World War I only two more tournaments were held. The first

85   *The Eglington Tournament (1839). Though the Eglinton Tournament was spoiled by a disastrous rainstorm on its first day, it eventually took place under clear skies. This artist's impression may record how things were when the weather improved, or it may simply be an idealized rendering of how the tournament was supposed to be.*

occurred at Parham in Sussex in 1875 and involved the notorious Wilfred Scawen Blunt, Lord Zouche and the latter's wife Doll. Doll, who was having an affair with Blunt, represented the Queen of Abyssinia. Attacked by Moors, who included Blunt, she was supposed to be rescued by Lord Zouche and his companion Lord Mayo. The jealousy between Zouche and Blunt erupted unpleasantly during the fighting and the next day Doll Zouche left her husband. The Victorians are unlikely to have thought such antics worth emulating, and this particular scandal, along with the Eglinton experience, seems to have put paid to any further similar events. There was, however, one further tournament before World War I. This was held some thirty-seven years later, on 11 July 1912, in the Empress Hall at Earls Court where, as part of a celebration of Shakespearean England, a number of aristocrats staged an Elizabethan-style tournament before an audience that included Queen Alexandria, Lord Curzon of Kedleston, Lord Rosebery, Sir Ernest Cassel, Winston Churchill and Pierpont Morgan.[7]

Yet, even with the end of the nineteenth century, chivalry did not die. As much of the rhetoric, the literature and the propaganda associated with World War I demonstrates, the continuous diet of chivalric ideals so warmly received by so many upper- and middle-class Britains during previous decades provided a ready-made incentive and elicited a predictable response to the call to arms. Manliness, heroic sacrifice, patriotic loyalty, and the defence of noble causes were now to have their day. Even the meanest clerk would have his great moment of glory in the tiltyard. Herbert Asquith put it this way in a poem that was much admired at the time:[8]

Here lies a clerk who half his life had spent
Toiling at ledgers in a city grey,
Thinking that so his days would drift away
With no lance broken in life's tournament.
Yet ever 'twixt the books and his bright eyes
The gleaming eagles of the legions came,
And horsemen, charging under phantom skies,
Went thundering past beneath the oriflamme.

And now those waiting dreams are satisfied;
From twilight to the halls of dawn he went;
His lance is broken; but he lies content
With that high hour, in which he lived and died.

Four years after war broke out, however, chivalry was dead. In spite of recurrent subsequent evidence to the contrary—the patriotic rhetoric that heralded World War II and most recently the Falklands War, Hollywood fantasies of King Arthur or Robin Hood, films such as *Scott of the Antarctic*, Olivier's *Henry V*, and dozens of Westerns—the smashed illusions of those who survived the unspeakable realities of World War I could never be put back together again. Today, the war poetry that shapes our consciousness is not that of a Herbert Asquith but the brutal nightmares of Sassoon, Owen, and Rosenberg. We have, too, the experience of the Holocaust (the ultimate product of the fascist potential inherent in chivalry) and the current threat that war, whether fought in an 'honourable' cause or otherwise, will lead inevitably to total doom.

Even so, the phenomenon of the tournament survives. Almost every summer weekend, the English public may observe the spectacle of knights in armour jousting and displaying their martial and equestrian skills. The centre for these activities is Chilham Castle in Kent, headquarters of the Jousting Association, a private association of medieval enthusiasts whose aim, according to one of their pamphlets, is 'to bring back the colour, pageantry and excitement of mediaeval days'. The founder of the Jousting Association is Max Diamond, otherwise known as The Black Gauntlet, an ex-stuntman who has led his knights to Canada, Australia, South Africa, and West Germany.[9] In August 1985, a new dimension was added to the career of this knight errant when a team of French knights crossed on to English soil to attend a tournament at Chilham as a kind of return match to follow the Field of Cloth of Gold 465 years previous.

Max Diamond's work is obviously in part a commercial enterprise that derives its profits from spectators' entry fees, from school educational visits, and from opportunities to advise film-makers and producers of various kinds of 'medieval' events. As such, he is closer to a William Marshal (see Chapter 1) than a Philip Sidney or a Henry Lee. More significant, however, is the fact that the tournaments at Chilham, however colourful and spectacular, lack two ingredients that were so evident and vital in the Tudor and Jacobean eras and in the Eglinton revival—they are not expressive of a chivalric code of values nor do they seem motivated by any polital purpose, unless the professed desire of the Association 'to upkeep our great heritage and to attract overseas visitors to Britain' be construed as somehow political. Apart from the Eglinton venture in 1839 and the tournaments of 1827, 1875 and 1912, the English tournament as an expression of the chivalric values of its organizers and participants ceased when Charles I turned his back on them in 1625.

If we accept that the chivalric code in some way contributed to the English Civil War, the American Civil War, World War I, the rise of fascism in the 1930s, the Falklands War, and the current behaviour of South Africa's white minority, then we should be content to see Max Diamond and his knights as engaged only in a delightful exercise in historical re-creation, with the need to earn a living the main motivation for acquiring their skills. If those are their goals, I wish them well.

Abbreviations used in Appendix and Notes

B.L. The British Library (London)

BEAL Peter Beal, 'Poems by Sir Philip Sidney: The Ottley Manuscripts', *The Library*, 5th series, 33 (1978), 284–95.

BIRCH, *ELIZABETH* Thomas Birch, *Memoirs of the Reign of Queen Elizabeth* (1754).

BIRCH, *JAMES* Thomas Birch, *The Court and Times of James I* (1849).

BROWN Sebastian Giustinian, *Four Years at the Court of Henry VIII*, translated and selected by Rawdon Brown, 2 vols. (London, 1854).

C.A. The College of Arms (London)

CSP *SPANISH* G.A. Bergenroth and others (eds.), *Calendars of Letters, Despatches, and State Papers, relating to the Negotiations between England and Spain, 1558–1607*, 13 vols. (London, 1862–1916); and M.A.S. Hume (ed.), *Calendar of State Papers, Spanish, Elizabeth,* 4 vols. (London, 1892–9).

CSP *VENETIAN* Rawdon Brown and others (eds.), *Calendar of State Papers and Manuscripts Relating to English Affairs Existing in the Archives and Collections of Venice, and in Other Libraries of Northern Italy,* 9 vols. (London, 1864–98, 1900, 1904, 1905).

CHAMBERLAIN *The Letters of John Chamberlain,* ed. Norman Egbert McClure, 2 vols. (Philadelphia, 1939).

COLLINS Arthur Collins, *Letters and Memorials of State,* 2 vols. (1746).

CRIPPS-DAY Francis Henry Cripps-Day, *The History of the Tournament in England and in France* (London, 1918).

FEUILLERAT, *ELIZABETH* Albert Feuillerat (ed.), *Documents Relating to the Office of the Revels in the Time of Queen Elizabeth* (Louvain, 1908).

FEUILLERAT, *MARY* Albert Feuillerat (ed.), *Documents Relating to the Revels at Court in the Time of King Edward VI and Queen Mary* (Louvain, 1914).

GTR Sydney Anglo, *The Great Tournament Roll of Westminster* (Oxford, 1968).

GAIRDNER James Gairdner (ed.), *Letters and Papers Illustrative of the Reigns of Richard III and Henry VII* (London, 1861–3). 2 vols.

GAWDY *Letters of Philip Gawdy,* ed. Issac H. Jeayes (London, 1906).

GOLDWELL Henry Goldwell, *A briefe declaration of the shews* (1581).

HMC *HATFIELD* *Historical Manuscripts Commission. Calendar of the Manuscripts of the Most Hon. The Marquis of Salisbury Preserved at Hatfield House,* vols. XI and XII (London, 1906 and 1910).

HMC *RUTLAND* *Historical Manuscripts Commission. The Manuscripts of His Grace the Duke of Rutland Preserved at Belvoir Castle,* vol. IV (London, 1905).

HALL *Hall's Chronicle; Containing the History of England,* ed. Henry Ellis (London, 1809).

HASS. 68 Quarto MS. Hass. 68 in Kassel Landesbibliothek und Murhardsche Bibliothek.

JONSON *Ben Jonson,* ed. C.H. Herford and Percy and Evelyn Simpson, 11 vols. (Oxford, 1925–52).

JORDAN W.K. Jordan (ed.), *The Chronicles and Political Papers of King Edward VI* (London, 1966).

KING'S WORKS *The History of the King's Works,* ed. H.M. Colvin, vol. IV (London, 1982).

KIPLING Gordon Kipling, *The Triumph of Honour: Burgundian Origins of the Elizabethan Renaissance* (The Hague, 1977).

L.P.   *Letters and Papers, Foreign and Domestic, of the Reign of Henry VIII, 1509–47,* vols. 2–21, ed. J.S. Brewer, J. Gairdner, and R.H. Brodie (London, 1862–1910).

LEE   E.K. Chambers, *Sir Henry Lee* (Oxford, 1936).

LELAND   John Leland, *De Rebus Britannicis Collectanea,* vol. II (1774).

LODGE   E. Lodge (ed.), *Illustrations of British History,* 3 vols. (1791).

MACHYN   *The Diary of Henry Machyn,* ed. John Nichols (London, 1848).

NICHOLS, *ELIZABETH*   John Nichols, *The Progresses and Public Processions of Queen Elizabeth,* 3 vols. (London, 1823).

NICHOLS, *JAMES*   John Nichols, *The Progresses, Processions, and Magnificent Festivities, of King James the First,* 4 vols. (London, 1828).

ORGEL & STRONG   Stephen Orgel & Roy Strong, *Inigo Jones: The Theatre of the Stuart Court,* 2 vols. (London, Berkeley, and Los Angeles, 1973).

PRO   The Public Record Office (London)

PEELE   *The Life and Minor Works of George Peele,* ed. David H. Horne (New Haven and London, 1952).

RORD   *Research Opportunities in Renaissance Drama.*

SEGAR (1590)   William Segar, *Of Honor and Armes* (1590).

SEGAR (1602)   William Segar, *Honor Militarie and Ciuil* (1602).

SPECTACLE   Sydney Anglo, *Spectacle and Pageantry and Early Tudor Policy* (Oxford, 1969).

SPEDDING   *The Works of Francis Bacon,* edited by James Spedding, Robert Leslie Ellis, Douglas D. Heath, vol. VIII (London, 1858).

STRONG   Roy Strong, *The Cult of Elizabeth: Elizabethan Portraiture and Pageantry* (London, 1977).

VALE   Juliet Vale, *Edward III and Chivalry: Chivalric Society and its Context, 1270–1350* (Woodbridge, 1982).

VON RAUMER   Frederick von Raumer, *History of the Sixteenth and Seventeenth Centuries Illustrated by Original Documents,* 2 vols. (London, 1835).

VON WEDEL   'Journey through England and Scotland Made by Lupold von Wedel in the Years 1584 and 1585', *Transactions of the Royal Historical Society,* n.s. 9 (1895), 223–70.

WALKER   J.D. Walker (ed.), *The Records of the Honourable Society of Lincoln's Inn: The Black Books,* 4 vols. (London, 1897).

WICKHAM   Glynne Wickham, *Early English Stages,* 3 vols. [vol. II in two parts] (London and New York, 1959, 1963, 1972, 1981).

WINWOOD   Sir Ralph Winwood, *Memorials of Affairs of State in the Reigns of Q. Elizabeth, and K. James I,* ed. Edmund Sawyer, 3 vols. (1725).

YOUNG (1)   Alan R. Young, 'Sir Philip Sidney's Tournament Impresas', *Sidney Newsletter,* 6 No. 1 (1985), 6–24.

YOUNG (2)   Alan R. Young, 'A Note on the Tournament Impresas in *Pericles*', *Shakespeare Quarterly,* 36 no. 4 (1985), 453–6.

Selected Glossary

à outrance jousts **à outrance** (later called **jousts of war**) employed the sharp edged and sharp-pointed weapons of war. As in real war, the combatants fought until one was disabled or killed.

à plaisance jousts **à plaisance** (later called **jousts of peace**) employed rebated weapons.

article petitions and challenges were usually accompanied by articles or a list of statements, setting out the rules governing the conduct of the proposed tournament.

attaint (or **atteint**) a blow. In the sophisticated scoring system that developed for the judging of jousts, points were awarded for the number of lances broken and for **attaints** (blows) on different parts of the body.

bard a term for horse armour. Originally consisting of a mail trapper, quilted cloth, or hardened leather, later horse armours were often made of plate. Horse armours could also include protection for the head, neck, and crupper (see **shaffron**, **crinet**, **crupper**). For tournaments, bards were sometimes merely ornamented cloth (see **caparison** and **trapper**).

barriers combat at barriers was a form of foot combat that eventually became a familiar event at most tournaments. Opponents, either singly or in groups, were separated by a waist-high wooden barrier and fought each other either with swords or long staves. In the 16th and 17th centuries, combats at barriers were frequently held indoors and accompanied by disguisings and the use of scenic devices and music.

bases usually made of fabric, but occasionally imitated in metal plate, **bases** were the deep skirts (often highly decorated) worn by knights from the waist to the knee.

burre (or **burr** or **bur**) a broad iron ring on a tilting lance just behind the place for the hand.

caparison a cloth or covering spread over the saddle or harness of a horse. It was often richly ornamented. At times the term appears to have been used for the defensive armour for a horse (see also **bard** and **trapper**).

challenge a summons or invitation to a combat. The challenge to a tournament frequently contained various (often fictional) assertions as to the challenger's (or his mistress's) superiority. It named a time and place for the combat and specified the types of contest and the weapons to be used. The proclamation of a challenge was one of the functions of heralds

chanfron (see **shaffron**).

coronel (or **colonel**, **cronall**, **curnall**, or **coronal**) a special tip added to the head of a tilting lance. It consisted of three or four short spreading points and thereby prevented any danger of a lance penetrating the armour of an opponent.

crinet (or **crinière**) part of the armour for a horse. It was attached to the top of the **shaffron** and protected the horse's neck and mane.

crupper the rear part of a horse. The term is often used to refer to the armour protecting that part of the horse's body.

garniture a large selection of matching pieces of armour which can be used to make up different types of tournament and field armour.

helm (or **heaume**) a large helmet that enclosed the entire head. Helms were of many types and special forms were developed solely for jousting, foot-combats, and other specialized combats.

impresa (or **imprese**) an emblematic device consisting of a brief motto and a symbolic picture. It alluded to its bearer in some personal fashion.

joust jousting was probably German in origin and is first seen in tournaments as a preliminary event in which knights or squires rode at each other, one on one, with lances. Initially, this event was quite distinct from the group combat, the main event of early tournaments. With increased emphasis on safety, the presence of female spectators, and the recognition that jousting offered considerable potential for the individual display of personal prowess and martial skill, this event supplanted tourneying as the main feature of tournaments. From the early 15th century, jousters commonly rode at each other separated by a wooden barrier (see **tilt**).

judgehouse the special viewing stand built to house the tournament judges at many Tudor and Jacobean tournaments.

lists the palisades enclosing the area designated for the events of a tournament. However, the term was frequently used for the space so enclosed and it is in this sense that the word is employed in this book.

locking gauntlet a steel gauntlet for the right hand, permitting a knight to lock his sword into his hand so that it could not be lost. Though often banned from earlier tournaments, it later became an accepted part of tournament equipment.

mail sometimes mistakenly referred to as 'chain' mail. An early form of armour made of interlinked metal rings.

manifer (or **main de fer**) a large steel gauntlet for the left hand and lower left arm (sometimes called a 'bridle gauntlet') that gave extra protection by covering the ordinary gauntlet on the exposed left side of a jouster.

morne the rebated head of a tilting lance.

petition the formal request made to the monarch, in the early Tudor period and before, asking for licence to hold a tournament.

pole-axe (or **pollaxe**) a weapon consisting of an axe-like head at the end of a handle.

punching stave (or **puncheon stave**) a spear or staff armed with a sharp point.

pursuivant an heraldic officer, ranking below a herald, who in turn ranks below a King of Arms in the English College of Arms.

rebated to be blunted or dulled. Rebated lances for tournaments had safety tips fixed to their points. Rebated swords had blunt edges and flat ends.

rondel a small round metal plate used on some helmets and gauntlets to protect vulnerable straps and catches.

Round Table from the early 13th century there are records of knights attending tournament-like events referred to as **Round Tables**. These sometimes involved the use of Arthurian costume and other imitations of Arthurian romance. In particular they appear to have emulated the festive character of Arthurian romance and were characterized by martial games, for which rebated weapons were used, and by an emphasis upon feasting and dancing. Historians are undecided as to whether Round Tables were actually derived from Arthurian romance or were themselves in existence before their romance counterparts. Such events continued to be held in the first part of the 14th century but thereafter are less and less frequently heard of.

running at ring the object of this sport was to catch a suspended ring on the point of one's lance. It was far safer than jousting, and hence often preferred. It was also a way of practising for jousting.

shaffron part of the armour for a horse. It covered the forehead, the front of the nose, and the cheeks of the horse. Often there were holes for the eyes, sometimes protected by flanges. Frequently the shaffron would have a sharp spike on the forehead.

tilt the **tilt** was a barrier, initially of cloth or canvas but later of wood, erected down the centre of the lists. It was a safety feature first used at tournaments early in the 15th century. Opponents jousted one on either side of the tilt and were thus prevented from colliding with each other. Their lances were necessarily pointed at an angle, making them more likely to break and less likely to cause injury.

tonlet a 'skirt' of armour protecting the hips and upper thighs.

tournament (or **tourneamentum, hastiludium, burdicia, ludi equestri**) a term often loosely used to refer to all types of mock mounted combat. Strictly speaking, it should be confined to cavalry combats involving opposing groups of antagonists in the manner of the earliest events known as 'tournaments'. In this book, however, the term has been used to refer to any meeting at which mock combats were held, the exact nature of such combats being specified by such terms as **joust**, **tourney**, combat at **barriers**, etc.

tourney a mock cavalry combat in which groups of knights fought against each other. At Tudor and Jacobean tournaments, the tourney came to consist of single combats, using swords as weapons. The tourney was usually the second event of an English tournament in the 16th and 17th centuries and followed the jousting.

trapper a covering for a horse made of cloth, mail, or plates. Cloth trappers could be elaborately decorated (see also **bard**, and **caparison**).

vamplate a circular metal plate on the jousting lance that protected the right hand where it held the lance.

Appendix

A CALENDAR OF TUDOR AND JACOBEAN TOURNAMENTS

[This Chronology includes only the principal documentary sources. In a number of instances these have subsequently been reprinted. See *GTR*, pp. 138–46; Anglo, 'The Court Festivals of Henry VII: A Study Based upon the Account Books of John Heron, Treasurer of the Chamber', *Bulletin of the John Rylands Library*, 43. 1 (1960), 12–45; Anglo, 'Archives of the English Tournament: Score Cheques and Lists', *Journal of the Society of Archivists*, 2 no. 4 (1961), 153–62; Anglo, 'Financial and Heraldic Records of the English Tournament', *Journal of the Society of Archivists*, 2 (1962), 183–95; W.R. Streitberger, 'Renaissance Revels Documents, 1485–1642', *RORD*, 21 (1978), 11–6; W.R. Streitberger, 'Court Festivities of Henry VII: 1485–1491, 1502–1505', *RORD*, 26 (1983), 31–54; C.E. McGee and John C. Meagher's checklists of Tudor and Stuart Entertainments in *RORD*, 24 (1981), 51–155; 25 (1982), 31–114; 27 (1984), 47–126; and see also the various works referred to in the prefatory 'Note on Sources'.]

Tournaments of Henry VII's Reign

13 Nov. 1485.
Coronation jousts for Henry VII. Palace of Westminster.
B.L. MS. Egerton 985, fol. 47b; PRO E.404/79, ♯58 and ♯90; PRO Lord Chamberlain's Series I, ♯424.

?Between 5 June and 20 Sept. 1486.
Jousts. Location unknown.
PRO E.403/2558, fol. 4b; and E.404/79, ♯4.

Nov. 1487.
Coronation Jousts for Queen Elizabeth. ?Palace of Westminster.
PRO E.404/79, ♯38.

21, 29, 30 Nov. 1489.
Creation of Arthur Prince of Wales. Mock Battle. London.
B.L. MS. Cotton Julius B. xii, fols. 58–61.

May 1492.
Tournament. Sheen.
B.L. MS. Add. 7099, fol. 3; B.L. Cotton Vitellius A. xvi, fol. 145b; B.L. MS. Harl. 69, fols. 3b–4a, 7a; Guildhall Library MS. 3313, fol. 225a; Segar (1590), p. 92. [Segar mistakenly dates this event in 1494.]

29 Oct., 9, 11, 13 Nov. 1494.
Jousts and tourney for creation of Henry Duke of York. Palace of Westminster.
B.L. MS. Cotton Julius B. xii, fols. 91–110; B.L. Cotton Vitellius A. xvi, fols. 150–52a; B.L. MS. Add. 7099; B.L. Add. 6113, fols. 67–8; B.L. MS. Harl. 69, fols. 6a–b, 7b–8a, 21b–22a; B.L. Add. 33,735, fol. 5b–6a; Guildhall Library MS. 3313, fols. 233b–35; C.A. MS. M. 6, fol. 58b; Walker, I, 104. [B.L. MS. Harl. 69 contains a proposal for jousts and tourney on 12 Nov. (fol. 7b).]

Thurs. 23 May 1494/or 1499/or 1504/or 1510.
Barriers. Greenwich.
B.L. MS. Harl. 69, fol. 5b. [The exact date of this event is uncertain (see Kipling, p. 137n; *GTR*, p. 21n, 138).]

May 1501.

Tournament. Tower of London.
B.L. MS. Egerton 2358, fol. 12a–b.

Nov. 1501.

Welcome for Katherine of Aragon. Jousts, tourney and barriers. Palace of Westminster.
B.L. MS. Cotton Vitellius A. xvi, fols. 184–98; B.L. MS. Cotton Vitellius F. xii; B.L. MS. Harl. 69, fols. 28b–32b; B.L. MS. Egerton 2358, fols. 24–42; B.L. MS. Add. 46455, fols. 4–10; C.A. MS. I M. 3, fols. 24–6a; C.A. MS. 1st M. 13, fols. 52a–7b; PRO E. 101/415/3; Middle Temple Library, *Minutes of Parliament* (1501); Archives of the Simancas, T. c. Y. 2.

1502.

Triumph. Tower of London. Possibly same event as May 1501.
Segar (1590), p. 92.
[Possibly a misdated reference to event of May 1501.]

24. Jan. 1502.

Tournament to celebrate proxy marriage of Princess Margaret to James IV of Scotland. London.
Houghton Library, Harvard MS. English 1095 (unfoliated).

Summer 1505.

Jousts. Richmond.
B.L. MS. Add. 21,480; B.L. MS. Add. 59899, fol. 93b.

Feb. 1506.

Jousts, tourney, and barriers to entertain Philip of Castile. Richmond.
B.L. MS. Cotton Vespasian C. xii, fols. 236–44a; Guildhall Library MS. 3313, fols. 59b–60b; PRO. E. 36/214 (entries for 20 Feb. and 3 April); Hall, p. 501.

14–21 May 1506.

Jousts, tourney, barriers and other martial sports in answer of challenge of Lady of May. Greenwich.
B.L. MS. Harl. 69, fols. 2b–3b. [For the dating of this event see Kipling, p. 132, n. 37.]

On and about 23 April (St George's Day) 1507.

Jousts and feasts. Carew Castle.
M.E. James, *The Life of Sir Rhys ap Thomas* (Tenby, n.d.), cited by Mark Girouard, *Life in the English Country House* (Harmondsworth, 1980), pp. 26–7.

May, June, 1507.

Jousts in honour of Queen of May. Kennington.
C.A. MS. R. 36, fols. 124a–5b; S.M.L. 29 (Ceremonies), fol. 21 (a later copy of MS. R. 36, fols. 124a–5b); PRO. *Revels*, E. 36/214, entry for 10 May; Anonymous, *Here begynneth the iustes of maye* (dated 12th year of Henry VIII's reign). This text is followed by *Here begynneth the Iustes and Tourney of ye moneth of Iune.*

June 1508.

'Hastiludia' and Running at Ring. Greenwich.
A.G. L'Estrange, *The Palace and the Hospital; or Chronicles of Greenwich* (London, 1886), I, 130. [L'Estrange does not cite his source.]

Dec. 1508.

Tourney to celebrate betrothal of Princess Mary and Archduke Charles. London (or Westminster).
Petrus Carmelianus, *The Solemnities & triumphes doon & made at the spousells and Mariage of the kynges doughter* (1508). An English translation in *The solempnities and triumphes* (STC 17558).

Tournaments in Henry VIII's Reign

25–6 June 1509.

Jousts to celebrate coronation of Henry VIII. Westminster Palace.
Guildhall Library MS. 3313, fols. 316 (69)–320a (73); PRO. *Revels*, LC 9/50, fols. 211–12; PRO. Rolls Office, Sp. Trans. I., 5, fol. 51; Inner Temple, *Acts of Parliament, 1509* (see F.A. Inderwick [ed.], *A Calendar of the Inner Temple Records* (London, 1896), I, 14; Walker, I, 154–5; Hall, pp. 510–2.

August 1509.

Tilting at the Ring. Westminster (?).
I Diarii di Marino Sanuto, ed. F. Stefani (Venice, 1879–1902), V, ix, 122; (*CSP, Venetian*, II, 5 (item #11); *L.P.*, I i, 75.

12 January 1510.

Jousts at Christmas. Richmond Palace.
Hall, p. 513.

18 January 1510.

Tournament. Location unknown.
L.P., I i, 156.

17 March 1510.

Tilting at the ring to entertain Spanish ambassadors. Location unknown.

PRO. *Revels*, E. 36/217, fols. 24–5; Hall, p. 514; *L.P.*, I i, 185.

23, 27 May and 1, 3 June 1510.
Barriers for Maying festival at Greenwich.
B.L. MS. Harl. 69, fol. 5b [this item may relate to an earlier event]; C.A. MS. L. 12, fols. 10–11; Hall, p. 515; *CSP Spanish*, II, 44 (item #45).

June–September 1510.
Jousts and tourney during summer. Oking.
Hall, p. 515.

October 1510.
Foot combats. Greenwich.
Hall, p. 515.

13 November 1510.
Jousts, tourney, and running at ring. Richmond Palace.
Hall, p. 516; *L.P.*, II ii, 1493.

12, 13 February 1511.
Jousts in honour of birth of Prince Henry. Westminster Palace.
Bodleian Library MS. Ashmolean 1116, fols. 109–10; B.L. MS. Add. 6113, fols. 79b–80, 201b–2, 208b; B.L. MS. Add 18,826, fol. 16; B.L. MS. Add. 12, 514, fols. 136ff; B.L. Cart. Harl. Antiq. 83 H. I; B.L. MS. Harl. 69. fols. 4b–5; B.L. MS. Harl. 6079, fol. 36b; C.A. MS. 'The Great Tournament Roll of Westminster'; C.A. MS. Jousting Cheques for 'Justs holden at Westminster'; Guildhall Library MS. 3313, fols. 94b–101; PRO. *Revels*, E. 36/217, fols. 41–55; PRO. *Revels*, E. 36/229, fols. 23–87; PRO. Rolls Office MS. 'The King's Book of Payments 1 May 1509–December 1518'; Hall, pp. 517–8; Segar (1602), p. 192.

1–3 May 1511.
Jousts and tourneys for Maying celebrations. Greenwich.
Guildhall Library MS. 3313, fol. 101b; Hall, p. 520.

15 May 1511.
Jousts for Maying celebrations. Location unknown.
Hall, p. 521.

1 January 1512.
Assault on mock castle (*Le Fortresse Dangerus*). Greenwich.
PRO. *Revels*, E. 36/229, fols. 175–205; PRO. *Revels*, SP 2/Fol. A, no. 4; PRO. Rolls Office MS. 'The King's Book of Payments 1 May 1509–

December 1518' (see payment dated April 1512 for Christmas expenses). Hall, p. 526.

1 June 1512.
Jousts preceded by pageant of a fountain and a coal black castle (*The Dolorous Castle*). Greenwich.
PRO. *Revels*, E. 36/217, fols. 163–9; PRO. Rolls Office MS. 'The King's Book of Payments 1 May 1509–December 1518'; Hall, pp. 533–4.

6 September 1513.
Tournament (exact nature unclear) during Henry VIII's military campaign in France. St Omers.
B.L. MS. Stowe 146, fol. 109.

18 October 1513.
Jousts to celebrate capitulation of Tournai. Margaret of Savoy was principal spectator. Tournai.
PRO. *Revels*, E. 36/217, fols. 72–3; PRO. *Revels*, SP. 1/7, fol. 74; *Calendar of State Papers (Milan)* (London, 1912), i, 669; Hall, p. 566.

May 1514.
Jousts. Probably to celebrate Maying at Greenwich.
Hall, p. 568.

3 February 1515.
Jousts to celebrate Candlemas. Greenwich.
PRO. *Revels*, E. 36/217, fols. 205–9; PRO. *Revels*, SP. 2/Fol. A, no. 7; Hall. pp. 580–1.

19 April 1515.
Jousts. Richmond Palace.
PRO. *Revels*, E. 36/217, fols. 210–2; PRO. *Revels*, SP. 2/Fol. A. no. 8; PRO. Rolls Office MS. 'The King's Book of Payments 1 May 1509–December 1518'; Hall, p. 581.

1 May 1515.
Jousts to celebrate Maying. Greenwich.
PRO. *Revels*, SP. 2/Fol. A. No. 8; Sanuto, *Diarii*, xx, 243 (see Brown, I, 75–6, 81).

29 January and 5 February 1516.
Running at the ring. Greenwich.
PRO. *Revels*, E. 36/229, fols. 159–73.

19, 20 May 1516.
Jousts to honour Queen of Scots. Greenwich.
PRO. *Revels*, E. 36/217, fols. 232–51; PRO. Rolls Office MS. 'The King's Book of Payments 1 May 1509–December 1518'; B.L. MS. Harl. 69, fol. 16b; C.A. MS. Jousting Cheque ('Justys att Grenewyche'); Letter from Thomas Allen to

Earl of Shrewsbury dated 1516, quoted by S.R. Meyrick, *A Critical Inquiry into Ancient Armour* (London, 1824), II, 262; Hall, pp. 584–5.

7 July 1517.

Joust to entertain Flemish ambassadors. Greenwich.

B.L. MS. Add. 21,116, fol. 40; PRO. *Revels*, E. 36/217, fols. 77–88; PRO. Rolls Office MS. 'The King's Book of Payments 1 May 1509–December 1518'; C.A. MS. M. 7, fol. 61; *CSP Venetian,* II, item ♯918; Brown, II, 97–8; Sanuto, *Diarii*, xxiv, 468 (see Brown, II, 101–3); Hall, pp. 591–2.

6, 7 October 1518.

Jousts to celebrate Treaty of Universal Peace and to entertain the French ambassadors. ?Greenwich.

PRO. *Revels*, E. 36/228, 1–6; PRO. Rolls Office MS. 'The King's Book of Payments 1 May 1509–December 1518'; *CSP Venetian,* II, 464–67; Brown, II, 224–5, 228–35; Sanuto, *Diarii*, xxvi, 136 (see Brown, II, 233–4); Hall, p. 595.

3, 8 March 1519.

Jousts to entertain the French hostages. Greenwich.

PRO. Rolls Office MS. 'King's Book of Payments 1519'; PRO. *Revels*, SP. 1/18, fols. 53–8; Hall, p. 598.

21, 27, 28 October 1519.

Jousts for Earl of Devonshire's wedding. Greenwich.

PRO. *Revels*, E. 36/217, fols. 97–100; PRO. Rolls Office MS. 'King's Book of Payments, 1519'.

1, 19 February 1520.

Jousts for Shrovetide. Greenwich.

PRO. *Revels*, E. 36/217, fols. 108–10; Hall, pp. 600–1.

11–23 June 1520.

Jousts, tourneys, barriers. Meeting between Henry VIII and Francis I. The Field of the Cloth of Gold (Guisnes).

PRO. *Revels*, E. 36/217, 132–62, 279–88; PRO. *Revels*, E. 36/229, fols. 89–123; Sanuto, *Diarii*, xxviii, xxix; Archivio Gonzaga (Mantua), B. 85, B. xxxiii. 10; Bodleian Library MS. Ashmole 1116; B.L. Cotton Caligula D. VII; *CSP Venetian*, III; C.A. MS. 1st M. 6, fols. 7b–12b, 67–73; Segar (1590), pp. 92–3; *Lordonnance et ordre du tournoy ioustes et combat a pied et a cheval* (Paris, 1520); *La description et ordre du camp, festins*

et joustes (Paris, 1520); *Chronicle of Calais*, ed. John G. Nichols (London, 1846); Hall. pp. 610–18.

10, 12 February 1521.

Jousts and tourney. Greenwich.

PRO. *Revels*, SP. I/29, fols. 211–5b; Hall, p. 622.

2 March 1522.

Jousts to entertain Imperial ambassadors. Greenwich.

PRO. *Revels*, SP. I/29, fols. 219–24; Hall, pp. 630–1.

4, 5 June 1522.

Jousts and tourney to entertain Charles V. Greenwich.

PRO. *Revels*, SP. I/24, 225, 235b–6; Hall, pp. 634–6; *CSP Spanish*, II, 420–5, 443–5; *CSP Spanish, Supplement*, pp. 135–40.

10 March 1524.

Jousts. Location unknown (probably Greenwich).

Hall, p. 674.

29 December, 2, 3, 5 January, 8 February 1524–5.

Jousts, tourney, barriers and assault on a castle called 'Loyal'. Greenwich.

PRO. *Revels*, SP. 1/32, fols. 271–6; B.L. MS. Add. 33,735, fol. 4b; B.L. MS. Harl. 69, fols. 20b–1; C.A. MS. M. 6, fols. 57b–8; C.A. MS. 'Tournaments Lists and Score Cheque Portfolio' (Box 37); Hall, pp. 688–91.

14 January 1526.

Barriers. Greenwich.

PRO. *Revels*, SP. 1/37, fols. 8–16.

13 February 1526.

Jousts on Shrove Tuesday. Greenwich.

Hall, pp. 707–8.

30 December, 3 January.

Jousts and tourney for Christmas. Greenwich.

Hall, p. 719.

19 February 1527.

Jousts (?for Shrovetide). Location unknown (probably Greenwich).

PRO. *Revels*, SP. 1/41, fols. 179–82b; Hall, p. 719.

6 May 1527.

Jousts to celebrate Anglo-French League and to entertain French ambassadors. Greenwich.

PRO. *Revels*, SP. 1/41, fols. 239–71b; Sanuto, *Diarii*, xiv, cols. 265–8 (see *CSP Venetian*, IV, 57–61 (item ♯105); Hall, p. 722.

10 November 1527.
Jousts to celebrate Henry VIII's investiture of the Order of St Michael and to entertain French delegation. Greenwich.
Hall, p. 734.

Christmas 1528/29.
Jousts and tourney to entertain Papal legates. Greenwich.
Hall, p. 756.

31 May 1533.
Jousts to celebrate coronation of Anne Boleyn. New tiltyard at Whitehall Palace.
Charles Wriothesley, *A Chronicle of England during the Reigns of the Tudors*, ed. William Douglas Hamilton (London, 1875); Walker, I, 235–56; Hall, p. 805; L.P., VI, item 601, p. 278.

January 1536.
Henry VIII jousted but possibly not in a tournament. Greenwich.
CSP Spanish, V, ii, 39 (item #21); L.P., X, 71 (item #200).

6 January 1540.
Jousts to celebrate coronation of Anne of Cleves. Probably at Whitehall.
Hall, p. 837.

1, 2, 3 May 1540.
Jousts, tourney and barriers to celebrate May Day. Whitehall.
PRO. Rolls Office MS (calendared in *L.P.*, XV, 300 (item #616); B.L. MS. Harl. 69, fols.18a–b; C.A. Partition Book I, fols. 80b, 126a; Segar (1590), p. 93. John Stow, *The Survey of London* (London, 1956), pp. 400–1.

Tournaments in Edward VI's Reign

21, 22 February 1547.
Jousts and tourney for coronation of Edward VI. Whitehall.
B.L. MS. Egerton 3026, fols. 30a–31b; Wriothesley, *Chronicle of England*, p. 183.

Shrovetide 1548.
Jousts and martial feats, including siege and assault of mock castle. Greenwich.
Stow, *Annales* (1631), p. 595.

January 1550.
Barriers on Candlemas Day. Location unknown.
Viscount Dillon, 'Barriers and Foot Combats',

Archaeological Journal, 61 (1904), 304.
Dillon does not cite a source for his information.

May 1550.
Running at the ring. Location unknown.
Jordan, p. 32.

June 1550.
Jousts and tourney. Richmond.
Jordan, pp. 32–3.

June 1550.
'Tilt and tourney on foot'. ?Whitehall.
Jordan, p. 33.

19 June 1550.
Water tournament. Deptford.
Jordan, p. 36.

1 April 1551.
Running at the ring and other martial feats. Location unknown.
Jordan, p. 57.

3 May 1551.
Running at the ring and tourney. Greenwich.
Jordan, p. 61; Machyn, p. 5.

6 July 1551.
Running at the ring. Blackheath.
Machyn, p. 7.

3, 6 January 1552.
Jousts, tourney and barriers. Greenwich.
Feuillerat, *Mary*, pp. 56, 63, 66–7, 76, 82–4; Jordan, pp. 97, 103–5.

17 January 1552.
Jousts. Greenwich.
Jordan, p. 106.

12 May 1552.
Running at the ring and other martial feats. Blackheath (near Greenwich).
B.L. MS. Cotton Vitellius F. v (Machyn, p. 18).

Tournaments in Queen Mary's Reign

4 December 1554.
Barriers. 'Before the Court gate' (?Greenwich).
C.A. MS. M. 6, fol. 59b; B.L. MS. Harl. 69, fols. 22b–3b; B.L. MS. Add. 33,735, fols. 6b–7a; Nichols, *Elizabeth*, II, 332–3.

18 December 1554.
Running 'on fott with spayers and swerds at the tornay'. 'At the court gatte' (?Greenwich).

B.L. MS. Cotton Vitellius F. v (Machyn, p. 79).

24 January 1555.
Jousts. Whitehall.
Machyn, p. 80.

12 February 1555.
Jousts and tourney to celebrate marriage of Lord Strange and Lady Cumberland. Location unknown.
B.L. MS. Cotton Vitellius F. v (Machyn, p. 82).

19 March 1555.
Jousts. Location unknown.
B.L. MS. Cotton Vitellius F. v (Machyn, p. 83); J. Strype, *Ecclesiastical Memoirs* (Oxford, 1822), III, i, 385.

25 March 1555.
Jousts. Whitehall.
B.L. MS. Cotton Vitellius F. v (Machyn, p. 84).

Shrovetide 1556.
'A tourney by six knights.' The great hall at Hatfield.
B.L. MS. Cotton Vitellius F. v (part of *Diary of Henry Machyn* destroyed by fire). Nichols *Elizabeth* reprints text of Strype who drew on the Cotton MS. (I, 16–7).

29 December 1557.
Jousts for Christmas. Hampton Court.
B.L. MS. Cotton Vitellius F. v (from portion destroyed fire); Nichols in *Elizabeth* gives Strype's versions of Cotton MS. (I, 18–9).

Tournaments in Queen Elizabeth I's Reign

1558.
Jousts, tourney and barriers. Whitehall.
Segar (1590), p. 94. Segar specifically says that this tournament was held in 1558 in Elizabeth's reign (this began on 17 Nov. 1558).

16, 17 January 1559.
Jousts, tourney and barriers to celebrate the coronation of Queen Elizabeth. Whitehall.
Bodleian Library MS. Ashmole 863, fol. 211; C.A. Portfolio, Jan. 1559; Machyn, p. 187; *CSP Venetian*, VII, 18–9; *CSP Domestic. Elizabeth*, XXXVIII (item ♯35).

3 July 1559.
Jousts. Greenwich.
B.L. MS. Cotton Vitellius F. v (Machyn, pp. 202–3); Nichols, *Elizabeth*, I, 71–2.

11 July 1559.
Jousts and tourney. Greenwich.
B.L. MS. Cotton Vitellius F. v (Machyn, pp. 203–4); John Strype, *Annals of the Reformation* (1723), I, 193.

5 November 1559.
Jousts. Whitehall.
C.A. Portfolio (score cheques); Machyn, pp. 216–7; John Strype, *Annals of the Reformation*, I, 196.

Shrovetide 1560 (?).
Tournament. Location unknown.
University Library, Cambridge, MS. Hengrave 88 (3) ♯22A.

21 April 1560 (?).
Jousts. Whitehall.
C.A. Portfolio (score cheque); C.A. Partition Book I, fol. 213b.

28 April 1560.
Jousts. ?Whitehall.
C.A. Portfolio (score cheque); Machyn, p. 233.

Christmas 1561–2.
Tilt and tourney. Inner Temple [?repeated at Whitehall on 18 January 1562].
Machyn, p. 275; Gerard Legh. *Accedens of Armoury* (1562), fols. 224b–5a. For a discussion of this event, see Marie Axton, 'Robert Dudley and the Inner Temple Revels', *The Historical Journal*, 13 (1970), 365–78.

10 February 1562.
Jousts. Whitehall.
Machyn, p. 276.

14 February 1562.
Running at the ring. 'Beyond sant James in the feld.'
Machyn, p. 277.

7 January 1565.
Jousts and tourney on Foot. ?Whitehall.
PRO. E. 351/3202; *CSP Spanish 1558–1567*, I, 403 (item ♯284).

5 March 1565.
Jousts tourney and foot tourney. ?Whitehall.
C.A. Portfolio (score cheques); *CSP Spanish*, I, 404–5 (item ♯286).

16 July 1565.
Tourney to celebrate marriage of Henry Knollys and Margaret Cave. Durham Place.
CSP Spanish, I, 452.

11, 12, 13 November 1565.
Jousts, tourney and barriers to celebrate wedding of Ambrose Dudley and Anne Russell. Whitehall.
C.A. Portfolio (score cheques); C.A. Partition Book I, fol. 268a–9b; Thomas Astle MS. (untraced but printed in Leland, II, 666–9); B.L. Donation MS. 4712, no. 8. Lib. W.Y. 193.

17 November 1569 or 1570.
Jousts to celebrate Elizabeth's Accession Day. Location unknown but in 1569 the Court was at Hampton Court because of the plague.
PRO. E. 351/3204; William Camden, *Annales Rerum Anglicarum, et Hibernicarum, Regnante Elizabetha* (1615), pp. 186–7.

7, 8 May 1571.
Jousts, tourney and barriers. Whitehall.
PRO. E. 351/3205; Bodleian Library MS. Ashmolean 837, fol. 245a, and 845, fol. 164a–b, 167a; C.A. Portfolio (score cheques); C.A. MS. M. 4, fols. 1a–3b; Segar (1590), pp. 94–5; Howes, *Annals* (1631), p. 669; *HMC Rutland*, I, 92; *Correspondance Diplomatique de Bertrand de Salignac de la Mothe Fenelon*, ed Charles Purton Cooper (Paris & London, 1840), IV, 88–9, 95.

14 June 1572.
Tourney at night by torchlight to entertain the Duke of Montmorency. Whitehall (not in tiltyard).
PRO. E. 351/3206; B.L. MS. Cotton Titus C. 10, fol. 16a; Segar (1590), pp. 96–7; *Correspondance Diplomatique*, V, 18.

17 December 1572.
Jousts to celebrate the marriage of the Earl of Oxford to Lord Burghley's daughter Ann. ?Whitehall.
C.A. MS. M. 4, fols. 4a and 5a.

1574 (month unknown).
Jousts and tourney. Location unknown.
C.A. MS. M. 4, art. 4.

September 1575.
Jousts. Woodstock.
C.A. Portfolio (Challenge for Jousts at Woodstock). B.L. MS. Add. 41499A, fols. 4a–5b (fragment of 'The Hermit's Tale'); B.L. MS. Royal 18A, xlviii, fols. 1–37; *The Queenes Maiesties Entertainment at Woodstock* (1585). For a discussion of the tilting that appears to have preceded the entertainment of Elizabeth, see Frances A.

Yates, *Astraea* (London & Boston, 1975), p. 95 n. 3; and *Lee*, pp. 85, 134, 282.

28 February 1576.
Jousts to entertain Frederic Perrenot, Sieur de Champagny. Greenwich.
B.L. MS. Add. 41499A, fol. 1a; PRO. E. 351/3211 (new Judge House possibly for this event); Segar (1590), p. 200.

17 November 1577.
Jousts for Accession Day. Whitehall.
C.A. MS. M. 4, art. 2; B.L. MS. Harl. 7392, fols. 37b–8, 48–9; PRO. 31/3. 27, fol. 185a; National Library of Wales (Adam Ottley Papers), see Beal, 284–95.

1578 (month unknown).
Jousts. Location unknown.
C.A. MS. M. 4, art. 3.

1579 Exact date and location unknown.
C.A. MS. 4, art. 7; PRO. E. 351/3214.

11 January 1579.
Barriers to entertain M. de Simier. ?Greenwich.
CSP Spanish, II, 627, 630; Feuillerat, *Elizabeth*, pp. 286–7, 292.

1, 2 February 1579.
Jousts and fight at barriers with swords on horseback to entertain Count Cassimer. Whitehall.
C.A. MS. M. 4, art. 7 (?tilting list for this occasion); Walter B. Devereux, *Lives and Letters of the Devereux, Earls of Essex*, I, 170; Lodge, II, 146.

17 November 1580.
Jousts for Accession Day, Whitehall.
PRO. 3/31. 28, fol. 203a.

22 January 1581.
Jousts in answer to Earl of Arundel's challenge. Whitehall.
C.A. Portfolio (score cheques); C.A. MS. M. 4, fol. 22a–b; PRO. E. 351/3215 (erecting of scaffold under royal window in the tiltyard); B.L. MS. Lansdowne 99, fols. 259a–64b; B.L. MS. Add. 41499A, fol. 6a; undated broadside proclaiming Callophisus' challenge (STC 4368.5); E. Spenser (trans.), *Axiochus* (1592), sigs. D1a–D4a (unique copy in Pforzheimer Library, Cat. 966); Segar (1590), pp. 95–6; Holinshed, *Chronicles* (London, 1808), IV, 434; Feuillerat, *Elizabeth*, p. 336.

15–16 May 1581.
Jousts (The Fortress of Perfect Beauty). Whitehall.
Bodleian Library MS. Ashmole 845, fols. 165b, 166a; PRO. E. 351/3216 (preparing tiltyard for this event); Feuillerat, *Elizabeth*, pp. 340–3; Goldwell; Holinshed, *Chronicles*, III, 1316–21; William Camden, *The History of the Most Renowned and Victorious Princess Elizabeth* (1688), Bk. III, 265; von Raumer, II, 431–4.

17 November 1581.
Jousts for Accession Day. Whitehall.
Bodleian Library MS. Ashmole 845, fol. 165a; C.A. MS. M. 4, art. 1 and 6; PRO. E. 352/3216; PRO. E. 351/542, fol. 31b; *CSP Spanish*, III, 222 (item ♯169).

1 January 1582.
Barriers. ?Greenwich.
PRO. AO. 1. 2045/7 (Revels); *Les Memoires de Monsievr le Duc de Nevers* (Paris, 1665), Pt. I, pp. 555–6; Feuillerat, *Elizabeth*, 344 (table); Segar (1590), pp. 98–9.

4 January 1582.
Combat involving prisoners in mock castle (part of Twelfth Night entertainment). ?Greenwich.
Memoires de Monsievr le Duc de Nevers, I, 557.

May 1583.
Jousts to entertain Count Albert of Alasco and French ambassador. ?Greenwich.
CSP Spanish, III, 474.

17 November 1583.
Jousts for Accession Day. Whitehall.
C.A. Portfolio (score cheques); C.A. MS. M. 4, fol. 30a (score cheques); C.A. Partition Book II, fol. 4a; PRO. E. 351/542, fol. 53b; PRO. E. 351/3218 (preparing Judgehouse, scaffolds and stairs).

17 November 1584.
Jousts for Accession Day. Whitehall.
C.A. Portfolio (score cheques); C.A. MS. M. 4, fol. 31a (score cheque); PRO. E. 351/3219 (stairs for Judgehouse, and stairs and scaffold under royal window); B.L. MS. Add. 41499A, fol. 6a; Von Wedel, 258–9 (see also V. von Klarwill, *Queen Elizabeth and Some Foreigners* (London, 1928), pp. 330–2.

6 December 1584.
Jousts ('hastiludium') between ten married men

and ten bachelors. Whitehall.
Bodleian Library MS. Ashmole 845, fol. 168a; C.A. MS. M. 4, fol. 32a; Von Wedel, 262.

17 November 1585.
Jousts for Accession Day. Whitehall.
C.A. MS. M. 4, fol. 33a; PRO. E. 351/3220 (preparing tilt and scaffolds).

Shrovetide 1586.
Barriers. Greenwich.
PRO. E. 351/3220 (setting up barriers in the hall).

23 April 1586.
Barriers on Feast of St George held by Earl of Leicester. Utrecht.
Nichols, *Elizabeth*, II, 457.

17 November 1586.
Jousts for Accession Day. Whitehall
C.A. MS. m. 4, fol. 34a; B.L. MS. Add. 41499A, fol. 7b; PRO. E. 351/3221 (setting up Judgehouse and repairing and painting tilt).

17 November 1587.
Jousts for Accession Day. Whitehall.
C.A. MS. M. 4, fol. 35a; PRO. E. 351/3222 (setting up Judgehouse and repairs); Gawdy, pp. 22–5.

26 August 1588.
Jousts to celebrate victory over Spanish Armada. ?Whitehall.
CSP Spanish, IV, 419; James Aske, *Elizabetha Triumphans* (1586), quoted by Nichols, *Elizabeth*, II, 574.

17 November 1588.
Jousts for Accession Day. Whitehall.
C.A. Portfolio (score cheque); C.A. MS. M. 4, fol. 36a; PRO. E. 351/3223 (repairs and painting); *CSP Spanish, 1587–1603)*, IV, 494 (item ♯485); B.L. MS. Lansdowne 59, fol. 40b (see Feuillerat, *Elizabeth*, p. 391).

19 November 1588.
Jousts for St. Elizabeth's Day and to celebrate victory over Spanish Armada. Whitehall.
CSP Spanish, IV, 494 (item ♯485); Nichols, *Elizabeth*, II, 538.

17 November 1589.
Jousts for Accession Day. Whitehall.
C.A. Portfolio (score cheque); C.A. MS. M. 4, fol. 37a; PRO. E. 351/542, fol. 139a; PRO. E. 351/3224 (new scaffold and stairs for royal window).

17 November 1590.
Jousts for Accession Day. Whitehall.
C.A. Portfolio (score cheque); C.A. MS. M. 4, fol. 38a; PRO. E. 351/542, fol. 152a; PRO. E. 351/3225 (setting up Judgehouse, new scaffolds, etc.); Lodge, p. 419; Segar (1602), pp. 197–200; John Dowland, *Second Booke of Songs or Ayres* (1600), sigs. D2b–F1a ('Tymes eldest sonne'); Bodleian Library MS. Rawlinson, Poetry 148, fol. 75b; Cumbria Record Office, Appleby Castle MS (Speech of Lord Cumberland'); B.L. MS. Add. 41499A, fol. 11b; B.L. MS. Add. 28,635, fol. 88b; B.L. MS. Add. 33,963, fol. 109; B.L. MS. Stowe, 276, fol. 2; Peele, I, 169–73.

19 November 1590.
Jousts for St Elizabeth's Day. Whitehall.
C.A. Portfolio (note under this date).

17 November 1591.
Jousts for Accession Day. Whitehall.
C.A. Portfolio (score cheque); C.A. MS. M. 4, fol. 40a; PRO. E. 351/542, fol. 165b; PRO. E. 351/3226 (setting up Judgehouse, new scaffold under royal window).

26 February 1593.
Jousts on Shrovetide in response to challenge issued by Earl of Essex and Earl of Cumberland (no evidence that jousts ever held). Location unknown.
B.L. MS. Egerton 2804, fol. 84b.

17 November 1593.
Jousts for Accession Day. Windsor.
C.A. Portfolio (score cheques); C.A. MS. M. 4, fol. 42a; Bodleian Library MS. Ashmole 1109, fol. 154b; PRO. E. 351/542, fol. 191b; Devereux Accounts (Longleat): Declared Accounts, 1592–93, fol. 76b and Household Accounts, 1592–3, fol. 78a–b; Birch, *Elizabeth,* I, 131; *Memoirs of Robert Cary*, ed. F.H. Mares (Oxford: Clarendon, 1972), p. 28; G.C. Williamson, *George, Third Earl of Cumberland* (Cambridge, 1920), pp. 122–3.

17 November 1594.
Jousts for Accession Day. Whitehall.
C.A. Portfolio (score cheques); C.A. MS. M. 4, fol. 43a; C.A. MS. Lant, fol. 32; PRO. E. 351/542, fol. 205b; PRO. E. 351/3229 (setting up scaffold and stairs beneath royal window, new horse stool, frame to hold staves, setting up Judgehouse); Longleat, Devereux MSS., Household Accounts, 1594–8, fols. 87, 91a–b.

19 November 1594.
Jousts for St Elizabeth's Day. Whitehall.
C.A. MS. M. 4, fol. 44a–b.

4 March 1595.
Barriers for Shrovetide. Whitehall.
Nichols, *Elizabeth*, III, 319–20; C.A. Portfolio (score cheque); C.A. MS. M. 4, fols. 45a–7a; PRO. E. 351/542, fol. 517b.

17 November 1595.
Jousts for Accession Day. Whitehall.
C.A. Portfolio (tilting list); C.A. MS. M. 4, fol. 48a; PRO. E. 351/3230 (making a new tilt, possibly for this event); *HMC Various* (London, 1907), IV, 163–4 (list of tilters from MSS. of F.H. T. Jervoise); Kent Archives Office, Maidstone, DeLisle MS. U1475, C12/26, fols. 229–30 (letter from Rowland White to Sir Robert Sidney, dated 22 Nov. 1595); PRO. E. 351/542, fol. 217b; PRO. S.P. 12/254, nos. 67, 68; Lambeth Palace MS. 936, no. 274; Lambeth Palace MS. 933, no. 118; Lambeth Palace MS. 652, no. 95; Alnwick Castle, Northumberland MS. 525 (Safe 4), fols. 47–53, 69; B.L. MS. Add. 4457, fols. 31–3; B.L. MS. Add. 40,838, fols. 24–7; Folger Library MS. V. b. 213, fols. 1–13; Folger Library MS. V. b. 214, fol. 200; Inner Temple Library MS. Petyt 538, Vol. 36, fols. 111–14; Pierpont Morgan Library MS. MA 1201, fols. 12–21; Queen's College, Oxford, MS. 121, pp. 405–7.

17 November 1596.
Jousts for Accession Day. Whitehall.
C.A. MS. M. 4, fol. 50a; PRO. E. 351/543, fol. 9a–b; PRO. E. 351/3231 (setting up Judgehouse, stairs and stage below royal window and removing them after jousts); Alnwick Castle, Northumberland MS. 525 (Safe 4), fol. 53.

19, 20 November 1596.
Jousts. Whitehall.
C.A. Portfolio ('The Judges booke made ready for her Ma[jes]te for the Challenge of the Earle of Essex'); C.A. MS. M. 4, fol. 51a–b.

17 November 1597.
Jousts for Accession Day. Whitehall.
C.A. MS. M. 4, fol. 52a; PRO. E. 351/543, fol. 24a. B.L. MS. Add. 41499A, fol. 1a–b (Speech of Restless Knight).

6 January 1598.
Barriers for Twelfth Night by members of Middle Temple. ?Whitehall.
Benjamin Rudyerd, *Le Prince d'Amour* (1660), p. 86.

17 November 1598.
Jousts for Accession Day. Whitehall.
C.A. MS. M. 4, fol. 53a; PRO. E. 351/543, fols. 37b, 38a; PRO. E. 351/3234 (standing and stairs below royal window, setting up Judgehouse, making new gate); Chamberlain, I, 54; E.M. Tenison, *Elizabethan England* (Leamington Spa, 1953), X, 432–3.

19 November 1598.
Jousts (Earl of Essex was chief challenger). Whitehall.
C.A. MS. M. 4, fol. 54a; B.L. MS. Add. 12,514 (list of jousters).

19 November 1599.
Jousts for Accession Day (postponed because of bad weather). Whitehall.
C.A. MS. M. 4, 54b–5b; PRO. E. 351/543, fol. 53b; Gawdy, pp. 96–7; Collins, II, 142; *HMC Penshurst*, II, 417.

21 November 1599.
Jousts. The Earl of Cumberland was chief challenger. Jousts deferred until Shrovetide because of Cumberland's sickness. Whitehall.
C.A. MS. M. 4, fols. 55b, 56a–b.

1 May 1600.
Jousts or martial exercises involving Earl of Cumberland. ?Greenwich.
F. Davison, *A Poetical Rhapsody* (1602), sig. L7b.

17 November 1600.
Jousts for Accession Day. Whitehall.
C.A. MS. M. 4, fol. 57a; PRO. E. 351/543, fol. 67a; PRO. E. 351/3236 (new frame for ambassadors 'againste the runninge daye', payments to night watchmen); Chatsworth, Bolton Abbey MSS, Sundry Documents 54 ('Speeche to ye Queene'); Lambeth Palace Library, Talbot Papers, MS. 3201 (formerly K 27); Winwood, I, 271, 274; *HMC Penshurst*, II, 485–6; Collins, II, 215–6. Nichols, *Elizabeth*, III, 516; *HMC Hatfield* (London: HMSO, 1904), X; Gawdy, pp. 103–5.

19 November 1600.
Jousts. Whitehall.
C.A. MS. M. 4, fol. 58a.

17 November 1601.
Jousts for Accession Day. Whitehall.
B.L. MS. Add. 10110, fol. 68b; PRO. E. 351/543, fols.. 78b, 79a, 82a; PRO. E. 407/59; *HMC Hatfield*, XI, 462, 540.

17 November 1602.
Jousts for Accession Day. Whitehall.
B.L. MS. Add. 10110, fol. 69b; B.L. MS. Harl. 5826, fol. 128; PRO. E. 351/543, fol. 91a–b; PRO. E. 351/3238 (taking down Judgehouse, work on standing below Queen's window, painting tilt pales, payments to night watchmen); PRO. E. 407/59; *HMC Hatfield*, XII, 438, 459, 574; Chamberlain, I, 172; *Diary of John Manningham*, ed. John Bruce (Westminster, 1868), pp. 86–7.

20 November 1602.
Jousts. Whitehall.
B.L. MS. Add. 10110, fol. 67b, 68b.

The Tournaments of King James I's Reign

June 1603.
Jousts at meeting of James I and Queen Anne. Grafton.
The Third Globe, ed. C. Walter Hodges, S. Schoenbaum and Leonard Leone (Detroit, 1981), p. 42.

January 1604.
Running at the ring. Hampton Court.
PRO. E. 351/543, fol. 110; PRO. E. 351/3239 (setting up a standing for the Queen to see running at the ring); MS. Diary in the library of Sir Richard Baker Wilbraham, Rhode Hall, Scholar Green, Stoke-on-Trent, Cheshire, notes running at the ring by the King and eight or nine lords 'for the honour of those goddesses' (H.S. Scott, ed., *The Journal of Sir Roger Wilbraham, Camden Society Miscellany*, X [1902], 66).

24 March 1604.
Jousts for Accession Day. Whitehall.
PRO. E. 351/543, fol. 110b; PRO. E. 351/2805 (31 Oct. 1603–31 Oct. 1604); PRO. E. 351/3239 (payments to watchmen in tiltyard); Henry Foley (ed.), *Records of the English Province of the Society of Jesus* (London, 1877), p. 59.

November 1604.
Jousts for wedding of William, Earl of Pembroke. Wilton.
John Aubrey, *The Natural History of Wiltshire*, ed. John Britton (London, 1847), p. 88. No other evidence for this event. The accuracy of Aubrey's statement must remain open to question.

24 March 1605.
Jousts for Accession Day. Greenwich.
PRO. E. 351/543, fol. 133a; PRO. E. 351/2805 (1 Nov. 1604–31 Oct. 1605); B.L. MSS. Add. 38139, fol. 192a (list of tilters); Winwood, II, 52, 54; *CSP Venetian (1603–7)*, X, 1605.

20 May 1605.
Jousts for Whitmonday (to celebrate birth and christening of royal child). Greenwich.
PRO. E. 351/543, fol. 133a; C.A. Talbot Papers, MS. L, fol. 15 (see Lodge, III, 162).

6 January 1606.
Barriers to celebrate marriage of Earl of Essex and Lady Frances Howard. Whitehall.
PRO. E. 351/543, fol. 1606; PRO. E. 351/3241 (erecting of wire screen to protect King and Queen at barriers); B.L. MS. Cotton. Julius. C. iii, 301; Orgel & Strong, I, 111–2.

24 March 1606.
Jousts for Accession Day. Whitehall.
PRO. E. 351/543, fol. 153a; Winwood, II, 205; *CSP Domestic*, XIX, 89 (8, 305); *CSP Venetian*, X, No. 503 (pp. 332–3).

May/June 1606.
Jousts. Greenwich.
PRO. E. 351/543, fols. 154b and 155a.

4 August 1606.
Running at the ring. ?Greenwich.
PRO. E. 351/2963 (payments for lances, etc.); H. Roberts, *England's Farewell to Christian the Fourth* (1606), rpt. Nichols, *James*, II, 79–81; B.L. MS. Add. 38,139, fol. 266b; B.L. MS. Add. 33,498, fol. 2; B.L. MS. Add. 22,601, fols. 7a–b; B.L. MS. Harl. 4888, art. 20; B.L. MS. Stowe, 610, fol. 24b; B.L. MS. Egerton 2877, fols. 162b–a; William Drummond, *Works* (1711), pp. 231–3.

5 August 1606.
Jousts in honour of James I's escape from Gowrie Conspiracy. ?Greenwich.
PRO. E. 351/2963 (payments for weapons, armour, etc.); PRO. E. 351/2805 (1 Nov. 1605–31 Oct. 1606); Nichols, *James*, II, 80–1, 88; *CSP Venetian*, X, No. 564 (pp. 390–1); La Broderie, *Ambassades* (1750), I, 260.

24 March 1607.
Jousts for Accession Day. Whitehall.
PRO. E. 351/543, fol. 174b; PRO. E. 351/2805 (1 Nov. 1606–31 Oct. 1607); B.L. MSS. Cotton. Vespasian. C. xiv, fol. 161; Arthur Wilson, *The*

History of Great Britain, being the Life and Reign of King James the First (1653), p. 54; La Broderie, *Ambassades* (1750), II, 144; *CSP Venetian (1603–7)*, X, 487.

25 May 1607.
Jousts at Pentecost in honour of Prince of Joinville. Whitehall.
PRO. E. 351/543, fol. 175a; de la Boderie, *Ambassades*, II, 247, 264.

24 March 1608.
Jousts for Accession Day. Whitehall.
PRO. E. 351/534, fol. 190a; PRO. E. 351/3243 (payments regarding Judgehouse, stairs below royal window, and gallery ceiling); *CSP Venetian (1607–10)*, XI, 116; de la Boderie, *Ambassades*, III, 195.

Shrovetide 1609.
Running at the ring (the King and followers and Prince Henry and his men). Whitehall.
PRO. E. 351/543, fol. 211a; *CSP Venetian*, XI, 243, 246, 254.

24 March 1609.
Jousts for Accession Day. Whitehall.
PRO. E. 351/543, fol. 211a; PRO. E. 351/2805 (1 Nov. 1608–31 Oct. 1609); *CSP Venetian*, XI, 255–6; Birch, *James* (1849), I, 89–92.

6 January 1610.
Prince Henry's Barriers. Whitehall.
PRO. E. 403/2730, fols. 27a, 34b, 61b, 154a, 181b, 182a; PRO. E. 351/543, fol. 227a; B.L. MSS. Cotton. Vespasian. C. xiv, Vol. II, fol. 285; B.L. MS. Add. 12,514 fols.. 132a–3b; *CSP Venetian*, XI, 401, 403, 406, 410–1, 414; Edmund Howes, *Annals* (1631), p. 897; Birch, *James*, I, 92; Orgel & Strong, I, 160–3.

27 March 1610.
Jousts for Accession Day (postponed from 24 March because of bad weather). Whitehall.
PRO. E. 351/543, fol. 228b; PRO. E. 351/2805 (1 Nov. 1609–31 Oct. 1610); PRO. E. 351/3244 (payments to watchmen in tiltyard); B.L. MS. Add. 14,417, fol. 11a; *CSP Venetian*, XI, 453, 460.

23 April 1610 (St George's Day).
Running at the ring. Chester.
B.L. MS. Add. 29,779, fol. 35.

6 June 1610.
Jousts to celebrate creation of Prince Henry as Prince of Wales. Whitehall.

C.A. Partition Book II, fol. 164b; *CSP Venetian*, XI, 503, 507–8; Winwood, III, 181; Howes, *Annales* (1631), p. 991; *HMC Report on Manuscripts in Various Collections* (London, 1904), III, 261–3.

25 March 1611.
Jousts for Accession Day (postponed because 24 March was Easter Sunday). Whitehall.
PRO. E. 351/543, fol. 247a; PRO. E. 351/2805 (1 Nov. 1610–31 Oct. 1611); B.L. MSS. Add. 14,417, fol. 23a.

October 1611.
Running at the ring. Whitehall.
PRO. E. 351/543, fol. 260a.

26 December 1611.
Running at the ring (part of Christmas celebrations). Whitehall.
PRO. E. 351/543, fol. 260b; PRO. E. 351/2805, fol. 2b (rpt. Peter Cunningham [ed.], *Extracts from the Accounts of the Revels at Court* (London, 1842), p. 211.

1 January 1612.
Running at the ring (part of Christmas/New Year's celebration). Whitehall.
Cunningham, *Revels at Court*, p. 211.

January 1612.
Joust, tourney, and barriers. Whitehall.
PRO. E. 351/3246 (preparing Banqueting House for barriers); *CSP Domestic*, LXVIII, 35 (9, 115) refers to 'tilt, turney and barriers'.

25 February 1612.
Running at the ring (part of Shrove Tuesday celebrations at which Prince Henry and others ran a match at the ring for a supper). ?Whitehall.
Chamberlain, I, 339–40; *CSP Venetian*, XII, 328.

24 March 1612.
Jousts for Accession Day. Whitehall.
PRO. E. 351/543, fol. 260b; PRO. E. 351–2805 (1 Nov. 1611–31 Oct. 1612); PRO. E. 351/3246 (payments to watchmen in tiltyard); Chamberlain, I, 342; *CSP Venetian*, XII, 329.

15 February 1613.
Running at the ring (celebrations for Shrovetide and for marriage of Princess Elizabeth to Count Palatine). Whitehall.
PRO. E. 351/544, fol. 10b; J.M. DeFranchis, *Of the Most Auspicious Marriage* (1613), pp. 69–70; John Finet, *Finetti Philoxenis*, p. 11; Nichols, *James*, II, 549–50.

24 March 1613.
Jousts for Accession Day. Whitehall.
PRO. E. 351/544, fol. 10b; PRO. E. 351/2805 (1 Nov. 1612–31 Oct. 1613); B.L. MS. Harl. 1368, fol. 44a; Bodleian Library, MS. Ashmole 38, p. 103; *Letters of Sir Henry Wotton to Sir Edmund Bacon* (1661), p. 6; Jonson, VIII, 382–3; Gawdy, p. 173; *HMC Rutland*, IV, 494; Chamberlain, I, 440.

26 or 27 March 1613.
Tilting, tourney and barriers (in answer to challenge issued by Sir Thomas Parsons). Whitehall.
Letters of Sir Henry Wotton to Sir Edmund Bacon (1661), p. 7.

1 January 1614.
Jousts to celebrate marriage of Earl of Somerset and Frances Howard. Whitehall.
PRO. E. 351/544, fol. 26b; Nichols, *James*, II, 716–8, 727–30.

24 March 1614.
Jousts for Accession Day, Whitehall.
PRO. E. 351/544, fol. 26b; PRO. E. 351/2805 (1 Nov. 1613–31 Oct. 1614); B.L. MS. Harl. 5176, fol. 217a; B.L. MS. Harl. 1653, fol. 19a; *HMC Rutland*, IV, 499.

Week of 25 July 1614.
Running at the ring (celebrations for second visit of King Christian of Denmark). Whitehall.
PRO. E. 351/544, fol. 26b; PRO. E. 351/2805 (1 Nov. 1613–31 Oct. 1614); Howes, *Annales*, p. 1012.

24 March 1615.
Jousts for Accession Day. Whitehall.
PRO. E. 351/544, fol. 44a; PRO. E. 351/2805 (1 Nov. 1614–31 Oct. 1615); B.L. MS. Harl. 1368, p. 45; B.L. MS. Harl. 5176, fol. 220b.

25 March 1616 (the 24th was a Sunday).
Jousts for Accession Day Whitehall.
PRO. E. 351/544, fols. 59b, 64a, 77a; C.A. MS. M. 4, fol. 58b; B.L. MS. Harl. 1368, p. 46; B.L. MS. Harl. 5176, fol. 221a; Bodleian Library, MS. Rawlinson, A 240, fol. 47a; *HMC Rutland*, IV, 508–9; Finet, *Finetti Philoxenis*, pp. 33–4.

5 November 1616.
Barriers by Gentlemen of Inns of Court to celebrate creation of Prince Charles. Whitehall.
PRO. E. 351/545, fol. 6a; B.L. MS. Harl 5176, fol. 225a; Middleton, *Civitatis Amor* (1616), quoted by Nichols, *James*, III, 215; Howes, *Annals*, p. 1026.

6 November 1616.
Running at the ring to celebrate creation of Prince Charles. Whitehall.
(Same sources as for 5 November.)

2 February 1618.
The Tilt of Henry Prince of Purpool, performed by students of Gray's Inn for Candlemas. Gray's Inn.
Nichols, *James*, III, 466.

24 March 1618.
Jousts for Accession Day. Whitehall.
PRO. E. 351/544, fol. 89a, 91a; B.L. MS. Harl. 5176, fol. 229a; Finet, *Finetti Philoxenis*, pp. 51-3; Nichols, *James*, III, 474.

January or February 1620.
Tilting. Whitehall.
PRO. E. 351/544, fol. 116a.

24 March 1620.
Jousts for Accession Day and first tournament of Prince Charles. Whitehall.
C.A. Partition Book II, fols. 225b, 227b, 246b, 248a, 253b; C.A. S.M.L. (Ceremonies III), pp. 14-6; PRO. E. 351/544, fols. 115b, 119a, 121b; PRO. E. 351/3253 (building pavilion for Prince Charles, repairs to tiltyard); PRO. E. 101 435/6; C.A. MS. Portfolio (Letter to Mr. Tilton); C.A. MS. M. 3, fols.. 1a-3b; C.A. MS. Heralds II, fol. 620; Bodleian Library, MS. Eng. Misc. C. 4, fols. 7-8; Bodleian Library, MS. Ashmole 837, fols. 129a-32a; Bodleian Library, MS. Add. C. 259, fol. 148; B.L. MSS. Add. 12,514, fol. 166a-b; B.L. MS. Add. 27,962, fol. A284a-b; Finet, *Finetti Philoxenis*, p. 64; *CSP Venetian (1619-21)*, XVI, 190; 225, 227, 241, 249; *HMC Rutland*, IV, 520; Chamberlain, II, 294, 298-9; F.F. Warner, *Catalogue of the Manuscripts and Muniments of Dulwich College* (London, 1881), p. 183; John Beaumont, *Bosworth-field* (1629), p. 147.

18 April 1620.
Running at tilt (or at the ring). Whitehall.
PRO. E. 351/544, fol. 116a; B.L. MS. Add. 27,962, fols. A287a, A293a; Chamberlain, II, 302; Camden, *Annals*, quoted by Nichols, *James*, IV, 604.

8 January 1621.
Running at the ring (Prince Charles and others entertain the French Ambassador Cadnet). Whitehall.
Finet, *Finetti Philoxenis*, p. 71; Chamberlain, II, 333.

24 March 1621.
Jousts for Accession Day. Whitehall.
C.A. MSS. 2. M. 3, fols. 6a-7b; PRO. E. 351/544, fols. 132a, 134b, 136b; B.L. MSS. Add. 12514, fol. 129a; B.L. MS. Add. 27,962, fol. A431b; B.L. MS. Harl. 5176, fol. 242b; Bodleian Library, MS. Ashmole 837, fol. 131b; Finet, *Finetti Philoxenis*, pp. 76-7; *CSP Venetian*, XVII, 4, 13; Chamberlain, II, 356, 359.

24 March 1622.
Jousts for Accession Day (prepared and then postponed on several occasions and finally cancelled). Whitehall.
C.A. Partition Book II, fol. 272b; PRO. E. 351/544, fols. 145a, 148a-b; PRO. E. 351/3255 (building pavilion for Prince Charles, a judge-house and stands for ambassadors); PRO. 101 435/15 20 Jac. I (expenses); PRO. AO. 1. 2047/23; B.L. MSS. Add. 12514, fols. 128a-b, 133a, 159a, 165; Finet, *Finetti Philoxenis*, pp. 94-5, 102-3; *CSP Venetian (1621-3)*, XVII, 452; Chamberlain, II, 428, 433.

24 March 1624.
Jousts for Accession Day (this event was postponed until a later date). Whitehall.
PRO. AO. I. 2047/24 (Revels); PRO. E. 351/2805 (1 Nov. 1623-31 Oct. 1626); B.L. MSS. Add. 27,962, fol. C133b; Diary of Archbishop Laud, quoted by Nichols, *James*, IV, 968-9.

Dec. 1624.
Running at the ring. Prince Charles was one of runners.
B.L. MSS. Add. 27,962, fols. C267b-8a.

The Reign of King Charles I

May 1625 or Feb. 1626.
Jousts and barriers to celebrate marriage of King Charles and Henrietta Maria and their entry into London. ?Whitehall.
B.L. MS. Add. 6297, p. 292; Marc Vulson de la Colombière, *Le Vray Theatre d'Honneur et de Chevalerie* (Paris, 1648), I, 222: 'En Angleterre, l'on fit des tres-belles joustes, & quantité de jeux & de combats à la Barriere, aux nosces du Roy Charles à present Regnant, auec Madame Henriette Marie de la France, soeur du Roy Louis XIII. apres la magnifique Entrée qu'on leur fit à Londres.' [London was not considered safe for the royal couple until the last week of January 1626. The coronation celebration and attendant festivities finally took place on 2 February 1626.]

Notes

1 To Them That Honour Desyreth

1 Roger of Hoveden, *Annals*. Quoted by Cripps-Day, Appendix I, p. v.

2 P. Meyer, *L'Histoire de Guillaume le Maréchal, Compte de Striguil et de Pembroke, Regent d'Angleterre de 1216 a 1219, Poème Français* (Paris, 1891–1901), I, 125.

3 The much-quoted English *Statua Armorum* of 1292 (fundamentally a document of 1267) is primarily concerned with preventing squires, footmen and spectators from getting out of hand.

4 Tournaments (combats between groups of persons) continued, but the term 'tournament' was also used generically for all types of combat. In the remainder of this book the term is used in this latter way and the term 'tourney' is used for group combats.

5 B.L. MS. Harl. 69, fol. 32a.

6 *L.P.*, III i, 307.

7 Cripps-Day, p. 93; Joseph Strutt, *The Sports and Pastimes of the People of England* (London, 1801), p. 124; Viscount Dillon, 'Tilting in Tudor Times', *Archaeological Journal*, 55 (1898), 297.

8 Cripps-Day, p. 30.

9 Richard Barbour, *The Knight and Chivalry* (1970; New York, 1982), p. 168.

10 On this matter, see Johan Huizinga's *The Waning of the Middle Ages* (1924; rpt. London, 1970), pp. 66–73.

11 Ruth Huff Cline, 'The Influence of the Romances on Tournaments of the Middle Ages', *Speculum* 20 (1945), 209. As Cline points out, a stock motif of romance was such an offer of a woman as prize at a tournament.

12 Vale, pp. 67–75.

13 Cline, 204–7.

14 Sydney Anglo's account in *The Great Tournament Roll of Westminster* (Oxford, 1968) is a notable exception to this.

15 Letter from John Paston, the Younger, to Margaret Paston (8 July, 1468) in *The Paston Letters*, ed. James Gairdner (Edinburgh, 1910), II, 318.

16 Kipling, *passim*.

17 Ibid. p. 118.

18 Anglo provides a fine apology for the Tudor tournament in *GTR*; and *Spectacle*.

19 C.A. MS. M. 3, fol. 24b; and C.A. MS. R36, fol. 124b.

20 *L.P.*, XV, 300.

21 *Spectacle*, p. 21. Anglo offers a masterly discussion of these matters, pp. 21–46.

22 See, for example, the description of Henry's meeting with Philip of Castile in B.L. MS. Cotton Vespasian C. xii, fols 236–44a.

23 Brown, I, 76.

24 See *Spectacle*, pp. 261–80.

25 Ibid. p. 299.

26 Giacomo Soranzo's report on English affairs in *CSP Venetian*, V, 535.

27. Jordan, p. 61.

28 Machyn, p. 5.

29 On this point, see *Spectacle*, p. 301.

30 On this matter, see Frances A. Yates, *The Valois Tapestries*, 2nd ed. (London, 1975), pp. 51–3; and Richard C. McCoy, 'From the Tower to the Tiltyard: Robert Dudley's Return to Glory', *The Historical Journal*, 27 (1984), 430.

31 B.L. MS. Harl. 69, fol. 22b.

32 Ibid.

33 Machyn, p. 79.

34 Ibid. p. 84.

35 *The Defense of Poesie*, ed. Albert Feuillerat in *The Prose Works of Sir Philip Sidney* (Cambridge, 1963), III, 24.

36 On this point, see Norman Council, 'Ben Jonson, Inigo Jones, and the Transformation of Tudor Chivalry', *English Literary History* 47 (1980), 267–9.

37 On this matter, see Richard C. McCoy, '"A dangerous image": The Earl of Essex and Elizabethan Chivalry', *Journal of Medieval and Renaissance Studies*, 13 no. 2 (Fall 1983), 316–7.

38 *HMC Penshurst*, II, 486.

39 Segar (1602), p. 197.

40 The epitaph is quoted in *Lee*, p. 304; Lee's speech is in B.L. MS. Add. 41499A, fol. 1.

41 *Annales Rerum Anglicarum, et Hibernicarum, Regnante Elizabetha* (1615), pp. 186–7.

42 Segar (1602), p. 196.

43 The most important treatment of these matters is to be found in Strong, pp. 117–62.

44 B.L. MS. Add. 41499A, fol. 3b. The latter part of this quotation appears to allude to Sir Henry Lee's famous vow 'during his life to present himselfe at the Tilt armed, the day aforesayd [i.e. 17 Nov.] yeerely' (Segar 1602, p. 197).

45 *CSP Spanish 1587–1603*, item 485, p. 494.

46 Lodge, II, 419.

47. H. Roberts, *England's Farewell to Christian the Fourth* (1606), sig. B4b.

48 That Henry occasionally ran at tilt, a more dangerous feat than running at ring or foot combats, is noted by his biographer Sir Charles Cornwallis in *A Discourse of the Most Illustrious Prince Henry* (1626), sig. C4b.

49 B.L. MS. Add. 12,514, fol. 132a.

50 From 'Tears on the Death of Moeliades' in *Works* (1711), p. 15.

51 Orgel & Strong, I, 160–3.

52 Strong, pp. 190–1. For the most recent study of Prince Henry, see Roy Strong's *Henry Prince of Wales and England's Lost Renaissance* (London, 1986).

53 *The Marriage of Prince Fredericke, and the Kings daughter, the Lady Elizabeth* (1613), sig. B3a.

54 D.S. Bland, 'The Barriers: Guildhall MS. 4160', *The Guildhall Miscellany* 6 (Feb. 1956), 9.

55 C.A. MS. 2. M. 3, fols. 1b–2a.

56 On 8 Jan 1621 he did joust with 'six or seven noblemen,' but the occasion was not a formal tournament. He also ran at ring in April 1620 and December 1624 (see Nichols, *James*, IV, 604, 646); and B.L. MS. Add. 27962, fols. C267b–8a.

57 *CSP Venetian 1619–21*, XVI, 227; *CSP Venetian 1621–3*, XVII, 4, 452.

58 Marc Vulson de la Colombière, *Le Vray Theatre d'Honneur et de Chevalerie* (Paris, 1648), I, 222.

59 Quoted Strutt, *Sports and Pastimes*, p. xxvii.

60 Orgel and Strong, I, 259, lines 349–50.

61 *HMC Report on Manuscripts in Various Collections* (London, 1904), III, 261; *CSP Venetian*, XI, 503.

62 Winwood II, 205; also printed in Chamberlain, I, 223.

63 Gawdy, p. 173; and Sir Henry Wotton, *Letters to Sir Edmund Bacon* (1661), pp. 5–6.

64 Chamberlain, II, 359.

65 This may, however, have been due to an outbreak of plague. See Quentin Bone, *Henrietta Maria, Queen of the Cavaliers* (Urbana, 1972), pp. 43, 52.

2 What Price Glory?

1 B.L. MS. Cotton Julius XII, B, fol. 91.

2 B.L. MS. Add. 46455, fols. 4–10. See Gordon Kipling, 'Henry VII and the Origins of Tudor Patronage,' in *Patronage in the Renaissance*, ed. Guy Fitch Lytle and Stephen Orgel (Princeton: Princeton Univ. Press, 1981), 160.

3 B.L. MSS. Add. 10110, fol. 69b.

4 B.L. MSS. Add. 12,514, fol. 144; MS. Harl. 1107, fol. 66b, 67a. Cf. C.A. MS. Portfolio (Tournament Cheques), 'A Letter to Mr. Tilton' (dated 20 Feb. 1618).

5 B.L. MSS. Add. 6297, pp. 291–2.

6 *HMC Hatfield*, XII, 438, 459, 574.

7 C.A. MS. M.4, fol. 1b. The tournament planned for 15 June 1581 was also postponed for a week.

8 C.A. MS. M.4, fol. 54b. The celebration of James I's Accession Day in 1610 was similarly disturbed 'by reason of the extraordinary fowle weather' and a proclamation was made postponing it (B.L. MS. Add. 14, 417, fol. 11a).

9 B.L. MS. Harl. 69, fols. 7a, 28b; *L.P.*, XV, 300; and Leland, II, 668.

10 See, for example, B.L. MS. Harl. 69, fol. 19; MS. Harl. 1354, fol. 13; MS. Harl. 1776, fol. 45; MS. Harl. 6064, fol. 86; B.L. MS. Add. 33,735, fol. 2b; B.L. MS. Stowe 1407, fol. 209; Bodleian Library, MS. Ashm. 763, fol. 148; MS. Ashm. 116, fol. 1086; C.A. MS. M.6, fol. 56, etc.

11 *Nugae Antiquae* (1779 ed.), III, 234.

12 Sydney Anglo, 'Archives of the English Tournament: Score Cheques and Lists', *Journal of the Society of Archivists*, 2 no. 4 (Oct. 1961), 155. What follows here is considerably indebted to Anglo's work.

13 *GTR*, pp. 38n, 112–5.

14 See the discussion in Anglo, 'Archives', 157–8.

15 Gairdner, I, 395; Guildhall Library MS. 3313, fol. 96b (see, *The Great Chronicle of London*, ed. A.H. Thomas and I.D. Thornley [London, 1938], p. 370); Hall, p. 566).

16 C.A. MS. Portfolio (Tournament Cheques), item 63.

17 C.A. M.4, fol. 3b; and Eric St. John Brooks, *Christopher Hatton* (London, 1946), p. 52.

18 C.A. MS. M.4, fol. 44b.

19 C.A. Partition Book I, fol. 121a.

20 *CSP. Dom. (Eliz.) 1547–1580*, Vol. XXXVIII, item 35.

21 The incident is recounted in Sir Anthony Wagner's *Heralds of England: A History of the Office and College of Arms* (London, 1967), p. 105.

22 C.A. Partition Book I, fol. 269a–b.

23 C.A. Partition Book II, fols. 225b, 227b, 248a.

24 Kipling, 'Origins,' 155–164. Cf. the articles by W.R. Streitberger on the financing of Tudor entertainments in *RORD*, 21 (1978), 11–6; 26 (1983), 31–54; 27 (1984), 21–45.

25 Kipling, 163.

26 See E.K. Chambers, *Notes on the History of the Revels Office Under the Tudors* (1906; rpt. New York, 1967), p. 5ff.

27 PRO. E. 36/217. The accounts for 12 and 13 February 1511 (fols. 41–55) are transcribed by Anglo in *Spectacle*, pp. 116–33.

28 PRO. Rolls Office MS. 'The King's Book of Payments 1 May 1509–December 1518' (total payment to Sir Henry Guildford dated August 1517). See *L.P.*, II ii, p. 1476.

29 PRO. E. 36/217, fols. 77–88. See *L.P.*, II ii, p. 1510.

30 Ibid., fol. 55. See *Spectacle*, p. 33.

31 Ibid., fols. 279–88.

32 Ibid., fols. 132–62.

33 Chambers, *Notes*, p. 7.

34 Feuillerat, *Mary*, pp. 53, 115, 129, 159, 178, 180–99.

35 Ibid., p. 188.

36 He did this for a tournament on 19 February 1520, one week after the Revels had outfitted him and his companions for another tournament

(PRO. E. 36/217, fols. 108–10).

37 Feuillerat, *Mary*, p. 56.

38 Ibid., pp. 83–4.

39 Feuillerat, *Elizabeth*, p. 72.

40 Eleven detailed but incomplete Audited Accounts exist for the period 1571–88 (PRO. A.O. 3/906, nos 1–12). Less detailed Declared Accounts for 1572-3, 1574-5, 1578-9, 1580-1, 1584-5 also exist (PRO. A.O. 1/2045, nos 1–6 and 9).

41 E.K. Chambers, *The Elizabethan Stage* (Oxford, 1923), I, 207; and Gerald E. Bentley, *The Jacobean and Caroline Stage* (Oxford, 1941–68), IV, 651, 657.

42 Feuillerat, *Elizabeth*, p. 391.

43 Gawdy, p. 25.

44 Feuillerat, *Elizabeth*, p. 336.

45 Ibid., p. 341.

46 Ibid., pp. 286–7, 292, 294, 301.

47 PRO. AO.1. 2045/7.

48 Leland, II, 668.

49 PRO. 31/3. 28, fol. 203a.

50 Chambers, *Notes*, p. 63.

51 PRO. E. 351/2805; and PRO. AO.1. 2046, 2047.

52 PRO. E. 403/2730, fols. 181b–2a.

53 PRO. E. 403/2730, fols. 181b–2a; and PRO. E. 402/2729, fol. 137.

54 PRO. E. 101/435/6.

55 PRO. E. 101/435/15.

56 *Accounts of the Lord High Treasurer of Scotland*, ed. Sir James Balfour Paul (Edinburgh, 1900), ii, p. lxv. See also, *GTR*, p. 11.

57 Claude Blair, *European Armour* (London, 1958), p. 114.

58 PRO. E. 101/517/23, No. 11; E. 36/215, fols. 459, 471, etc.

59 Blair, *European Armour*, p. 115. The album is in the custody of the Victoria and Albert Museum.

60 *L.P.*, II ii, p. 1479; PRO. SP. Dom. Jac. I, Warrants IV, 29.

61 *CSP. Dom. Eliz.*, XXXIV, 33; and *CSP. Dom. Eliz. (1601–3)*, CCLXXXVII, item 70, p. 305.

62 Lee, p. 106.

63 PRO. E. 404/79, items 38, 58, 90; B.L. MS. Add. 7099.

64 B.L. MS. Egerton 2358, fols. 38a, 42b–44b; PRO. E. 36/214.

65 Joycelyne G. Russell, *The Field of Cloth of Gold: Men and Manners in 1520* (London, 1969),

pp. 120–1; and *L.P.*, III ii, p. 1539; III i, pp. 412–3.

66 PRO. AO.1 2299/1.

67 PRO. AO.1. 2299/4.

68 PRO. 403/2730, fol. 34b.

69 B.L. MS. Harl. 7457, fols. 9a, 12a, 19a–b.

70 PRO. SP 14/64, fol. 112a–b.

71 See Gabrielle A. Macdonald, 'Horsemanship as a Courtly Art in Elizabethan England', Diss. University of Toronto, 1982, pp. 7, 34.

72 Ibid., p. 7.

73 Brown, II, 102.

74 MacDonald, pp. 35–6; and Reese, p. 123.

75 M.M. Reese, *The Royal Office of Master of the Horse* (London, 1976), p. 116.

76 Ibid., pp. 152, 160.

77 Ibid., p. 163.

78 J.L. Nevinson, 'Portraits of Gentlemen Pensioners Before 1625', *Walpole Society*, 34 (1952–4), 2; and Hall, p. 512.

79 Machyn, pp. 203–4. In May 1552 Edward VI had participated with his Pensioners in Greenwich Park and on Blackheath, and the day had ended with a running at ring, but this latter event does not appear to have included the Pensioners (Machyn, p. 18).

80 PRO. E. 407, Box 1.

81 On the Zinzans and their professional status, see Herbert Berry's 'The Globe: Documents and Ownership' in *The Third Globe*, ed. C. Walter Hodges, S. Schoenbaum, and Leonard Leone (Detroit, 1981), pp. 40–3, 56–7.

82 Berry (see previous note) states that Sir Robert was an infrequent tilter but the extant records show otherwise.

83 Berry, p. 43.

84 Sydney Anglo. 'The Court Festivals of Henry VIII', *Bulletin of the John Rylands Library*, 43 no. 1 (Sept. 1960), 18.

85 M.E. James, *The Life of Sir Rhys ap Thomas* (Tenby, n.d.), cited by Mark Girouard, *Life in the English Country House* (Harmondsworth, 1980), pp. 26–7.

86 Von Wedel, 255; *A Journey into England by Paul Hentzner in the Year 1598*, ed. H. Walpole (Edinburgh, 1881), p. 33. For further evidence, see W.B. Devereux, *Lives and Letters of the Devereux* (London, 1853), I, 403; and Collins, II, 219–20.

87 Collins, II, 216; Winwood, II, 52.

88 Birch, *Elizabeth*, I, 131; and *HMC Calendar of the Manuscripts of the Most Honourable The Marquess of Bath*, Vol. V (London, 1980), 254.

89 Longleat: Devereux Declared Accounts, 1594–8, fol. 78.

90 Longleat: Devereux Household Accounts, fols. 87, 91; Collins, I, 362. On Bacon's possible authorship, see J. Spedding (ed.), *The Works of Francis Bacon* (London, 1858), VIII, 371–91.

91 Collins, II, 216.

92 *HMC Rutland*, IV, 494.

93 Ibid. IV, 499.

94 Ibid. IV, 508–9.

95 Ibid. IV, 520.

96 Longleat: Devereux Household Accounts, fols. 87, 91.

97 *Memoirs of Robert Cary*, ed. F.H. Mares (Oxford, 1972), p. 28.

98 Ibid. p. 29.

3 Such a Noble Theatre

1 B.L. MS. Harl. 69, fol. 28b; Rawdon Brown, II, 101; and PRO. P.S. O. 2/44/14; and Bodleian Library, MS. Tanner 89, fols. 58a–b.

2 *L.P.*, II, ii, 1510.

3 Payment to Sidrake Brice for building a new tilt at Greenwich (PRO. E. 351/3265).

4 PRO. E. 351/3253. In 1619–20 both sides were painted, a total area of 427 square yards. If one assumes that the tilt was approximately two yards in height, this would make it approximately 107 yards long.

5 *Spectacle*, p. 149.

6 B.L. MS. Lansdowne 285, fol. 39b. *Cf.* Marc Vulson de la Colombière's *Le Vray Theatre d'Honneur et de Chevalerie* (Paris, 1648), in which he stresses the importance of taking the sun into account when arranging '*combats à outrance*' (II, 140).

7 B.L. MS. Harl. 69, fol. 28b.

8 Joycelyne G. Russell, *The Field of Cloth of Gold* (London, 1969), p. 111.

9 B.L. MS. Harl. 69, fol. 32b; Hall, p. 618.

10 Although the term 'lists' generally appears to have been used to refer to the open rectangular area where the various combats took place, the term on occasion also appears to refer to the fences enclosing that area.

11 Mounting steps were a necessity in any tiltyard and they are several times referred to in the Works Office accounts (see, for example, PRO. E. 351/3229, 3233, 3237, 3242).

12 *King's Works*, IV, 287.

13 PRO. E. 315/3229. Ed[mund] Spenser

(transl.), *Axiochus* (1592), sig. D 1a.

14 PRO. E. 36/217, quoted in *L.P.*, II, ii, 1510.

15 B.L. MS. Harl. 69, fol. 28b.

16 B.L. MS. Lansdowne 285, fol. 39a.

17 *The Marriage of Prince Fredericke* (1613), sig. B2b.

18 John Stow, *A Survey of London*, ed. Charles L. Kingsford (Oxford, 1908), II, 32.

19 B.L. MS. Add. 35, 819, fol. 135a.

20 The Field of Cloth of Gold measurements are given by the Earl of Worcester in a letter to Henry VIII (*The Chronicle of Calais,* ed. John G. Nichols [London, 1846], p. 86). Hall gives an estimate of 300 × 106 yards (p. 611).

21 King René, *Traite de la Forme et devis d'un Tournoy*, reprinted in Cripps-Day, p. lxxiv.

22 I refer here to the tournament ground at Chilham Castle in England, the headquarters of the British Jousting Centre. See Max Diamond's *Joust a Minute!* (London, 1982), p. 164.

23 The stand for spectators facing the royal gallery at the Field of Cloth of Gold may have had three viewing levels. One source described it as 'iij galaryes made in length x' score paces (C.A. MS. M. 6, fol. 9b).

24 B.L. MS. Harl. 69, fol. 28b.

25 Stow, I, 268.

26 *Holinshed's Chronicles of England, Scotland, and Ireland* (London, 1808), IV, 434.

27 B.L. MS. Harl. 69, fol. 28b. See also the account of the expenditure of the Clerk of the King's Works for setting up scaffolding and various other tasks (B.L. MS. Egerton 2358, fols. 38a–42a).

28 B.L. MS. Add. 33,735, fol. 2a.

29 Walker, I, 104. The custom was apparently well-established for the members had paid for tournament stands at Smithfield in 1443–4 and 1466–7.

30 *Minutes of Parliament of the Middle Temple*, trans. and ed. Charles T. Martin (London, 1904), I, 2.

31 Ibid. I, 7–8; Walker, I, 154, 164, 168, 235–56, 283; *A Calendar of the Inner Temple Records*, ed. F.A. Inderwick (London, 1896), I, 14.

32 Von Wedel, p. 258.

33 Raumer, II, 431–2; and B.L. MS. Add. 41499A, fol. 3b.

34 F.F. Warner, *Catalogue of the Manuscripts and Muniments of Dulwich College* (London, 1881), p. 183.

35 On wages in late sixteenth-century London and how they related to the cost of theatre admission (much lower than for tournaments), see Ann J. Cook, *The Privileged Playgoers of Shakespeare's London, 1576–1642* (Princeton, 1981), 228–36, 277–81, and *passim*.

36 When the Inns of Court paid for their own separate stands in 1547, their fees went to the 'Keper of the Paleys at Westminster' (Walker, I, 283).

37 PRO. E. 351/3239.

38 Leopold G. Wickham Legg, *English Coronation Records* (Westminster, 1901), p. 216.

39 PRO. E. 351/3236, 3238.

40 PRO. E. 351/543, fol. 79a.

41 Segregation by sex, which is amply demonstrated in surviving illustrations, is discussed in Wickham, I, 36.

42 *CSP. Spanish 1558–67*, I, p. 403.

43 *Finetti Philoxenis* (1656), p. 53.

44 Ibid. p. 53.

45 Ibid. p. 76.

46 Ibid. p. 76.

47 Ibid, p. 64.

48 PRO. E. 351/544, fols. 132a, 116a.

49 B.L. MS. Cotton. Vitellius. A. XVI, fol. 198; and C.A. MS. 1st M. 13, fols. 56b and 57a.

50 PRO. Revels E. 36/217, fol. 41.

51 Birch, *James*, I, 92.

52 Hall, p. 517.

53 Membrane 24. See *GTR*, p. 96.

54 Gairdner, I, 396.

55 *L.P.*, III i, item 869, p. 306; and Hall, pp. 566, and 611.

56 *L.P.*, II, ii, 1510.

57 Pierpont Morgan Library MS. M. 775, fol. 122b.

58 Oxford's tent is described in the preface to his 1581 tournament speech, the unique copy of which is contained in the Pforzheimer Library copy of Spenser's translation of *Axiochus* (1592).

59 Segar (1602), p. 197.

60 Peele, I, 242.

61 Nichols, *James*, II, 269–70.

62 C.A. MS. 2. M. 3, fol. 1a.

63 Ibid, fol. 2a.

64 PRO. E. 351/3253.

65 'Account of the Tyltying Expenses by John Viscount Purbeck,' PRO. E. 101/435/6.

66 C.A. MS. 2. M. 3, fol. 6a; and 'The first accompt of Spencer Lord Compton'. PRO. E. 101/435/15.

67 *Finetti Philoxenis*, pp. 102–3.

68 C.A. MS. M. 6, fol. 56. The inferior copy of this drawing in B.L. MS. Harl. 69 shows only three judges, while the original shows five.

69 C.A. MS. M. 6, fol. 62.

70 PRO. E. 351/3242.

71 PRO. E. 351/3231, 3243.

72 PRO. E. 351/3219, 3243.

73 B.L. MS. Harl. 69, fol. 28b.

74 PRO. E. 36/229. Quoted in *L.P.*, II, ii, 1495.

75 *The Great Chronicle*, ed. A.H. Thomas and I.D. Thornley (London, 1938), p. 372.

76 PRO. E. 351/3216, 3229, 3231.

77 Von Wedel, pp. 258–9.

78 Segar (1602), pp. 198–9.

79 See Strong, p. 153.

4 From Westminster to Whitehall

1 Hall, p. 513.

2 Ibid. pp. 516, 581.

3 Jordan, pp. 32–3.

4. Segar (1590), p. 92; and B.L. MS. Egerton 2358, fol. 12a–b. This latter alludes to events at Kennington, Billingsgate, and Barnes (fols. 42b–4b). There was also a tiltyard at Eltham as late as 1517 (PRO. T.R. Misc. Book 215).

5 Hall, p. 515.

6 *Spectacle*, p. 299; and Machyn, p. 18.

7 B.L. MS. Cotton Vitellius F. V: in section destroyed by fire. John Strype's version is quoted in Nichols, *Elizabeth*, I, 16–7.

8 Nichols, *Elizabeth*, I, 442. See also *Lee*, pp. 85, 134, 282.

9 The draft challenge for jousts at Woodstock, endorsed 1575, is in the College of Arms (C.A. Portfolio, formerly Box 37).

10 C.A. MS. M. 4, fol. 42a. The phrase 'Course att ffeilde' differs from the usual heralds' phrase of 'Justes att . . .' and may indicate that no tilt barrier was used.

11 Strong, p. 168.

12 B.L. MS. Egerton. 2358, fols. 38a–42a.

13 The gate is described by Stow, *Survey of London*, ed. Kingsford, II, 122.

14 Ibid., II, 119.

15 B.L. MS. Harl. 69, fol. 28b.

16 Stow, II, 121–2.

17 Penelope Hunting, *Royal Westminster* (London, 1981), p. 143.

18 Ibid.

19 Hall, pp. 510–1. Anglo in *Spectacle*, p. 111 and *GTR*, p. 46, has associated this chivalric *mise-en-scène* with the royal viewing stand, but Hall's phrasing implies that the stand and the 'curious Fountain' were two different structures.

20 Quoted from John Nedcham's accounts in *King's Works*, IV, 291.

21 Stow, II, 122.

22 B.L. Harl. MSS. 69, fol. 28b. The measurement is from the plan of 'The Medieval Palace of Westminster' appended to *King's Works*.

23 PRO. E. 101/470/18; B.L. Harl. MSS. 69, fol. 28b.

24 Ibid. fol. 31b.

25 Hall, p. 520.

26 Stow, *Annales* (1631), p. 595; Machyn, pp. 5, 18; Jordan, pp. 103–6.

27 The dimensions of the tiltyard are from the plan of Greenwich Palace in *King's Works*, IV, 98.

28 Bodleian Library, MSS. Rawl. D775, fols. 16b, 68a, 77b; PRO. E 101/504/2, fol. 29a.

29 Bodleian Library, MSS. Rawlinson, D775, fols. 9a, 55a, 56b.

30 PRO. E 351/3244.

31 During the Commonwealth period the buildings and land were divided and sold. A Greenwich man, Henry Henn, bought part of the tiltyard for £224. See Beryl Platts, *A History of Greenwich* (Newton Abbot, 1973), pp. 172–3.

32 For a discussion of banqueting houses and what was meant by the term 'banquet' in this context, see Mark Girouard, *Life in The English Country House* (Harmondsworth, 1980), pp. 76, 78, 104–7.

33 PRO. LC 5/132, p. 49; *The Travels of Cosmo III through England*, ed. L. Magalotti (London, 1821), p. 331; and *Victoria County History of Middlesex*, II, 350.

34 B.L. MS. Cotton Vitellius F. v: from the portion destroyed by fire and quoted in John Strype's version by John Nichols in *Elizabeth*, I, 18–9.

35. Raumer, II, 431–4.

36 PRO. E 351/3239; E 351/543, fol. 110b.

37 *Spectacle*, p. 113.

38 Evidence that such items were built in London and then transported by barge to Greenwich for such occasions may be found in the Revels Office accounts. See *L.P.* III ii, 1558; and *L.P.* IV i, 419.

39 *L.P.*, VI, item 601, p. 278.

40 There was a tradition that Holbein had designed the gate but early records do not support the idea.

41 PRO. E 351/3258, 3262.

42 Stow, II, 102.

43 PRO. E 36/251 and 252. See also PRO. E 351/3228, 3261.

44 Von Wedel, p. 235.

45 PRO. E 36/252, p. 625; and Westminster Abbey Muniments, quoted in *King's Works*, IV, 310.

46 *Finetti Philoxenis*, p. 64.

47 PRO. E 351/543, fol. 79a.

48 Fisher's plan is reproduced by Hunting in *Royal Westminster*, p. 155. It shows a divergence of about twenty degrees, but the more reliable plan of 'Whitehall Palace circa 1670' appended to *King's Works* shows an angle of about eight degrees.

49 Machyn, p. 269. Per Palme in *Triumph of Peace* (Stockholm, 1956) claims that Elizabeth enclosed the tiltyard 'with galleries and degrees' (p. 106) but offers no source.

50 George S. Dugdale *Whitehall Through the Ages* (London, 1950), p. 29.

51 See *LCC Survey of London*, XVI, 28ff.

52 *Records of the English Province of the Society of Jesus* (London, 1877), ed. Henry Foley, Vol. I, 59–60.

53 PRO. E 351/544, fol. 115b; and *Finetti Philoxenis*, pp. 63–7.

54 'Whitehall Palace circa 1670' appended as Plan VII to *King's Works*; and fig. 24 in *King's Works*, IV, 309.

55 Leland, II, 669.

56 PRO. E 351/543; PRO. E 351/3239; B.L. MS. Harl. 1653, April 1614.

57 PRO. E 351/3274; PRO. Works 5/2, 1661–2 and 5/4, 1663; B.L. Add. MS. 10116, fol. 134.

5 Curious Devices

1 *Remains Concerning Britain*, ed. R.D. Dunn (Toronto, Buffalo, London, 1984), p. 177.

2 For a detailed discussion of the emblem and emblematic theory, see Peter M. Daly, *Literature in the Light of the Emblem* (Toronto, Buffalo, and London, 1979). See especially, pp. 3–9.

3 *Dialogo dell' Imprese militari e amorose* (Lyons, 1559), p. 8.

4 *The Worthy Tract of Paulus Iouius* (1585), sig. A 3b.

5 Vale, pp. 64–5.

6 C.A. MS. M. 3, fols. 12–3. Quoted in *GTR*, pp. 33–4.

7 Gairdner, I, 396, 399.

8 Hall, pp. 511, 591; and *L.P.*, III ii, 1551.

9 Hall, pp. 630–1.

10 See, Hall's description, pp. 611–4.

11 See *Spectacle*, pp. 113, 261–80.

12 *L.P.*, IV ii, 1393.

13 Hall, p. 722.

14 Ibid.

15 See Feuillerat, *Mary*, pp. 9, 56, 63, 66, 67, 82–4, 188.

16 C.A. MS. M. 6, fols. 56b–7a. For a discussion of these drawings and the full situation of the Dudley family early in Elizabeth's reign, see Richard C. McCoy, 'From the Tower to the Tiltyard', *Historical Journal*, 27, no. 2 (1984), 425–35.

17 McCoy identifies the family crests in 'From the Tower to the Tiltyard', 432–3. McCoy believes the pictures memorialize the Dudleys' achievement in the November 1559 tournament. He appears to have been unaware of the sources of the impresas, apart from the 'Te Stante Virebo' impresa.

18 Beal, 287–8. Beal discusses the probable authorship of the entertainment, pp. 285–9. See also, Young (1), 6–24.

19 Bernard M. Wagner suggested that the date of the poems was 17 November 1577 or 1583 (*PMLA*, 53 [1938], 120), but since Sidney did not appear in the 1583 tournament (see C.A. MS. M. 4, fol. 30a), 1577 would appear to be the more likely date.

20 Beal, 288. This impresa may have been used on a different day of the same tournament (its bearer on this occasion appeared as 'a desert knighte') or at a different tournament altogether.

21 Elena Povoledo, 'Le théâtre de tournoi en Italie' in *Le lieu Théâtral à la Renaissance*, ed. Jean Jacquot (Paris, 1964), p. 98.

22 Feuillerat, *Elizabeth*, p. 346; PRO. E 351/3215 and 3216.

23 B.L. MSS. Add. 41499B, fol. 31.

24 Goldwell, sigs. B. ia, B vb.

25 Chamberlain, I, 121.

26 Arthur Wilson, *The History of Great Britain, being the Life and Reign of King James the First* (1653), p. 54.

27 Collins, II, 216.

28 *HMC Rutland*, IV, 494. See, Young (2), 453–6.

29 *Jonson*, XI, 136.

30 Epigramme No. XXIX in *Jonson*, VIII, 36. Cf. Epigramme No. LXXIII in *Jonson*, VIII, 51.

31 Segar (1590), p. 102.

32 Von Wedel, 236.

33 PRO. E 36/251: fifth payment.

34 *Travels in England* (London, New York & Melbourne, 1889), p. 33: '*Emblemata varia papyracea, clypei formam habentia, quibus, adiectis symbolis, nobiles in exercitiis equestribus & gladiatoriis uti sunt soliti, hic memoriae causa suspensa.*

35 *Travels in England 1599*, trans. Clare Williams (London, 1937), p.164.

36 *The Compleat Gentleman* (1622), p. 199.

37 *The Diary of Samuel Pepys*, ed. Robert Latham and William Matthews (Berkeley and Los Angeles, 1970), I, 181, 238.

38 *CSP Venetian (1610–3)*, XII, 196; and *CSP Domestic, James*, p. 59. The compiler of the travel diary was almost certainly Johann Georg Dehn-Rotfelser, the adopted son of Caspar Widmarck-ter (one of the Hessian ambassadors in the party).

39 The three other manuscripts in the Kassel library are: Octavo MS. Hass. 6; Quarto MS. Hass. 66; Quarto MS. Hass. 67. A transcript of this last is in the British Library (B.L. Add. MSS. 33,838).

40 Quarto MS. Hass. 68, fol. 85b. For details concerning Otto's visit to England, see Philipp Losch, 'Die Reise des Landgrafen Otto von Hessen nach England und den Niederlanden im Jahre 1611', *Hessenland*, 42 (1931), 289–96.

41 *Letters of Sir Henry Wotton to Sir Edmund Bacon* (1661), p. 6.

42 B.L. Add. MSS. 41499A, fol. 7b.

43 'Love is curable with plants'. *Remains*, p. 184. See, Ovid, *Metamorphoses*, I. 523.

44 'Vpon my Lord of Buckingham's Shield at a Tilting, his Imprese being a Bird of Paradise' in *Bosworth-Field* (1629), p. 147. Buckingham was Beaumont's patron.

45 C.A. MS. M. 4, art. vii; Lodge, II, 146; Camden, *Remains*, p. 190.

46 Emma Marshall Denkinger, 'The *Arcadia* and "The Fish Torpedo Faire,"' in *Studies in Philology* 28 (1931), 177.

47 George Whetstone, *Sir Philip Sidney, his honourable life, his valiant death* (1587), sig. B3a.

48 C.A. MS. M. 4, fol. 22a–b; and B.L. MS. Landsdowne 99, fols. 259–64.

49 For Dudley's impresa, see above p. 126. Montgomery's is given without any accompanying description of the picture in Quarto Hass. MS. 68, fol. 141b.

50 Hass. 68, fol. 139a.

51 For a description of the impresa in the Shield Gallery, rather than the drawing in the College of Arms manuscript, see Hass. 68, fol. 132a.

52 These are all taken from Hass. 68, fols. 130b, 131a, 138a, 129a respectively.

53 Ibid. fol. 140a.

54 See, for example, Sir Henry Wotton, *Reliquae Wottonianae* (1651), p. 21. Wotton also praised Essex 'inventions of entertainment; and above all [. . .] his darling piece of love, and self-love', this last being Essex' 1595 Accession Day tilt entertainment.

55 Peele, I, 235.

56 B.L. Add. MSS. 41499A, fol. 7b.

57 Collins, I, 362. For a summation of available information on this portrait, see Strong, *Artists of the Tudor Court*, pp. 136–7.

58 Manningham, *Diary*, p. 4; Camden, *Remains*, p. 190; *Jonson*, I, 148; and Hass. 68, fol. 131a.

59 For a discussion of the work, see Roy Strong *Artists of the Tudor Court* (London, 1983), pp. 134–5.

60 Similar in some respects is the portrait of a young man (possibly Dudley North in 1601), partially in armour, and with a pink scarf tied around his left arm, reputedly 'put there by the Queen after a tournament'. See *Walpole Society*, 3 (1913–4), Plate XV, and 37.

61 The painting is discussed in Strong, pp. 157–9.

62 Peele, I, 274.

63 Harington (trans.), *Orlando Furioso* (1634 edition), p. 349.

6 Winged Words

1 B.L. MS. Harl. 69, fol. 7a.

2 Ibid. fol. 6a.

3 Ibid. fol. 5b.

4 Ibid. fols. 3b, 7a, 5b.

5 Ibid. fol. 2b.

6 See, for example, the challenge for the *Pas de l'Arbre d'Or* of 1468 discussed in Kipling, p. 131.

7 On these matters see D. Sandberger, *Studien über das Rittertum in England vornehmlich wahrend des 14. Jahrhunderts* (Berlin, 1937); and Vale's chapter on '"Ludi" and "Hastiludia",' pp. 57–75.

8 C.A. MS. R36, fols. 124a–5b. Quotations are from Gordon Kipling's 'The Queen of May's Joust at Kennington and the *Justes of the Moneths of May and June*', *Notes and Queries*, n.s. 31, no. 2 (June 1984), 158–62.

9 *Iustes of the moneth of Maye*, sig. A iia. The challenge specifically stated that each course would

last 'the space of halffe an our, as trewly as shal be accompted by an horloge ther present in the gard and kepyng of a damysell of our courte'.

10 *Iustes and tourney of ye moneth of Iune*, sig. A vib. On Mary's possible role in the May tournament, see Kipling, p. 133.

11 Ibid. p. 134. See also Kipling's 'The Queen of May's Joust', 162.

12 Hall, p. 688.

13 B.L. MS. Harl. 69, fol. 20b.

14 Hall, pp. 688–91; PRO. Revels, SP 1/32, fols. 271–6.

15 Hall, p. 689.

16 Jordan, p. 105.

17 Hall, p. 511. Cf. Wolsey's Shrovetide banquet in 1522, during which a castle defended by ladies with allegorical names was besieged. The attackers threw dates and oranges at the defenders who threw back rose water and candies.

18 Goldwell, sig. A iva–b.

19 Ibid. sig. A iiib (incorrectly designated as B iiib).

20 See E.G. Fogel, 'A Possible Addition to the Sidney Canon', *MLN*, 75 (1960), 389–94; and Jean Wilson (ed.), *Entertainments for Elizabeth I* (Woodbridge and Totowa, N.J., 1980), pp. 62–3.

21 B.L. MS. Add. 41499A, fol. 6a.

22 B.L. MS. Lansdowne 99, fols. 259a–64b. The speeches have been reprinted in *Malone Society Collections*, I pt. 2 (London, 1908), 181–7.

23 Ibid. fol. 263a. The White Knight's response is dated 15 January.

24 Ibid. fol. 264a.

25 Ed[mund] Spenser (trans.), *Axiochus* (1592), sigs. D 1a–D 4a.

26 F. Davison, *A Poetical Rapsody* (1602), sig. L7b.

27 *Diary of John Manningham of the Middle Temple*, ed. John Bruce (Westminster, 1868), p. 1. No record of any court masque is extant for this date, but it is known that the Accession Day tournament was held at Whitehall as usual.

28 *The Great Chronicle of London*, edited by A.H. Thomas and I.D. Thornley (London and Aylesbury, 1838), p. 372; and Hall, p. 518.

29 For an account of this manuscript and of the related but now lost Ferrers Manuscript, see Clifford Leech, 'Sir Henry Lee's Entertainment of Elizabeth in 1592', *MLR*, 30 (1935), 52–5; and *Lee*, pp. 268–75.

30 Printed by J.W. Cunliffe as part of his article on 'The Queenes Majesties Entertainment at Woodstocke', *PMLA*, 26 (1911), 132.

31 *The Queenes Entertainment at Woodstocke* (1585), sig. B3b.

32 Ibid. sig. B2b.

33 C.A. MS. M. 3. 12a.

34 *The Great Chronicle*, p. 313; and Hall, p. 568.

35 This interpretation was questioned by Chambers in 1936 and Prouty in 1942 but is accepted by Wilson, in *Entertainments for Elizabeth I*, pp. 119–22.

36 See, Cunliffe, 'The Queenes Majesties Entertainment at Woodstocke', 130. There may have been a somewhat similar Leicester entertainment at Christmas 1561–2 (Marie Axton, 'Robert Dudley and the Inner Temple Revels', *The Historical Journal*, 13 [1970], 371–2).

37 *The Queenes Majesties Entertainment at Woodstocke* (1585), sig. C3a.

38 See James M. Osborn, *Young Philip Sidney, 1572–1577* (New Haven and London, 1972), p. 348.

39 In the *New Arcadia* Sidney describes the ladies in the tiltyard gallery, among whom 'was the *Star*, wherby his [Philisides'] course was only directed' (Book II, ch. 21). Sidney's name for Penelope in his sonnet sequence was, of course, Stella (star).

40 In the *Old Arcadia*, Sidney described his life prior to 1575 in the character of Philisides, a melancholy knight disguised as a shepherd, but the Philisides in the *New Arcadia* seems closer to the Sidney of 1577–86.

41 *The Poems of Sir Philip Sidney*, ed. W.R. Ringler, Jr. (Oxford, 1962), p. 356–7 (AT 19). 'Singe neighbours singe' is given by Ringler on pp. 357–8 (AT 21).

42 On the dating of this event, and the ascription of the texts and the impresa to Sidney, see Beal, 284–95.

43 Three years earlier, a 'Mr Sidney' had fought in a tournament (C.A. MS. M. 4, art. 4), but in 1574 Philip Sidney was still away in Europe on his educational tour.

44 For a more complete discussion of this and other impresas by Sidney, see Young (1), 6–24. In June 1610, Lord Compton also appeared disguised as a shepherd (see *HMC Report on Manuscripts in Various Collections*, III, 261–2).

45 *The Countesse of Pembrokes Arcadia* (1590), Book II, ch. 21, ed. Albert Feuillerat in *The Prose Works of Sir Philip Sidney* (Cambridge, 1969), I, 284–6.

46 The identification of Philisides as Sidney and Lelius as Lee was first made by James L. Hanford and Sara R. Watson in 'Personal Allegory in the *Acadia*', *MP*, 32 (1934), 1–10.

47 Roger Howell, *Sir Philip Sidney* (Boston, 1968), pp. 10–1.

48 For a different explanation of Elizabeth's response to the outcome of Sidney's mission, see James M. Osborn, *Young Philip Sidney* (New Haven, 1972), pp. 492–5.

49 Printed in Beale, 288. The most obvious 'desert' received by Sidney was his being made Cup-bearer to the Queen in 1576.

50 Goldwell, sigs. A viiia–b.

51 Both songs have generally been accepted as being by Sidney, see Ringler (ed.), pp. 345–6.

52 Goldwell, sig. B 1a.

53 *Astrophel and Stella*, Sonnet 41, Ringler (ed.), p. 185.

54 B.L. MS. Add. 41499A, fol. 6a.

55 Ibid. fols. 6b–7a.

56 Ibid. fol. 3b.

57 This latter was perhaps Lee whose motto was *Fide et Constantia*.

58 B.L. MS. Add. 41499A, fols. 7a–b.

59 Ibid. fol. 1b.

60 *Hatfield Papers*, XII, 438. Cf. pp. 459 and 574.

61 Strong, p. 154; and Frances A. Yates, *Astraea: The Imperial Theme in the Sixteenth Century* (London and Boston, 1975), pp. 57–8.

62 B.L. MS. Stowe 276, fol. 2; B.L. MS. Add. 33,963, fol. 109; B.L. MS. Add. 28,635, fol. 88b; John Dowland, *First Booke of Songs or Ayres* (1597), no. xviii.

63 There is no complete manuscript version of this work. Wilson in *Entertainments for Elizabeth I* has created a conflated text based on B.L. MS. Add. 41499A and William Hamper's edition of the Hamper MS. Quotations are from Wilson's edition.

64 Cf. the poem 'Farre from triumphing Court' ascribed to Lee in Robert Dowland's *A Musical Banquet* (1610). The subject of the poem is the familiar knight-turned-hermit. Lee may have composed it when Queen Anne visited him in 1608.

65 *Second Booke of Songs or Ayres*, sigs. D 2b–F 1a; and Bodleian Library, MS. Rawlinson. Poetry 148, fol. 75b.

66 B.L. MS. Add. 41499A, fol. 1a.

67 John Lee also appeared on the score cheque for 18 November, 1598 (B.L. MS. Add. 12,514,

fol. 158a). For biographical details concerning John Lee, see *Lee*, pp. 223–4.

68 B.L. MS. Add. 41499A, fol. 6.

7 Apt Words Have Power

1 Cumberland's speech is reprinted in G.C. Williamson, *George, Third Earl of Cumberland* (Cambridge, 1920), pp. 108–9.

2 For some qualifications regarding Tudor Arthurianism, see Sydney Anglo, 'The British History and Early Tudor Propaganda', *Bulletin of the John Rylands Library*, 44 no. 1 (Sept. 1961), 17–48.

3 *Lordonnance et Ordre du tournoy* (Paris, 1520), sig. F 1b; see also C. B. Millican, *Spenser and the Round Table* (Cambridge, Mass., 1932), pp. 23–4. Anglo, however, argues that the Arthurian motif at Calais is not evidence of a Tudor cult of Arthur (see *Spectacle*, p. 162).

4 The pageant, with its obvious compliment to Henry, seems to have been intended to balance another earlier one that alluded to Charles' alleged descent from Charlemagne (see *Spectacle*, pp. 192–6).

5 Camden, p. 149.

6 *Polyhymnia*, in Peele, I, 232.

7 Ibid.

8 The speech is printed in Williamson, *George, Third Earl of Cumberland*, pp. 122–3. The reference to the 'Loyon' is either to Elizabeth, the lion of England, or to the *Golden Lion*, the ship she had placed at Cumberland's disposal.

9 *Anglorum Feriae*, in Peele, I, 270.

10 Williamson, *George, Third Earl of Cumberland*, p. 242.

11 Spenser, *Prothalamion*, line 151.

12 Peele, I, 226–7.

13 Longleat, Devereux MSS., Household Accounts, 1594–8, fols. 87, 91a–b.

14 Collins, I, 362.

15 Spedding, VIII, i, 376–91. Spedding's text is derived from various manuscripts at Lambeth Palace.

16 *Reliquae Wottonianae* (1651), p. 21.

17 Cf. the conjectural sequence given in Strong, p. 209.

18 PRO. S.P. 12/254, no. 68.

19 Lambeth Palace MS. 936, no. 274. See, Spedding, VIII, i, 376–7.

20 Lambeth Palace MS. 933, no. 118. See, Spedding, VIII, i, 378.

21 Lambeth Palace MS. 936, no. 274. See, Spedding, VIII, i, 376–7.

22 Collins, I, 362.

23 Lambeth Palace MS. 936, no. 274. See, Spedding, VIII, i, 376–7.

24 Alnwick Castle, Northumberland MS. 525 (Safe 4), fol. 69. Printed in F.J. Burgoyne, *An Elizabethan Manuscript Preserved at Alnwick Castle* (London, 1904), p. 57.

25 There was a brief reconciliation in 1594 (Conyers Read, *Lord Burghley and Queen Elizabeth* [London, 1960], p. 500).

26 Printed in J. Payne Collier's *The History of English Dramatic Poetry* (London, 1831), I, 285–8. Cecil's house was Pymms at Edmonton, some six miles from Theobalds.

27 Printed in Nichols, *Elizabeth*, III, 75. The charter, the only extant property from any Elizabethan court or theatrical entertainment, was sold at Sotheby's on 16 December 1980.

28 Bodleian Library, MS. Rawlinson D. 692, fols. 106–9.

29 B.L. MS. Harl. 286, fols. 248a–9a. The precise date of this piece is uncertain.

30 PRO. S.P. 12/254, no. 67. See, Spedding, VIII, i, 388–90.

31 According to White, some courtiers believed the soldier to be modelled on Sir Roger Williams, a military man who had risked his own career to help Essex join the expedition to Portugal in 1589.

32 Collins, I, 362.

33 See D. J. Gordon, 'Hymenaei: Ben Jonson's Masque of Union', *Journal of the Warburg and Courtauld Institutes*, 8 (1945), 117, 121–8.

34 *Prince Henry's Barriers*, in Orgel & Srong, I, 161 (lines 166–70).

35 Ibid. I, 161 (lines 205–8).

36 Ibid. I, 162 (lines 347–50).

37 Ibid. I, 160 (line 100).

38 Ibid. I, 163 (lines 384–93).

39 Charles Cornwallis, *The Life and Death of our Late most Incomparable and Heroique Prince Henry, Prince of Wales* (1641), pp. 14–5.

40 *Challenge at Tilt at a Marriage*, in *Jonson*, VII, 391 (Lines 67–75).

41 Ibid. VII, 394 (lines 184–5).

42 Ibid.

Epilogue

1 For this point and for a number of matters touched upon below, I am indebted to Mark Girouard's *The Return to Camelot: Chivalry and the English Gentleman* (New Haven & London, 1981), *passim*.

2 Ian Anstruther, *The Knight and the Umbrella: An Account of the Eglinton Tournament 1839* (London, 1963), p. 115.

3 Girouard, p. 93.

4 Anstruther, p. 12.

5 Ibid. pp. 246–8; and Mario Tosi, *Il torneo di Belvedere in Vaticano e i tornei in Italia nel cinquecento* (Rome, 1946), pp. 26, 40, 67.

6 Rollin G. Osterweis, *Romanticism and Nationalism in the Old South* (New Haven, 1949), pp. 9, 17, 48–9; and John Fraser, *America and the Patterns of Chivalry* (Cambridge, 1982), pp. 7–9, 234n–5n.

7 F.H. Cripps-Day, *The Triumph holden at Shakespeare's England* (London, 1912).

8 'The Volunteer' (1915), in *A Treasury of War Poetry*, ed. George Herbert Clare (Boston & New York, 1917), p. 153.

9 Diamond's unique understanding of tournament skills, derived from his training of horses and men, provides the subject matter for portions of *Joust a Minute*, written with Jeremy Huxley Ward (London, 1982). Another revival of tournament skills is represented by the series of 'medieval' tournaments arranged by the Plantagenet Society at locations throughout England during the summer of 1986.

Index